"Francis Grimké has long deserved the kind of well-researched and carefully pre-sented book that Drew Martin has written. Grimké's half-century career at one of the leading Black churches in Washington, DC, was marked by unusual commit-ment to the gospel message combined with unusual discernment in addressing the social, domestic, and racial realities faced by his congregation. Martin's accessible account of Grimké's 'holistic, yet differentiated, vision of the Christian life' also shows that some important historical figures knew how to promote both faith in the private sphere and responsible Christianity in public. For historical and con-temporary purposes, this is a timely and important book."

Mark Noll, author, *America's Book: The Rise and Decline of a Bible Civilization, 1794–1911*

"I have long awaited this book—a thorough exploration of Francis Grimké's theo-logical, ethical, and pastoral commitments. Drew Martin has sifted a range of materials in a compelling fashion to produce a readable, engaging, and thought-provoking treatment of this great Black Presbyterian pastor-theologian. In doing so, he demonstrates that Grimké was thoroughly committed to the whole counsel of God, which was why he preached racial justice. Martin's book is not just an ex-amination of the past but also a word for the present. Buy a copy for yourself, and a second for your pastor!"

Sean Michael Lucas, Chancellor's Professor of Church History, Reformed Theological Seminary

"Drew Martin's *Grimké on the Christian Life* is a book for all times, but an especially welcome one in ours. Bearing the name of his enslaver-father, the resilient and brilliant Francis Grimké served as a faithful pastor of the Fifteenth Street Church in Washington, DC, cofounded the NAACP, and consistently offered an embodied rebuke of racism in the northern Presbyterian church. All the while, he insisted on the truth of the gospel and its power to transform hearts and society. Martin combines Grimké's personal story and theological teachings to create a text that's historically important and devotionally rich. In a time when many see American Christianity as hopelessly compromised and unconstrained, Grimké's ministry continues to exemplify both bold witness and patient reform work within institu-tions. This book's portrayal of his life and thought is a valuable resource to the Presbyterian tradition and the Christian church."

Ansley L. Quiros, Associate Professor of History, University of North Alabama; author, *God with Us: Lived Theology and the Freedom Struggle in Americus, Georgia, 1942–1976*

"Francis Grimké is an important figure not only in African American church history and Presbyterian church history but in all of church history. His ministry seems especially relevant in our time. Drew Martin shows us that Grimké's faith and teaching on the kingdom of God often cut across 'cultural categories and sensibilities, challenging them all.' He believed that his vocation was to 'preach the gospel of grace,' on the one hand, and to 'fight race prejudice,' on the other. Martin's work is balanced and fair, affirming the many great aspects of Grimké's life and legacy while also giving helpful critique in the few places where Grimké's ministry and statements weren't fully consistent. You will be blessed by this book."

Thurman Williams, Director and Assistant Professor of Homiletics, Covenant Theological Seminary; Church Planter and Senior Pastor, New City Fellowship Church West End, St. Louis, Missouri

"I'm heartened that evangelicals are rediscovering the life and legacy of Francis Grimké. In this helpful book, Drew Martin shows how Grimké articulated a vision of the Christian life that was theologically conservative, confessionally Reformed, contextually sensitive, and socially progressive in matters of racial equality. Many will find Grimké a wise guide for navigating the theological and ethical tensions of our own culture. *Grimké on the Christian Life* is a great addition to a stellar series."

Nathan A. Finn, Professor of Faith and Culture, North Greenville University; Senior Fellow for Religious Liberty, The Ethics and Religious Liberty Commission

"Drew Martin skillfully and gracefully takes us into the remarkable life and ministry of Francis Grimké, whose witness to peace and hope in a world—and a church—riven with strife and injustice stands as relevant to our time as ever before."

John Inazu, Sally D. Danforth Distinguished Professor of Law and Religion, Washington University in St. Louis

"Francis Grimké played a significant role not just in southern Presbyterianism but also in African American and United States history. His advocacy for the rights of African Americans, as well as his passion for justice, dovetails with his commitment to biblical fidelity, theological rigor, and pastoral care. This kind of pastoral work is sorely missing from evangelicalism today, and Drew Martin has done an excellent job highlighting why we need to examine the lives and pastorates of men like Grimké more closely. An excellent book for anyone doing ministry in twenty-first-century America."

Otis W. Pickett, Affiliated Scholar, Clemson University; author, *Southern Shepherds, Savage Wolves*

GRIMKÉ

on the Christian Life

THEOLOGIANS ON THE CHRISTIAN LIFE

EDITED BY JUSTIN TAYLOR AND THOMAS KIDD

Grimké on the Christian Life:
Christian Vitality for the Church and World,
Drew Martin

EDITED BY STEPHEN J. NICHOLS AND JUSTIN TAYLOR

GRIMKÉ

on the Christian Life

CHRISTIAN VITALITY FOR
THE CHURCH AND WORLD

DREW MARTIN

FOREWORD BY IRWYN INCE

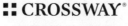

CROSSWAY®

WHEATON, ILLINOIS

Grimké on the Christian Life: Christian Vitality for the Church and World

© 2025 by Andrew J. Martin

Published by Crossway
        1300 Crescent Street
        Wheaton, Illinois 60187

Cover design: Josh Dennis

Cover image: Richard Solomon Artists, Mark Summers

First printing 2025

Printed in the United States of America

Unless otherwise indicated, Scripture quotations are from the King James Version of the Bible, public domain, or from Francis Grimké's near quotation of the King James Version.

Trade paperback ISBN: 978-1-4335-8234-9
ePub ISBN: 978-1-4335-8237-0
PDF ISBN: 978-1-4335-8235-6

Library of Congress Cataloging-in-Publication Data

Names: Martin, Andrew Joseph, author.
Title: Grimké on the Christian life : Christian vitality for the church and world / Andrew J. Martin ; foreword by Irwyn Ince.
Description: Wheaton, Illinois : Crossway, [2025] | Series: Theologians on the Christian life | Includes bibliographical references and index.
Identifiers: LCCN 2024029759 (print) | LCCN 2024029760 (ebook) | ISBN 9781433582349 (trade paperback) | ISBN 9781433582356 (pdf) | ISBN 9781433582370 (epub)
Subjects: LCSH: Christian life. | Church and the world. | Grimké, Francis J. (Francis James), 1850–1937.
Classification: LCC BV4501.3 .M27545 2025 (print) | LCC BV4501.3 (ebook) | DDC 248.4—dc23/eng/20241115
LC record available at https://lccn.loc.gov/2024029759
LC ebook record available at https://lccn.loc.gov/2024029760

Crossway is a publishing ministry of Good News Publishers.

VP		34	33	32	31	30	29	28	27	26	25
15	14	13	12	11	10	9	8	7	6	5	4	3	2	1

Let us stop worrying about the future of Christianity and get down to the hard work in carrying out the instructions of the Lord.

FRANCIS J. GRIMKÉ, "CHRIST'S PROGRAM
FOR THE SAVING OF THE WORLD" (1936)

CONTENTS

SERIES PREFACE

Some might call us spoiled. We live in an era of significant and substantial resources for Christians on living the Christian life. We have ready access to books, videos, online material, seminars—all in the interest of encouraging us in our daily walk with Christ. The laity, the people in the pew, have access to more information than scholars dreamed of having in previous centuries.

Yet, for all our abundance of resources, we also lack something. We tend to lack the perspectives from the past, perspectives from a different time and place than our own. To put the matter differently, we have so many riches in our current horizon that we tend not to look to the horizons of the past.

That is unfortunate, especially when it comes to learning about and practicing discipleship. It's like owning a mansion and choosing to live in only one room. This series invites you to explore the other rooms.

As we go exploring, we will visit places and times different from our own. We will see different models, approaches, and emphases. This series does not intend for these models to be copied uncritically, and it certainly does not intend to put these figures from the past high upon a pedestal like some race of super-Christians. This series intends, however, to help us in the present listen to the past. We believe there is wisdom in the past twenty centuries of the church, wisdom for living the Christian life.

Justin Taylor and Thomas Kidd

FOREWORD

On March 3, 1991, Rodney King was mercilessly and tragically beaten by officers of the Los Angeles Police Department. Less than a year later, on April 29, 1992, a jury acquitted all four officers involved in the brutal incident of assault, and three of the four were acquitted of using excessive force. For the next six days the city exploded in riots over the inability of the justice system to convict White officers of police brutality against African Americans. For his part, Rodney King called for an end to the violence on May 1, 1992: "I just want to say—you know—can we, can we all get along? Can we, can we get along?"

"Can we all get along?" is a simple yet telling question on the matter of race in the history of the United States. From one vantage point, the answer is also simple: no. Or not permanently. From another angle, the question is theological. The only reason our getting along matters at all is that humanity is made in God's image (Gen. 1:27). Thus, Jesus's church and her ministers in this country have always had something to say on the matter. The work you have in your hands, or are viewing on your screen, or are listening to, *Grimké on the Christian Life*, details the life, legacy, and teaching of "an unyielding advocate of righteousness."[1]

Francis J. Grimké (1850–1937), as Drew Martin reminds us, was one of the most gifted and remarkable preachers of the Christian life in American history. Born enslaved in Charleston, South Carolina, to an enslaver, Henry W. Grimké, and an enslaved woman, Nancy, Francis would know full well the seemingly intractableness of racism. This life experience, and the fact that the intractableness of racism was also present in the church,

---

[1] Carter G. Woodson, introduction to *The Works of Francis J. Grimké*, vol. 1, *Addresses Mainly Personal and Racial*, ed. Carter G. Woodson (Washington, DC: Associated Publishers, 1942), xiii.

did not cause Grimké to turn from faith in Jesus Christ. It had the opposite effect. He found that the only solution was in the gospel. Thus, he labored in ministry to keep presenting to people, in word and by example, the Lord Jesus Christ and their need for his saving power.

Dr. Grimké rooted the biblical mandate for reconciliation in creation. He preached that "God hath made of one blood all nations that dwell upon the face of the earth" (see Acts 17:26). He insisted that since all people were made of one blood, they should live as brothers and worship one God together.[2] It should be no surprise that he expected this gospel he preached to compel a life commensurate with its teaching. "Dr. Grimké was the eternal enemy of ministers who preached on thing and lived another."[3]

Carter G. Woodson notes that one of the White ministers who responded to Dr. Grimké's teaching on this point claimed that he was being inconsistent, because in the attempt to "uproot the argument in favor of segregation," he failed to quote all of Acts 17:26. He neglected to include the fact that God "hath appointed to them their metes and bounds."[4]

Indeed, some Presbyterian ministers were still making this argument in support of the separation of the races when my denomination was founded in 1973. The White minister argued that "the Negro was created and placed in Africa, the white man in Europe, and the yellow man in Asia. The church, in segregating the Negro, was doing the will of God."[5]

What was Dr. Grimké's response?

> If God appointed to each race its metes and bounds, by what right did the white man come from Europe and take possession of the Red Man's land in America? By what right did the white man compel the Negro to come to America to labor for him on the plantations and in the mines? By what right can the white man go to Africa today and deprive the natives of their most fertile land and corner them on reserves where they have to starve or leave to labor like slaves in the mines and on the plantations?[6]

I only wish that I had a book like *Grimké on the Christian Life* when I was a seminary student or early in my pastoral ministry. Throughout my seminary education and the first few years of my pastorate in the Presby-

---

[2] Woodson, *Works*, 1:xvi.
[3] Woodson, *Works*, 1:xiii.
[4] Woodson, *Works*, 1:xvi.
[5] Woodson, *Works*, 1:xvi.
[6] Woodson, *Works*, 1:xvi.

terian Church in America (PCA), I remained ignorant of the rich history of Black Americans in Presbyterianism. When my denomination formed, we declared ourselves to be "A Continuing Presbyterian Church." In this proclamation, the founders were declaring a connection to historic Presbyterianism in America and a belief that it was "preserving what was best from the PCUS."[7] This connection and preservation, however, has rarely included any focus on the biblical writings and teachings of Black American men and women within the Presbyterian tradition. The typical experience of students in theologically conservative seminaries often involves learning from authors who also defended American slavery and supported racial and ethnic hierarchies. I, and many others, too infrequently heard from figures like Grimké, who unabashedly preached historic Reformed theology while pushing back against unbiblical positions on race and class.

During one of my seminary courses, the professor posed the question of why we thought there were no Black American Presbyterian denominations. In the history of the United States, you find the formation of other distinctly Black denominations: African Methodist Episcopal Church, African Methodist Episcopal Zion Church, Colored Methodist Episcopal Church, National Baptist Convention, Progressive National Baptist Convention, Church of God in Christ. No Presbyterians. In my ignorance I believed the answer was found in the racist ideology of southern Presbyterianism. I thought that this was too much for Blacks to bear and made them unwilling to self-identity as Presbyterian. I was sorely mistaken—not about the racist ideology of southern Presbyterianism but about the historic willingness for Blacks to self-identity as Presbyterian.

Black Presbyterians in American history like Francis J. Grimké did not form separate Black Presbyterian denominations because they chose to remain in the majority White Presbyterian denominations, seeking interracial cooperation and integration. In addition, they "fought to hold their White brothers accountable to biblical norms of justice and love in the context of shared mission."[8]

In American Presbyterianism today we are still far from reflecting the fullness of the kingdom. Our racialized legacy continues to bear down on our present demographics. What can we learn from Grimké here? He was

---

[7] Sean Michael Lucas, *For a Continuing Church: The Roots of the Presbyterian Church in America* (Phillipsburg, NJ: P&R, 2015), 3.
[8] Sean Michael Lucas, "Lost Legacies: African American Fathers and Brothers in Presbyterian History" (PCA General Assembly Workshop, Greensboro, NC, 2017).

called to the pastorate of Fifteenth Street Presbyterian Church, Washington, DC, in 1878 as a young man. Fifteenth Street (founded as First Colored Presbyterian Church in 1841) was a prominent and influential church in the city. It was a remarkable post for a young minister. From this post he would serve Howard University and help found the NAACP. Additionally, he would serve as the first African American moderator of the presbytery at just thirty years old. Remarkably, as you will read in the pages that follow, in 1879 the presbytery had eleven ministerial candidates under care, nine of whom were associated with Fifteenth Street Presbyterian Church! We would do well in twenty-first-century Presbyterianism to learn from this father in the faith about raising up and training young men of color for gospel ministry in the Presbyterian church.

We owe Drew Martin a debt of gratitude for writing *Grimké on the Christian Life.* It is high time that Dr. Grimké's wisdom, faithfulness, and ministry insight be brought forward to a church that still struggles to proclaim and live out the implications of the gospel along the lines of race, ethnicity, culture, socioeconomics, and politics. The question remains: Can we all get along? Grimké would tell us that in Christ the answer is yes and amen.

Irwyn Ince
Coordinator of Mission to North America
Adjunct Professor of Pastoral Theology
Reformed Theological Seminary

PREFACE

As a pastor, historian, and theologian, I am grateful for the opportunity to write about Francis Grimké and his view of the Christian life. I have learned so much from studying Grimké and the world in which he lived. He is one of the most underappreciated figures of American religious history, and it gives me great joy to bring his teaching to a broader audience.

Two historical books have been written on his family, two on his famous abolitionist aunts (Sarah and Angelina), and one on his brother Archibald and his role in the early civil rights movement. There is even a famous work of historical fiction that imagines the Grimké family and the shape of their lives (Sue Monk Kidd's *The Invention of Wings*). I am glad that now people can hear more about the pastor in the family, Francis (or Frank, as he was more affectionately known).[1]

My interest in this book originally grew out of my work as a pastor. Before coming to teach at Covenant Theological Seminary, I helped to plant a church in Charlotte, North Carolina. Our mother church (Christ Central Church) is an intercultural Presbyterian congregation on the east side of the city, and the vision for our church was to follow a similar path on the historically Black west side. Our young church had a dedicated and diverse launch team, and we were a diverse, young, energetic, and inexperienced team of pastors. We went looking for theological resources that could help us to think about planting and pastoring an intercultural church in a

---

[1] On his family, see Kerri K. Greenidge, *The Grimkes: The Legacy of Slavery in an American Family* (New York: Liveright, 2022); Mark Perry, *Lift Up Thy Voice: The Grimké Family's Journey from Slaveholders to Civil Rights Leaders* (New York: Viking, 2001). On his aunts, see Gerda Lerner, *The Grimké Sisters from South Carolina: Pioneers for Women's Rights and Abolition* (Chapel Hill: University of North Carolina Press, 2004); Katharine DuPre Lumpkin, *The Emancipation of Angelina Grimké* (Chapel Hill: University of North Carolina Press, 1974). On Archibald, see Dickson D. Bruce, *Archibald Grimké: Portrait of a Black Independent* (Baton Rouge: Louisiana State University Press, 1993).

predominantly African American community in a city with a notoriously difficult history related to race relations. Our search took us to Francis Grimké. I am pleased to say that many aspects of Grimké's theological vision are alive and well at West Charlotte Church at Freedom today.[2]

As a historian, the more I read Grimké and the more I learned about his life, the more I realized how much work is still needed to recover the full picture of American religious history. As a student of history, I already knew this, but as I studied Grimké's life, it truly was shocking to me that he is not better known. It will be obvious from this book that we can hardly understand the history of the early civil rights movement, the history of Christianity in America, the history of the Presbyterian denominations, or even the history of public schooling in the nation's capital without knowing something about Francis Grimké. My hope is that this book will inspire more historical studies of his life and work.

Reading Grimké also made me very grateful for the historians already working hard to paint a fuller picture of American religious history. They are too many to name, but I have learned particularly from a few whom readers interested in knowing more about Grimké's context will want to explore as well. Curtis Evans's *The Burden of Black Religion* and Barbara Savage's *Your Spirits Walk Beside Us* both invite deeper reflection upon, as Evans puts it, the diversity of the "varied religious motives and activities of black religious persons."[3] Additionally, Mary Beth Swetnam Mathews's *Doctrine and Race* and Daniel Bare's *Black Fundamentalists* both demonstrate that the labels *liberal*, *evangelical*, and *fundamentalist* are less useful than many historians have claimed and most Americans assume.[4] These labels also frequently marginalize or mischaracterize minority voices. Here I am thinking not only of racial and ethnic minorities but of theological ones as well. Historic, orthodox Christian theology has not always fared well in America or in histories about American religious life.

Reflection on these themes shaped this book in at least two very practical ways. First, I have included plenty of Grimké's own words in this book, and I hope readers will appreciate the many quotations. It felt important

---

[2] Readers on a similar journey can find many of Francis Grimké's writings online. The four-volume collection of his works and the recently published collection of some of his meditations on preaching are full of insights.

[3] Curtis J. Evans, *The Burden of Black Religions* (New York: Oxford University Press, 2008), 279; Barbara Savage, *Your Spirits Walk Beside Us: The Politics of Black Religion* (Cambridge, MA: Belknap, 2008).

[4] Daniel R. Bare, *Black Fundamentalists: Conservative Christianity and Racial Identity in the Segregation Era* (New York: New York University Press, 2021); Mary Beth Swetnam Mathews, *African American Evangelicals and Fundamentalism between the Wars* (Tuscaloosa: University of Alabama Press, 2017).

to allow him to speak for himself as much as possible. Second, it seemed important to point out the various ways in which voices like Grimké's have been left out or grossly mischaracterized by the dominant narratives of American religious history. Readers interested in those details can find them in the footnotes, but in a few chapters the themes are so unavoidable, they appear in the text itself. I hope that readers appreciate the historical dimensions of this book, as well as the devotional ones. It seemed impossible to write about the latter without including at least some of the former.

In addition to the help Grimké offers to the pastor and the historian, I also have learned a great deal from him as a public theologian. I save those observations for the book's conclusion, and I pray that readers enjoy the journey in between.

Drew Martin
Covenant Theological Seminary
St. Louis, Missouri

VOLUMES IN

THE WORKS OF FRANCIS J. GRIMKÉ

Sources abbreviated *Works*, followed by volume and page numbers, are from *The Works of Francis J. Grimké*, ed. Carter G. Woodson, 4 vols. (Washington, DC: Associated Publishers, 1942). Individual volumes are as follows:

Vol. 1   *Addresses Mainly Personal and Racial*

Vol. 2   *Special Sermons*

Vol. 3   *Stray Thoughts and Meditations*

Vol. 4   *Letters*

INTRODUCTORY
CHAPTERS

CHAPTER I

FRANCIS J. GRIMKÉ'S LIFE AND LEGACY

One of the most gifted and remarkable preachers of the Christian life in American history grew up enslaved.

Childhood, Slavery, Freedom, and Education

Francis Grimké was born in 1850 on a plantation just outside Charleston, South Carolina. His father was Henry Grimké, the owner of the plantation, and his mother was Nancy Weston, a biracial slave. Henry took Nancy as his mistress after his wife, Selina, died, and they had three sons, including Francis, his older brother, Archibald, and his younger brother, John. Nancy also functioned as the de facto mistress of the plantation.[1] Nevertheless, she and the three boys continued to live in a small cabin that served as the slave quarters, and not in the big house. Needless to say, this was a morally complicated relationship.

When Francis was two years old, life became even more complicated when his father, Henry, died of yellow fever. South Carolina law at the time prohibited the manumission of the enslaved upon the death of their owners, so Henry had arranged in his will that ownership of Nancy and the children would be passed on to Montague, his White son by marriage. The plantation was sold, and Nancy was given enough money to purchase a tiny three-room

---

[1] Henry Justin Ferry, "Francis James Grimké: Portrait of a Black Puritan" (PhD diss., Yale University, 1970), 7.

house in Charleston. Technically still enslaved, Nancy and the boys never-theless lived with a significant degree of freedom for the next eight years. She earned money by laundering clothes, and the boys helped her in the work. South Carolina law prohibited schooling for Black people, so Nancy made major sacrifices in order to provide private tutoring for her children. The family also attended a Presbyterian church with a strong ministry to children. The boys learned the Bible at church, but in Archibald's memoirs it seems that their mother's example of devotion left the strongest impression on them. Nancy Weston was a remarkable mother, and her example of prayer stood out to the boys. Francis's childhood was hard, but the boys had a good home, where they learned the importance of faith in God and hard work.[2]

That all changed in 1860 when Montague married Julia Hibben, who had grown up on an Alabama plantation and expected her husband to provide her with slaves to attend to her personal needs. Archibald (age eleven) and Francis (age ten) were taken from their mother to serve their half brother's household. When Nancy objected, Montague had her thrown into a work house for a week, and she became so sick she nearly died. Even at that age, the boys had such a strong sense of justice that they would not submit to such an immoral arrangement. They frequently received merci-less beatings for their acts of protest. Archibald quickly escaped and lived in hiding until the end of the Civil War, but it took Francis longer as he was captured after his escape attempts, beaten and whipped, locked in a room, and sent to a notoriously harsh master to be "broken"—without success. Francis Grimké endured this treatment stoically. We can only imagine how those years shaped the young boy.

After the war the boys were emancipated and attended the new schools set up for freed slaves. They were noticed quickly by one of their teachers, who arranged for them to move up north to be mentored and educated. They began at Lincoln University, where Francis became the valedictorian of his class. Archibald went on to attend Harvard Law School, and Francis also studied law at Howard University in Washington, DC, before sensing a call to the ministry and moving to Princeton Theological Seminary to complete his studies. According to James McCosh, president of the Col-lege of New Jersey (later named Princeton University), Charles Hodge "reckoned him equal to the ablest of his students."[3] Benjamin B. Warfield,

---

[2] Archibald H. Grimké, "A Madonna of the South," *The Southern Workman* 29, no. 7 (1900): 392.
[3] James McCosh to unnamed addressee, October 18, 1879, in *Works*, 1:x.

another well-known professor at Princeton Seminary, had a "high regard" for Grimké as well.[4] The young Francis developed quite a reputation for his theological acumen and remarkable rhetorical gifts.

Early Ministry

Upon graduating from Princeton in 1878, Grimké took a call to Fifteenth Street Presbyterian Church, in Washington, DC. That same year he married Charlotte Forten of Philadelphia, whose family was well known for their social activism. During his early years of ministry at Fifteenth Street, Grimké became known for his preaching gifts. He also had the opportunity to use his gifts to advance numerous other important institutions and causes. He served as an influential member of the board for Howard University, where he was instrumental in helping the university to develop leadership more reflective of its student body. Alongside his brother Archibald, and in cooperation with other significant leaders like W. E. B. Du Bois, Grimké also helped to found the NAACP. In these and many other ways, he worked closely with key leaders who laid the groundwork for the civil rights movement.

Yet, while his wisdom and success in these endeavors led to numerous offers to teach as a professor and to extend his leadership abilities to a host of other organizations, Francis Grimké's commitment to the ministry of the gospel and devotion to his congregation set him apart. He refused to let these other undertakings prevent him from performing his vocation as a pastor. As he wrote in his own notebooks, "The Christian ministry is no place for one who does not see that his supreme mission is to call [people] to repentance and faith, and who is not fully determined to make everything else in his life subservient to that end." Grimké believed it absolutely necessary to make what was most important to God most important to himself. Speaking of the gospel minister, he wrote, "The kingdom of God, in seeking the salvation of [people], must be first with him, and must be kept first, high above every other interest."[5]

In light of Grimké's strong gifts for ministry, it is not surprising that he was called to be the pastor of Fifteenth Street Presbyterian Church despite his youth. Alongside churches like Berean Baptist, Lincoln Temple Congregational, Metropolitan African Methodist Episcopal, 19th Street

---

[4] Ethelbert D. Warfield to Francis J. Grimké, December 28, 1922, in *Works*, 4:357.
[5] *Works*, 3:420.

Baptist, and St. Luke's Episcopal, Fifteenth Street Presbyterian was home to some of the most prominent Black leaders in Washington at that time. The young Francis Grimké's ministry to his prominent church members consisted of a focus on active church membership, preaching, church discipline of wayward or noncommittal members, visitation of the sick, and personal growth in biblical holiness. This ministerial emphasis on rigorous accountability indicates that Grimké demonstrated little if any deference to the wealthy and prominent members of his congregation. In fact, it seems that Grimké communicated that a church with many gifts should see itself as having a deep obligation to utilize those gifts sacrificially for the good of the kingdom of God.

The church experienced tremendous growth during these early years and was a model of leadership development. According to one newspaper report, the church witnessed eighty conversions to the faith in 1879 alone. In the same year, according to church records, of eleven ministerial candidates under the care of the Presbytery of Washington City, fully nine were associated with Fifteenth Street Presbyterian Church. In 1880, just a few years into his first pastorate, Francis Grimké was elected as the moderator of the presbytery, becoming not only the first African American to serve in that role but also, at the age of just thirty years old, the youngest person ever to hold the position. His early years in the church were exceedingly fruitful.[6]

Not only did Fifteenth Street Presbyterian Church actively develop leaders for Christian ministry, but Grimké's growing reputation led him to develop relationships with other significant leaders in Washington. Soon after Grimké became a pastor, he developed a close friendship with Frederick Douglass (1818–1895), the famous African American abolitionist and leader. In 1884, two years after the death of his first wife, Anna, Douglass asked Grimké to officiate his wedding to Helen Pitts, who was White. The ceremony took place in the Grimké's home. Opposition to interracial marriage made the wedding controversial, and Grimké himself was caught up in the storm of opposition. Many years later, as he recounted the privilege of officiating the ceremony, he brushed off critics with his characteristic combination of clarity and nuance. He not only expressed distaste for the criticisms of White racists but also criticized those of his own race who held it against Douglass that he would marry a White woman. According to

---

[6] *People's Advocate*, May 3, 1879 (Washington, DC); Presbytery of Washington City, "Records," 2:119, cited in Ferry, "Francis James Grimké," 138, 139, 145.

Grimké the matter was simple, for their "right to marry" was "God-given," and therefore no one could "rightfully forbid it."[7]

The next year, Grimké was involved in a second controversy. Once again, he was called upon to serve as a lonely advocate. In 1875, Howard University had entered a formal partnership with the Presbytery of Washington City in order to provide theological education for ministerial candidates. In 1884, Grimké served not only on the board of trustees at the university but also as the chairman of the presbytery committee designated to oversee the relationship. That year, at the request of the presbytery, Grimké recommended that four young men who were members of his congregation continue to receive financial aid in their further ministerial studies at Howard. However, the dean of the theological department, James Craighead, who was White, recommended that the students lose their financial aid, accusing them of lying. He did so by writing to the financial aid board without informing Grimké, as the board's rules required.

Grimké became aware of the situation only when the students' aid did not come as expected, and when he wrote to the financial aid board to discover the reason, they informed him of Craighead's report. The students ultimately were exculpated of the charges, which raises more than a few questions about Craighead's motivations. The situation left a bad taste in the mouth of the presbytery, but even more so with Grimké. The next spring Grimké voted with a special committee of the presbytery to end the relationship with the university.[8] The decision to sever the relationship weighed deeply on him as a member of the board of trustees at Howard. Just a few months later, citing health concerns and the need for a different climate, Grimké petitioned his presbytery to dissolve his pastoral relationship with the Fifteenth Street Presbyterian Church so that he could take another pastoral call, in Jacksonville, Florida. Dealing with such controversies in his early years of ministry took quite a toll on the young pastor.

A Developing Voice

Grimké's stay in Florida proved brief, for he felt rejuvenated enough to return to Fifteenth Street after just four years, but he spent his brief sojourn there gaining valuable experience and developing a twofold approach to

---

[7] Francis J. Grimké, "The Second Marriage of Frederick Douglass," *Journal of Negro History* 19, no. 3 (1934): 326.
[8] Ferry, "Francis James Grimké," 149–54.

culture and race. On the one hand, when it came to speaking to his congregation or others in the African American community, he was not afraid to address matters of moral improvement. One particularly noteworthy example would be his frequent sermons on temperance. Grimké took the abuse of alcohol to be one of the most significant issues confronting his people, contributing to poverty, social degradation, and the mortality rate.[9] For Grimké, his people possessed a "sad inheritance" as a result of the injustices of slavery. The abuse of alcohol only compounded the realities Black people faced as a result of their White oppressors. Whatever circumstances led to excessive drinking, it was unhealthy, both physically and economically.[10]

While Grimké was willing to touch on moral improvement when speaking to members of his own church or race, during this period of his ministry he also began to write and speak out more boldly against the oppressive tendencies of White supremacy present not only within his own tradition but in American Christianity more broadly. When the famous evangelist Dwight L. Moody came to Jacksonville during Grimké's tenure there, Moody followed the advice of a local committee and held segregated evangelistic meetings. Moody's willingness to embrace segregation in the work of the gospel infuriated Grimké. Moody's attitude was "evil," "wicked," and "Anti-Christian in character," and it could find "no sanction in the word of God." Moody neglected "the duty of all Christians, and especially those who are in high and responsible positions, to bear witness to the truth, and to testify against evil." John the Baptist, Grimké wryly observed, "might have saved his head," if "he had been as discreet as Mr. Moody" on the subject. "Perhaps one day," Grimké concluded, "Mr. Moody may learn that God is no respecter of persons," and that "Christ died for all alike, and that the soul of the Negro is as precious in his sight as that of the white man."[11] While Grimké wrote vehemently against Moody's racial cowardice, in his own journals he could also express appreciation for Moody's work of evangelism, writing that his "tremendous work" and "wonderful success" were the result of his single-minded devotion to that same blood of Christ "that cleanses from all sin."[12]

---

[9] Ferry, "Francis James Grimké," 165.
[10] Francis J. Grimké, "The Attitude of the Home on the Temperance Question" (1898), in *Works*, 2:488, cited in Ferry, "Francis James Grimké," 166.
[11] Francis Grimké, "Mr. Moody and the Color Question in the South," 3, 7, 8, Digital Howard, Manuscripts for the Grimke Book, 27, accessed, March 3, 2021, http://dh.howard.edu/.
[12] *Works*, 3:420.

On the issue of racial segregation in the church, Grimké took the same prophetic public approach to matters in his own denomination. At the centennial General Assembly of the (northern) Presbyterian Church of the United States of America (PCUSA) in 1888, the reunification of the northern denomination with its (southern) Presbyterian Church in the United States (PCUS) counterpart was a central concern of debate. The northern Presbyterians in particular were anxious for unity, but the southern church pressed the northern denomination to embrace their practice of segregating churches and presbyteries by race as a condition of the merger. In the months leading up to the assembly, Grimké published a letter in which he did not hold back his criticism of either southerners or northerners who supported the plan. He accused southern segregationist churches of "caste prejudice" and "anti-Christian" views. However, when it came to northerners, Grimké went on to say, "I speak from experience" that "the Southern white man is precisely the same as the Northern white man, with the exception of his prejudices." And sadly, "in ninety-nine cases out of a hundred even in these the difference is so slight as to be scarcely appreciable." For Grimké, "organic unity" between the denominations was a good thing, but it was "by no means the most important thing." In simple terms, "it is better to do right than to be organically united with any branch of the church."[13]

Francis Grimké's brief sojourn in Florida gave him the opportunity to develop a voice that was increasingly clear and gracious, but also increasingly uncompromising. On fundamental matters, he refused to back down or mince words. And yet he also demonstrated a willingness to extend forgiveness and even respect. In spite of Dwight Moody's racial compromises, Grimké communicated respect for him and even celebrated his evangelistic work. Despite the racist past of the southern church, Grimké communicated a willingness to reunite with southerners if they would embrace Black people as equals moving forward. He chose his words carefully and with precision in order to maximize agreement and constructively clarify areas of disagreement. The need for his prophetic voice only grew in the years ahead. The southern church refused to give up its segregation in 1888, and though the northern church technically welcomed Black pastors and members, its churches remained segregated, to borrow Grimké's language, in "ninety-nine cases out of a hundred."

---

[13] Francis J. Grimké, "It Is Drawing the Color Line," 3, 4, Digital Howard, Manuscripts for the Grimke Book, 28, accessed, March 3, 2021, http://dh.howard.edu/.

Mature Ministry

When Francis and Charlotte returned to Fifteenth Street Presbyterian Church in 1889, he was thirty-eight years old and seasoned by his years in ministry. His experience proved crucial. If the post-Reconstruction years of his early ministry had been difficult, the circumstances for Black people in America now arguably were even worse. The hope and idealism of the Reconstruction era lay solidly in the past. Racially motivated violence was commonplace. The race riots in Brownsville, Texas (1906); Atlanta, Georgia (1906); and Springfield, Illinois (1908) drew special attention from Francis Grimké for the racial injustices that sparked them and the danger they posed to Black victims. The 1919 race riot in Washington itself brought those realities even closer to home.[14] These post-Reconstruction years also had the greatest numbers of lynchings in American history, and the victims were overwhelmingly Black people. Between 1880 and 1940, White mobs in the South killed at least 3,200 Black men alone.[15] Obviously these grievous circumstances weighed on Grimké as he ministered in the nation's capital.

In addition to the racial violence, racial segregation was not only tolerated but even endorsed by members of Christian groups with significant influence. In 1916 the American Bible Society celebrated its centennial in Washington by hosting a series of events including a pageant entitled "The Bible and Human Life." According to Grimké, twenty-five Black pastors attended a conference where one of the members of the society suggested that the pageant be segregated.[16] The irony of a segregated Bible conference on human life was outrageous, and White members of such societies too often did too little to rectify similar egregious offenses. The Black pastors protested and refused to attend.[17]

This racial prejudice hurt all the more when it not only was tolerated but even advocated in Grimké's own denomination. His clarion call against formally segregated churches and presbyteries won the day in 1888 when the northern Presbyterian church refused to concede to the southern church's demands for a denominational merger. In 1904, how-

---

[14] Ferry, "Francis James Grimké," 272–86.

[15] Amy Louise Wood, *Lynching and Spectacle: Witnessing Racial Violence* (Chapel Hill: University of North Carolina Press, 2011), 3.

[16] Francis J. Grimké, "The American Bible Society and Colorphobia," cited in Ferry, "Francis James Grimké," 323.

[17] Grimké himself received at least one letter downplaying the incident: Wallace Radcliffe to Francis Grimké, May 24, 1916, in *Works*, 4:165.

ever, things did not go so well. That year the General Assembly took up the matter of another merger with the Cumberland Presbyterians. The Cumberland Presbyterians separated from the mainline church in 1810 as a result of theological disagreements, and then in 1869 their new denomination segregated itself by encouraging its Black members to leave to form yet another denomination of their own. Needless to say, Grimké was not impressed by what he took to be the theological fuzziness of his would-be brethren, but in particular he was appalled by the willingness of his own denomination to change church bylaws to allow for segregated presbyteries at their request. With his tongue firmly planted in his cheek, Grimké affirmed that a change to church bylaws was needed indeed, but it was the segregated Cumberland Presbyterians who needed to make the change and not the unsegregated PCUSA.[18] In spite of Grimké's relentless protest, the merger between the denominations passed. Somehow the organic unity of denominations received higher priority than the Christian unity of brothers and sisters in Christ.

Given these circumstances, it is not hard to see why Francis Grimké believed that his vocation was to "preach the gospel of grace," on the one hand, and to "fight race prejudice," on the other.[19] He believed that the Christian church needed to preach the whole counsel of God in order that people might find eternal hope in Christ. He also believed that the American church's failure to obey God's commands regarding human equality not only contributed to the prevalent evils of racial prejudice and violence but also left a hypocritical stain that made it difficult for people to believe in the gospel of Jesus Christ. To preach the gospel effectively, it was necessary to preach God's law clearly. God's moral law enables people to see their sin and need for Christ. It also teaches believers in Christ how to live. The Christian church's failure to teach and follow God's moral law regarding the equality of all human beings was *the* chief hindrance to effective ministry.

If the church's failure to confront racial prejudice was an affront to gospel ministry, it is obvious why Grimké poured himself into a litany of initiatives and institutions that sought to address and rectify racial inequalities and inequities. In 1893, along with forty-six other ministers in the northern Presbyterian church, he formed the Afro-American Council.

[18] Francis J. Grimké, "Organic Union between the Cumberland Presbyterian Church, and the Presbyterian Church in the United States of America" (1904), box 40-8, folder 420, 10, Francis J. Grimké Papers, Howard University Library.
[19] Francis J. Grimké to the members of the class of 1878 of Princeton Theological Seminary, April 27, 1918, in *Works*, 4:215.

The council would offer fellowship and training to ministers who were formally members of the denomination but functionally excluded from the informal networks of collegiality and partnership that White ministers took for granted.[20] Grimké also spoke at the first conference at the Hampton Institute in 1897. In the years that followed, he continued to participate in its activities alongside Booker T. Washington, W. E. B. Du Bois, William Tunnell, and a range of other influential African American leaders. Grimké served as the institute's chair for the Committee on Religion and Ethics from 1898 to 1902.[21] He also served as the treasurer and was a longtime member of the executive board for the American Negro Academy, founded by Alexander Crummell to advance African American scholarship and promote literature, science, art, and higher education. Grimké, Du Bois and a select group of other significant figures contributed scholarly papers to the academy.[22] As a result of his respected service as a longtime member of the Board of Trustees of Howard University, his name was put forward to be the next president, a role Grimké declined in order to focus his energies on his calling as a pastor.[23]

Perhaps most importantly, Grimké was involved with the Niagara Movement and helped to establish the NAACP. Alongside Ida B. Wells-Barnett and Du Bois, Grimké was one of six African American signers of the call for the Emancipation Conference that led to the formation of the NAACP. As a pastor, Grimké elected not to take on a leadership role in the organization, however, and instead his brother Archibald served on the committee that established the organization and went on to serve as a vice president. Francis also made personal financial contributions to the NAACP and promoted it regularly at Fifteenth Street Presbyterian Church.[24] Francis Grimké took nearly every opportunity he could to work diligently and advocate prophetically for the just treatment of Black people.

Grimké engaged in these works of social activism in part because he believed that the American church's racial failures were an affront to the gospel of Jesus Christ and a hindrance to the kingdom of God. Why should anyone believe in a God whose people denied the basic equality of all human beings? Why should anyone believe in a gospel of salvation by

---

20 Ferry, "Francis James Grimké," 195.
21 Ferry, "Francis James Grimké," 204, 207.
22 Ferry, "Francis James Grimké," 214–15.
23 Ferry, "Francis James Grimké," 267.
24 Ferry, "Francis James Grimké," 287–90. Francis J. Grimké, "The National Association for the Advancement of Colored People: Its Value, Its Aims, Its Claims" (1921), in *Works*, 1:618–27.

grace when its advocates and their leaders mercilessly turned a blind eye to the reality of racial violence? Why would anyone want to associate with a God whose people continued to actively pursue segregation and exclusion, not only in society in general but in their own churches? Francis Grimké refused to separate the Christian faith from the Christian life. Both were necessary and mutually reinforcing. It was impossible to have one without the other.

Life Vision

Grimké finally retired from his pastorate at Fifteenth Street Presbyterian Church in 1927 after fifty years of faithful ministry. He previously attempted to retire in 1923, but his beloved congregation refused to receive his letter of resignation and begged him to stay on a few more years.[25] But finally, at the age of seventy-seven, it was time. His retirement did not stop his pen, though, as he continued to write prolifically until his death in 1937, the day after his eighty-seventh birthday. The prominent historian of African American history Carter Woodson collected Grimké's works and, in 1942, published four volumes of his writings, a collection that remains valuable to this day.

A sermon that Francis Grimké distributed widely the year before he died is just one of the many writings not included in those volumes. Entitled "Christ's Program for the Saving of the World," it served as a fitting summary of his own approach to ministry and the Christian life. In his introduction he explained that the sermon dealt "with a matter that is of vital importance to the progress of the kingdom of God." It was a sermon on the Great Commission of Matthew 28:18–20 and Mark 16:15.[26]

Grimké began the sermon by identifying "the great task" for which Christ had come and for which "his kingdom was set up on the earth." That task was "to redeem the world; to set things right; to bring about changes for the better in all the relations of life." Grimké pointed out that Jesus too had lived during a difficult time in human history—perhaps, in fact, "the darkest period morally." Society "in all its branches was rotten to the core" and "steeped in iniquities of every kind." And yet, Grimké pointed out, Jesus believed that such a world "could be redeemed." Perhaps even more

---

[25] Ferry, "Francis James Grimké," 342–45.
[26] Francis J. Grimké, "Christ's Program for the Saving of the World" (1936), box 40-6, folder 309, Francis J. Grimké Papers, Howard University Library.

incredibly, Jesus "committed the execution of His plan" for the world's redemption to his followers, who had "believed in Him," who had "accepted
Him as the Messiah," and "who had associated themselves with Him to
carry on the glorious undertaking after He was gone."[27]

How were Jesus's followers to execute this program for saving the
world? They were to do so by going out into the world and preaching the
gospel of Jesus Christ. Specifically, they were to proclaim that human beings are sinners who stand under the judgment of God unless they turn
in faith to Jesus Christ, the Son of God, for the forgiveness of their sins.
Grimké acknowledged that there are "some who still feel that this way
of saving the world is foolishness. They have other schemes to suggest
which they think are better." Despite the apparent foolishness of the gospel message, however, Grimké declared that the gospel of Jesus is our
only hope.[28]

Having laid the foundation of the plan, Grimké continued to develop
another key aspect. The "next element" in Christ's program for "saving the
world, for bettering conditions," was teaching. For Grimké the relentless
social activist, it "is not secular knowledge" that Jesus is "particularly concerned about, important as that kind of knowledge may be." Rather, the
knowledge Jesus has in mind is "that which is contained in the Old Testament Scriptures," together with the inspired record of Jesus's own life and
his disciples' teachings in the New Testament. "In the campaign for saving
a lost world, for bettering conditions, the contents of this Book must be
carefully studied and taught, line upon line, precept upon precept, here a
little, there a little, in season and out of season." Grimké went on to emphasize that this message of salvation from the Bible should be taken to
all peoples, that God promises to be with his people as they carry out the
mission, and that the mission cannot fail because it depends on the power
of God and not human power.[29]

Grimké concluded by underlining that "Christ's program for saving
the world, for bringing about changes for the better of individuals and in
communities—in the whole structure of human society, in all human relationships"—is carried out by preaching the gospel of salvation. It is not accomplished through "philosophy, or science, or any special department of
human knowledge; but teaching what is written in the Scriptures, the Word

---

[27] Grimké, "Christ's Program for the Saving of the World," 1–2.
[28] Grimké, "Christ's Program for the Saving of the World," 4.
[29] Grimké, "Christ's Program for the Saving of the World," 4–5.

of God." For Grimké, the darkness of the world and the failures of God's people were saddening, but they were not reasons for hopelessness. Christianity could easily withstand "competition with other religions" and any ideology, whether "Communism, Nationalism, Capitalism," or any other "antagonistic forces." Therefore, Grimké concluded, "Let us stop worrying about the future of Christianity, and get down to hard work in carrying out the instructions of our Lord." Francis Grimké devoted his life to following this program.[30]

Legacy

Francis Grimké's legacy confounds and confronts overly simplistic visions of the Christian life. How many Christian leaders today would preach such a sermon about Christ's program for saving the world after devoting their lives to ministry *and* social activism as Grimké did? Francis Grimké's voice is needed today as much as ever. This book attempts to listen to his voice and offers a portrait of the Christian life that cuts across today's debates on Christian living that tend to polarize so-called conservative and progressive Christians.

Along these lines, Grimké's treatment of the Christian life is essential not so much for its disorienting potential but as a resource for reorientation. Contemporary Christians need to hear the voice of a theologian who was *both* an adamant advocate for the centrality of the church's spiritual mission of preaching the gospel of salvation through Christ alone *and* one of the founders of the NAACP. Francis Grimké was one of the most important and influential pastor-theologians in America a century ago, and the teachings of his life and ministry remain incredibly relevant in our present cultural moment.

The neglect of figures like Grimké calls out to us to recognize just how deficient our telling of history has been. How could one of the most well-known pastors in America be forgotten so soon? Grimké was the pastor of Fifteenth Street Presbyterian Church in Washington, DC, for nearly fifty years. When his works were collected and published by Carter Woodson in 1942, the volumes contained only a fraction of his writings. Grimké's essays and articles were published widely and regularly commented on by notable figures. He corresponded with Presidents Theodore Roosevelt,

---

[30] Grimké, "Christ's Program for the Saving of the World," 9, 12, 13.

William Howard Taft, and Woodrow Wilson. He was a close personal friend of Frederick Douglass and officiated his wedding. Grimké was intimately connected with some of the most important social activists of the early twentieth century, including both Booker T. Washington and W. E. B. Du Bois, as well as abolitionists like William Lloyd Garrison. He was a longtime trustee of Howard University. He was looked to as the de facto leader of African American Presbyterians, and he regularly was invited to speak at a host of institutions. The historical neglect of such an influential and significant pastor and theologian tells us more than a little about how church history in America has been recorded.

But while it is important for history's sake to remember Grimké properly, it is important for *our* sake to pay attention to his voice because he both *taught* and *embodied* truths that are both *crucial to the ministry of the gospel* and *relevant to our own cultural moment*. Grimké captured these truths well in a letter he wrote to the alumni of Princeton Theological Seminary toward the end of his ministry in 1918:

> During these forty years two things I have tried to do with all my might: (1) To preach the gospel of the grace of God, to get men to see their need of a savior, and to accept of Jesus Christ as the way, the truth, the life. If I had to live my life over again I would still choose the ministry, I could not be satisfied in any other calling. (2) I have sought with all my might to fight race prejudice, because I believe it is utterly un-Christian, and that it is doing almost more than anything else to curse our own land and country and the world at large. Christianity, in its teachings, and in the spirit of its founder, stands for the brotherhood of man, calls us to do by others as we would be done by, to love our neighbor as ourselves.[31]

With characteristic passion and clarity, this letter points to perhaps one of the most significant aspects of Grimké's approach to the Christian life. He made careful distinctions, but he did not divide the Christian life. He distinguished between preaching the gospel and fighting race prejudice, but he did not separate the two. He distinguished sacred from secular knowledge, vocations, and issues, but he did not oppose them. He valued both the individual and the corporate aspects of Christian life and piety. He saw the importance of Christian work in the church, in society, and in the state, but he did not confuse or collapse the different spheres. Perhaps

---

[31] Grimké to the class of 1878 of Princeton Theological Seminary, April 27, 1918.

most importantly, when it came to racial issues, he was one of the most radical critics of racism and the insidious White supremacy that infected the church as it did the nation of his day, *and* he relentlessly encouraged the cultural development of his Black brothers and sisters. He believed in racial pride and solidarity, and also racial humility. He called racists to repent, and he willingly offered forgiveness and reconciliation. This book explores the complexities and nuances of Francis Grimké's both–and approach to the Christian life.

Holistic Christian Life: Vital Christianity

Thus, this book is organized according to the basic spheres of the Christian life. The following introductory chapter navigates the contours of Grimké's careful emphasis on the role of God's law and God's gospel in shaping believers for Christian living. Part 1 then investigates key themes related to the individual Christian life. Part 2 in turn surveys Grimké's emphasis on the role of the Christian family. Next, part 3 wrestles with the mission of the Christian church and the importance of the body of Christ. Then part 4 considers Grimké's nuanced vision of the public life of the believer, giving particular attention to the role of the state and the relationship between faith and politics. The book concludes with reflections on the practical benefits of a more well-rounded historical understanding of the development and shape of contemporary Christianity.

A healthy Christian life pays close attention to each of these spheres in order to live for God's glory. Grimké referred to this holistic vision of the Christian life as "Vital Christianity."

> Vital Christianity is Christianity that controls the life, that makes its influence felt in all that we do or undertake to do. It stands over against a dead Christianity, a Christianity that has little or no influence over us. And, unfortunately, that is the kind of Christianity that most of us possess.
>
> The thought[s] of God and of his revealed will for our government have little or no influence over even the great majority of professing Christians. Such a Christianity is absolutely of no value to us or to any one. The great need of the world today is vital Christianity. Christianity that puts God in the forefront, and keeps Him there, a Christianity that

reflects the sentiment, "Not my will, but Thine be done." A Christianity like that would work wonders in us and in the world.

For such a Christianity, let us pray, and pray earnestly. Without it things will simply go on from bad to worse.[32]

Amen! Let us consider more deeply what such "Vital Christianity" looks like through the life and lessons of Francis Grimké.

---

[32] Francis J. Grimké, "Vital Christianity" (undated), box 40-10, folder 508, Francis J. Grimké Papers, Howard University Library, 1–2.

CHAPTER 2

LAW, GOSPEL, AND THE WHOLE COUNSEL OF GOD

When it comes to the central themes of Francis Grimké's life and ministry, his emphasis on preaching *both* the law and the gospel stands out as one of the most important.

The Gospel of God as Humanity's Greatest Need

Regarding the gospel, he expressed his concern that "much is being said about what is necessary on the part of religion or the church to meet the demands of this modern scientific age."[1] Grimké's response emphasized that even if the world had changed, the central need of humanity had not, for "the great need . . . in this age is the same as it has ever been, the need of salvation, of being saved from the guilt and power of sin." If humanity's central problem had not changed, neither had the solution to that problem, for "there is only one way of meeting it." That way is the one "set forth in the inspired record, in the Scriptures of the Old and New Testament[s]." To put it in the simplest and most direct terms, the best way to meet humanity's central need is "by preaching the gospel."[2]

Grimké appealed to Paul's language in the New Testament to emphasize that this preaching of the gospel should be carried out in clear and understandable language, "not with enticing words of man's wisdom" but

---

[1] *Works*, 3:452.
[2] *Works*, 3:452.

rather "in demonstration of the Spirit and power" (1 Cor. 2:4). He concluded his point by affirming the full continuity of the needs of the early church with those of his own day. The conditions of the early church "were just as difficult as the present," and therefore the church's need in every age was "to get hold of the truth, as set forth in the Word of God, and fearlessly and faithfully proclaim it." Grimké made these claims about the gospel's centrality forcefully and adamantly. "There is no other way, and it is foolish and futile to think of any other."[3]

Though the preaching of the gospel is what people need more than anything else, Grimké elsewhere wrote that the church of his day was too focused on other concerns, and he lamented that the gospel message of Jesus was either taken for granted or forgotten. "We speak to people very seldom about their soul's salvation; and, when we do, as a general thing, it is done in such a perfunctory way, that It shows that we have no real sense of the seriousness of the task to which we have set ourselves." How could something so important be taken so lightly? Grimké suggested that one answer to this question involves underestimation of the stakes. "We do not speak as if we realized the tremendous issue at stake, the issue of life and death,—death, spiritual and eternal." If those who profess to believe the gospel genuinely realized the true nature of unbelievers' peril apart from the person and work of Christ, then "we would approach them in a very different spirit; and we would not be content to speak to them only once, we would keep after them until they heeded the call."[4] The church does not focus on the good news of the gospel enough, because it does not take the reality of sin and judgment seriously enough.

The Law of God in Both Evangelism and Discipleship

As a result, when Grimké championed the preaching of good news as the answer to humanity's greatest need, he frequently pointed out that it is impossible to preach this gospel without also preaching God's law. Therefore, it is essential for the church to reclaim the importance of preaching not only the good news but also the law of God that will make people appreciate the beauty and significance of that gospel message.

In fact, Grimké sharply criticized the church of his day for failing to appreciate the importance of preaching the whole counsel of God's word and

[3] *Works*, 3:452.
[4] *Works*, 3:420.

for failing to call for repentance as a central aspect of gospel proclamation. In 1916, the General Assembly of the Presbyterian Church hosted an Institute of Evangelism at the New York Avenue Presbyterian Church. After attending that institute, Grimké gave an address in which he expressed these concerns. He noted the ineffectiveness of the "evangelism that is current in this country." He attributed this ineffectiveness to the failure to include "accepting Jesus Christ in the sense of adopting His standard of living," "His principles of conduct," and the demand that all believers make "an earnest and honest effort to conform the character and life to the spirit and teachings of Jesus Christ."[5]

Preaching the "gospel" without preaching the need for repentance and commitment to following Christ in all of life is preaching cheap grace. The result is "men and women who come into the church through these evangelistic efforts" who, "in the great majority of cases, have no more idea or intention of doing what Jesus wants them to do, except qualifiedly, than they have of butting their heads against a stone wall."[6] In the society of his day, preaching cheap grace often was characterized by the failure to preach against the evils of racism. As a result, converts of such evangelism came into the church with a faulty understanding of the implications of the gospel for their lives as Christians. As Grimké put it:

> They come into the church and bring with them all their colorphobia. Their acceptance of Jesus Christ does not change, in the least, their attitude towards the Negro; their prejudice towards him continues just the same as before they made a profession of religion. And, they do not feel, in accepting Jesus Christ, that a change in this regard is necessary; nor does the evangelism that is preached by the white people in this country assume that a change is necessary. It is an evangelism that makes them feel that they can still hold onto their prejudice and yet be good Christians, yet be followers of the Lord Jesus Christ. Evangelism of that kind is of no real value, counts for nothing in the sight of God; evangelism of that kind is an insult to Jesus Christ; accepting Jesus Christ in that way is nothing but sheer hypocrisy—hypocrisy on the part of those who profess to accept, and on the part of those who are content with that kind of acceptance.[7]

---

[5] Francis J. Grimké, "Evangelism and Institutes of Evangelism" (1916), in *Works*, 1:523.
[6] Grimké, "Evangelism and Institutes of Evangelism," 523–24.
[7] Grimké, "Evangelism and Institutes of Evangelism," 523.

Grimké went on to point out that this problem came from the top down, for one of the very people being considered to chair the denominational General Evangelistic Committee had expressed in a private conversation that he did not "care to have anything to do with a colored man" who felt that he was his "social equal."[8] Not only that, but similar racist attitudes were central to the very institutions that prepared pastors for ministry. Though Grimké championed his alma mater, Princeton Theological Seminary, as "not only the oldest, but the greatest of our theological schools," and though he championed J. Ross Stevenson, the seminary's president and moderator of the denomination's General Assembly, as one of the "few strong men" of the denomination willing to "stand up" and protest "against the drawing of the color line in the church," he also had to point out the blatant hypocrisy of the racism that was tolerated and allowed to grow at the seminary. Grimké noted that when he himself had been a student at the seminary forty years previously, he and the other students of color had been allowed to live in the dormitories alongside the White students. Now, however, Black students were not allowed in those dormitories.[9] With this kind of training for ministry, it is no wonder that the church was failing to preach the whole counsel of God in calling people to faith and repentance.[10]

Proper evangelism needs to include a clear call to both repentance and faith. The call for repentance should not ignore the most prevalent sins of the day. A proclamation of the gospel that does not include a rigorous declaration of God's law cannot be expected to produce genuine repentance, and therefore cannot constitute effective evangelism. But Grimké not only offered a critique of poor evangelistic proclamation; he also took the time to carefully describe in positive terms what a proper evangelistic communication of both the law and the gospel entails:

> There is an evangelism that is genuine, an evangelism for which the great Presbyterian Church in the United States of America should stand, but for which it does not stand—an evangelism that means accepting Jesus Christ in reality and not in pretense—an evangelism that carries along

---

[8] Grimké, "Evangelism and Institutes of Evangelism," 525.

[9] Grimké, "Evangelism and Institutes of Evangelism," 525–26.

[10] On a similar note, two years later Grimké wrote a critical response to Billy Sunday's segregated evangelism campaign, taking him to task for his willingness to offer a "vigorous denunciation of many sins," while studiously avoiding the sin of racial prejudice, one of the most controversial issues of the day. Francis J. Grimké, "'Billy' Sunday's Campaign in Washington, DC" (1918), in *Works*, 1:559.

with it brotherhood, that so presents Jesus Christ that [people] see, and see plainly, what is involved in accepting Him.[11]

Failure to preach the law, and especially the selective proclamation of God's law, results in ineffective evangelism and flawed discipleship. Without the preaching of God's law, people are not given the opportunity to see their need for the forgiveness of Jesus. Inviting people to come to Christ without allowing them to count the cost of faith and repentance is not treating them with dignity and respect. It is foolish to expect discipleship and growth in the Christian faith to happen when the full picture of the Christian life is held out of view. Therefore, Grimké was not surprised at the sorry state of the American churches. They merely were reaping what they were sowing. Hiding God's law also meant leaving the good news of the gospel in the shadows. How could people appreciate the beauty of God's forgiveness if they did not know their sin and need for God's grace?

The Law of God as Both "Mirror" and "Guide"

By contrast, Grimké's understanding of gospel ministry was shaped according to his embrace of the trajectory from guilt to grace to gratitude. The good news of the grace of the gospel cannot be appreciated without a healthy understanding of personal guilt. Only those who truly recognize their need for forgiveness can begin to appreciate the depths of God's mercy. Similarly, the necessary response to the good news of grace and forgiveness includes a life of gratitude. Thankfulness for God's work of salvation should lead to the enjoyment of God's ongoing work of sanctification in the life of the believer. Gratitude to God leads to the joyful pursuit of personal holiness.

Therefore, Grimké's trust in the Scriptures led him to focus not only on the importance of the moral law's function as mirror that reveals the sinner's need for Jesus, but also on that law's role as a guide to thankful living. "I believe in the Bible as the Word of God," Grimké wrote, and therefore "the work of the minister mainly is to expound it with a view of developing character of the type set forth in the Scriptures." Citing Paul's exhortation to Timothy to "rightly divide the word" (see 2 Tim. 2:15), Grimké appealed to the Bible for its "great truths" and its "lofty ideals and principles" as "material for building up character of the noblest type." The proclamation

---

[11] Grimké, "Evangelism and Institutes of Evangelism," 524.

and work of the gospel should not only "bring [people] to Christ" but also "develop in them a Christly character." Grimké characterized this joint task of evangelism and discipleship as "the main business of the minister." Speaking of the pastor who fails to carry out this joint task, Grimké did not mince words: "He is a failure, and the sooner he gets out of [ministry], the better."[12] Christian ministry necessarily includes the proclamation of the law as part of the call to faith and repentance, the declaration of the gospel as the grace of God for the forgiveness of sins, and training in righteousness as the proper thankful response to the reception of God's grace. The law by itself leads to judgment, but for those who have experienced God's grace, it is the path of a renewed life.

Grimké also liked to emphasize that faithfulness in the Christian life cannot come without the work of the Holy Spirit. "Human nature left to itself, never can be made conformable to the law of God." In fact, "no amount of education, of human culture can ever make [human nature] to be other than it is, or lift it to the high level required by the character and laws of God." Human beings cannot please God by relying on their natural or unaided capacities. Therefore, "the work of the Spirit cannot be ignored, or minimized, or relegated to a subordinate place. Every step of advance towards the measure of the stature of the fullness of Christ can come only as the Spirit is back of it." The true Christian life ought to be marked by the fruits of good works, but Grimké was quick to emphasize that these works are themselves dependent on the Holy Spirit.[13]

The Law of God in Both Scripture and Nature

Francis Grimké believed that God's special revelation in the Christian Scriptures and God's general revelation imprinted on nature itself are both essential to a healthy view of God and of the Christian life. Grimké's many years of preaching demonstrated not only his devotion to God's word but also his belief in the reliability of biblical commands. Given his commitment to the whole counsel of God, it is not surprising to see him affirming and defending the usefulness of the Ten Commandments and other famous biblical passages as summaries and expositions of the path for Christian living. But in addition to the law of God revealed in the Scriptures, Grimké frequently appealed to the "law of nature" as equally revealed by God and

---

12 *Works*, 3:443.
13 *Works*, 3:431.

binding on all human beings. Grimké believed that all truth belongs to God and commands the conscience, whether that truth is revealed in the Christian Scriptures or in nature.

Concerning God's law revealed in the Scriptures, Grimké placed a particular emphasis on the second table of the Ten Commandments. In March of 1903 he delivered an address titled "The Things of Paramount Importance in the Development of the Negro Race." Grimké lamented that the advice being given to his Black congregants by many of their contemporaries focused predominantly on wealth and property. He acknowledged the importance of these material concerns and affirmed that it was right to value and pursue them. He even cited detailed statistics on the current state of African American wealth and property ownership in America. Yet, having demonstrated his intimate familiarity with the latest research regarding the standing of his people, Grimké went on to declare that when we encounter the problems of life, whether as individuals or as a particular race, "there is no book to which we can go with greater certainty of being properly directed, than the Word of God." Material development is important, but moral development even more so. Grimké went on to quote a whole host of Scripture passages to demonstrate this point, and he brought home his message by appealing to the second half of the Ten Commandments, on loving one's neighbor. The strongest and best social activism would focus on "rooting and grounding" people in the great principles of honoring parents and refusing to kill, commit adultery, steal, bear false witness, or covet. Material development without this moral development could not bring true success.[14]

At the same time, though he frequently affirmed the central importance of the special revelation of God in the Scriptures—in particular, the Ten Commandments—for gaining moral knowledge, Grimké also made frequent impassioned appeals to God's natural law. On the need to condemn racism and defend equal rights, Grimké expected that all people, Christians in particular, should recognize the laws imprinted on the human conscience and revealed in the natural order itself.

In 1906, a race riot broke out in Atlanta after local newspapers sensationalized accusations of sexual assault of White victims by alleged Black perpetrators. While the case itself was complicated, the outcome of the riots

---

[14] Francis J. Grimké, "The Things of Paramount Importance in the Development of the Negro Race" (1903), in *Works*, 1:379–80, 381, 385.

was not in doubt. Several days of violence left more than twenty African Americans dead. Only two White people were reported to have died, and one of those suffered a heart attack upon witnessing the violence.[15] Given the opportunity to address the riots, Grimké lamented the sexual assault of a White woman. He expressed sympathy for the sadness and anger felt by White family members and neighbors. He then proceeded to condemn the unlawful, violent riots and to lament the spirit of retribution that led to the grievous murders of innocent Black people by the White rioters.

After carefully identifying the social and moral issues at stake, Grimké closed his address by offering three pieces of advice. He encouraged the Black people of Atlanta and their supporters around the country not to become discouraged, to be discreet and cautious in their words and deeds, and finally to be prepared to defend themselves if necessary. In this temporal world, the protection of life sometimes requires the use of force. If public authorities could not be trusted to protect the lives of Black people, then Black people were justified in taking up arms to defend themselves. With very carefully chosen words, Grimké emphasized a duty of self-defense that was "in harmony with the dictates of nature, and of morality, and of religion."[16] For Grimké, "the dictates of nature" were a distinct fountain of moral knowledge revealed by God to all people. This fountain was in "harmony" with the Scriptures but not identical with them.

These principles also frequently led Grimké to base his public arguments upon natural law rather than Scripture. If natural law and Scripture were harmonious with one another and equally given by God, then the real question was which source of divine revelation would be more convincing to a particular audience. For example, in 1909 Grimké gave an address titled "Equality of Rights for All Citizens, Black and White Alike." He dealt extensively with the differences between the founding principles of the United States, on the one hand, and the Southern Confederacy, on the other. Quoting extensively from Alexander Stephens, the vice president of the Confederacy, Grimké contrasted the views of the founders and authors of the Constitution of the United States with Stephens's statement that the "cornerstone" of the Confederate government "rests upon the great

---

[15] David Fort Godshalk, *Veiled Visions: The 1906 Atlanta Race Riot and the Reshaping of American Race Relations* (Chapel Hill: University of North Carolina Press, 2006), 13–34.

[16] Francis J. Grimké, "The Atlanta Riot" (1906), in *Works*, 1:412, 414–15, 417. See Malcolm Foley, "'The Only Way to Stop a Mob': Francis Grimké's Case for Lynching Resistance," in *Every Leaf, Line, and Letter: Evangelicals and the Bible from the 1730s to the Present*, ed. Timothy Larsen (Downers Grove, IL: InterVarsity Press, 2021), 196–217.

truth that the Negro is not equal to the white man." Grimké argued that Stephens's racist ideas were contrary to the "laws of nature" even in the eyes of figures like Thomas Jefferson.[17] Of course, Grimké believed that racist ideas also were contrary to the Scriptures, but here an appeal to natural law was equally valid and rhetorically more effective.

Natural law was useful not only for making public arguments; Grimké also thought it useful in defending the Christian faith and shaping personal ethics. "The works of nature" and the "operations of nature's laws" had an apologetic use in defending belief in God, for "no one can study" these laws of nature "without realizing that some wonderful being or entity is back of it all."[18] God is revealed in nature itself. Therefore, drawing attention to the beauty and workings of nature is a good way to encourage people to consider the reality of a Creator God. In addition to this apologetic use, the natural law also can serve as a source of moral reflection. Grimké frequently relied on the natural law to infer a moral right and duty of self-protection. Speaking in 1919 at a special Thanksgiving service in Washington, DC, he affirmed that this right to self-protection is "inherent in every human being," is "God-given," and is a "right to be exercised when there is no other way of escaping the danger which threatens."[19] Therefore, it is possible to derive ethical principles by considering God's law revealed in nature.

The Gospel of God Considered Broadly and Narrowly

Clearly Francis Grimké possessed a nuanced approach to the law of God. The moral law of God is essential to evangelism because it serves as a mirror to help people see their sin and need for a Savior in Jesus Christ. God's moral law also is essential to discipleship because it serves as a guide to help people know how to live as Christians. Aspects of this moral law are revealed in both Scripture and nature. Because of this twofold revelation, Grimké could rely on the Bible to make moral arguments while, at other times, finding it useful to appeal to God's law revealed in nature through the human conscience. In many ways his profound skills as a public theologian depended on these categories for God's law.

His careful and sophisticated approach to God's law also enabled him to be very precise about the relationship between the law and the gospel.

---

17 Francis J. Grimké, "Equality of Rights for All Citizens, Black and White Alike" (1909), in *Works*, 1:424.
18 Francis J. Grimké, "A Special Christmas Message" (1918), in *Works*, 1:578–79.
19 Francis J. Grimké, "The Race Problem as It Respects the Colored People and the Christian Church, in the Light of the Developments of the Last Year" (1919), in *Works*, 1:607.

The law of God is inseparable from the gospel, and yet Grimké frequently emphasized—as noted above—that the good news of Jesus Christ is humanity's greatest need. Because the law and the gospel are inseparable, there is a broad sense of the gospel in which the law and the gospel are included together. At the same time, because the law by itself is incapable of bringing a person into a saving relationship with the Father through the work of Jesus, there is another, more narrow sense in which the gospel needs to be carefully distinguished from the law. Both senses were extremely important to Grimké's public teaching ministry.

Concerning the broad sense of the gospel—which involves the proclamation of God's legal demands, including love for neighbor—one of the most powerful illustrations is an address Grimké gave in 1899 regarding the best strategy for alleviating racial tensions in the southern states. He declared that "the gospel that teaches the fatherhood of God, the brotherhood of man, the spirit of sympathy, of love, of the strong bearing the infirmities of the weak, of the more fortunate coming to the help of the less fortunate, cannot be faithfully preached in the South without being blessed of God." Grimké acknowledged that such a gospel "may not be popular at first." Nevertheless, he continued, "It is bound sooner or later to triumph, if persisted in," because "God has promised that his word shall not return unto him void." Grimké expressed confidence in God's ability to bring true change through the preaching of the gospel in this broad sense that included a declaration of God's law. "I have the greatest faith in the efficacy of God's truth to win its way and bear down all opposition, if it is faithfully presented," he stated.[20]

Here it is clear that for Grimké there is a sense in which the gospel includes the command to love one's neighbor as oneself. In fact, he attributed the sorry state of social affairs to the refusal to receive this "gospel of love." In so doing, he offered a stinging indictment of the hypocritical "gospel of hate" that was believed and proclaimed in the White church:

> Nineteen hundred years have rolled away since this glorious gospel of good will broke upon the world; and yet we are still preaching the gospel of hate, and still living it. If you have any doubt of it, all you have got to do is to go out on these streets, get on the street cars, go to any of the theaters, any of the restaurants, go to any even of the white so-called Christian

---

[20] Francis J. Grimké, "The Remedy for the Present Strained Relations between the Races in the South" (1899), in *Works*, 1:317–33.

churches, if you want to see what kind of gospel white America has been educated on; what kind of gospel it believes in. You will be confronted everywhere with anything but a kindly, brotherly, loving spirit. You will be told as plainly as possible by look, gesture, act that your presence is not wanted, that you are not regarded with favor. It is in the air; you feel it wherever you go,—wherever you come in contact with the white man with very rare exceptions. The gospel of hate, the gospel of race hatred, is the gospel that is being most strenuously preached,—in the churches, in the homes, in the places of business, in public conveyances. In one form or another the accursed business of sowing that kind of seed is steadily going on, without abatement, without interruption, day in and day out, week in and week out, month in and month out, year in and year out.[21]

This "gospel" of race prejudice was a false gospel that needed to be replaced with the unifying gospel of Jesus Christ. The broad sense of the true gospel includes the good news of Jesus's person and work as well as the proclamation of the moral law of God.[22]

At the same time, Francis Grimké relentlessly sought to protect the narrow sense of the gospel of God, which is the preaching of the person and work of Christ alone for salvation. Grimké referred to this message of Jesus as the "pure, unadulterated Gospel." It can be believed with confidence because of the divine "inspiration of the Scriptures," which led to their "infallibility" and "sufficiency as a rule of faith and practice." The preaching of the gospel includes the "incarnation" of Jesus, his "Virgin Birth or supernatural origin," "the efficacy of His atoning sacrifice as an offering for our sin," his "resurrection from the dead," and his "miracles." Saving faith and repentance for sins depend on the work of God through this "pure, unadulterated Gospel."[23] In fact, as Grimké elsewhere preached, "Jesus Christ came into the world to preach just that gospel to every poor wandering, sin-cursed child of God" in order to "set in operation the agencies" of recovery for sinners.[24]

For Grimké, the proclamation of God's word is the "supreme" and "only" mission of the pulpit. Therefore, it is necessary for Jesus Christ to be kept "steadily to the front" and "spiritual things ever in the ascendancy." The

21 Grimké, "A Special Christmas Message," 586.
22 This true gospel of Jesus Christ clearly had social implications, and the question of whether this made Grimké a preacher of "the social gospel" will be considered below.
23 Francis J. Grimké, "Anniversary Address," delivered on the seventy-fifth anniversary of the Fifteenth Street Presbyterian Church, Washington, DC, November 19, 1916, in *Works*, 1:547–48.
24 Francis J. Grimké, "Sermon on Luke 15:3–4, 8" (1923), in *Works*, 2:275.

"people need to know not what we think, what we have to say," as Grimké put it, "but what God thinks, what He has to say."[25] The preaching and winning of people to Christ is the minster's "only business." All other things are "secondary or subsidiary." For Grimké, the "Christian ministry is no place for one who does not see that his supreme mission is to call [people] to repentance and faith." He cited the nature of God's kingdom in support of this conviction, for the "kingdom of God, in seeking the salvation of [people], must be first" with the minister of the gospel, "and must be kept first, high above every other interest."[26] When it came to identifying the "reason why so little is being done" and why "so little zeal is shown in trying to reach" people with the "gospel message," Grimké cited ignorance of "the reality of sin" and ignorance of "the fact" that salvation comes "through Christ alone." Therefore "to preach the gospel" is both a "great responsibility" and a "great privilege."[27]

Clearly, the preaching of the gospel in this narrow sense, which entails the message about Jesus for the salvation of sinners, was the center of Grimké's ministry. As he wrote in his meditations, "What the world needs is the Gospel of the grace of God in Christ Jesus; and that Gospel preached by men who believe it, and who know from personal experience that it has power to save."[28] The great need of humanity is the "need of salvation, of being saved from the guilt and power of sin." According to Grimké, there is "only one way of meeting" this great need. That is "preaching the gospel." Not only is there "no other way," but it is "foolish and futile to think of any other."[29]

The Law and the Gospel: Distinguishable but Inseparable

In many ways, the remainder of this book consists of an exposition of the implications of the principles identified in this chapter.

First, the gospel of God is humanity's greatest need, and the moral law of God is essential to bring people to belief in that gospel and to help believers in God grow in the Christian life. In other words, God's moral law functions as both the mirror that enables human beings to see the reality of their sin and need for a Savior and a guide for following Jesus as Lord.

---

25 *Works*, 3:350.
26 *Works*, 3:420.
27 *Works*, 3:559–60.
28 *Works*, 3:26.
29 *Works*, 3:452.

Second, this moral law is revealed both in the Scriptures and in nature and nature's laws. The Scriptures alone proclaim the solution to sin and brokenness in the world, but the creation itself powerfully declares God's truth, beauty, and way.

Third, because of the law's inseparability from the gospel, both in bringing people to faith and helping them grow in faith, it is possible to speak of the gospel in a broad sense and a narrow sense. The broad sense includes the proclamation of all God's word—law and gospel—and the narrower sense refers specifically to the person and work of Jesus to save fallen sinners. While the rest of this book will explore the implications of these principles in Francis Grimké's teaching and practice regarding the individual, family, church, and society, a few preliminary observations are worth making here.

First, Francis Grimké clearly distinguished between spiritual things and things he considered natural or material. When it came to conversations about race, he lamented that not enough attention was given to spiritual concerns, and that too much attention was given to material concerns. Contrary to this tendency, as he put it, "In the management of a church spiritual things should always be kept in ascendancy, should never be subordinated to material things."[30] Clearly, in light of the observations above regarding the importance of following God's law and love for neighbor, Grimké thought that material concerns were important and worthy. More will be said on this in a moment. At the same time, it is essential to observe that Grimké distinguished between the material and the spiritual, that he emphasized the importance of the spiritual in general, and that he particularly emphasized the spiritual nature of the church and its ministry.

Second and notwithstanding, Grimké also expressed and practiced a deep appreciation for the material aspects of the created order. Most obviously, he worked, wrote, and spoke tirelessly for the material advancement of Black people in America. Perhaps less famously but also significantly, his material concerns transcended moral issues and led to his deep appreciation for the arts, including the artistic expressions of non-Christians. At the personal level, Francis wrote of the importance of cultivating "the habit of reading good books," and Francis and Charlotte enjoyed reading poetry together, including Tennyson, Longfellow, Whittier, and Lowell.[31] More

---

30 *Works*, 3:290.
31 *Works*, 3:547; Henry Justin Ferry, "Francis James Grimké: Portrait of a Black Puritan" (PhD diss., Yale University, 1970), 116–17.

publicly, for more than thirty years during the winter months, the Grimkés hosted an "Art Club" in their home on Friday evenings for family members and friends. Together they explored painting, literature, architecture, and sculpture. On Sunday evenings they turned their attention to music, focusing on classical music during the first portion of the evening and then on hymns later. After enjoying renditions of Chopin, Beethoven, and Mendelssohn, the evenings typically closed with Francis's favorite hymn, "Lead, Kindly Light."[32] Thus, while he clearly distinguished between what he took to be spiritual concerns and what he variously referred to as "natural," "material," or "secular," Francis Grimké in no way rejected the engagement with the world. In fact, he enjoyed and advocated for temporal morality and temporal beauty. Spiritual concerns were of ultimate importance, but this did not mean that material concerns were insignificant.

Third, and drawing from these two observations, by now it should be clear that Francis Grimké rejected a "social gospel" that focused exclusively on material concerns. It should also be clear that he avoided separating the sacred from the secular in the manner of the fundamentalists of his day. His rejection of the social gospel did not lead him to neglect the social obligations of God's law. The chapters that follow will demonstrate that he willingly partnered not only with advocates of the social gospel but also with social activists who questioned and even rejected the Christian faith. This partnership was not haphazard, and it required a careful weighing of the costs and benefits, which will be explored further in the pages that follow. Neither did his rejection of the social gospel lead him to reject the true teachings among social gospel advocates. Francis Grimké willingly used their language when it was true. The fatherhood of God and the brotherhood of man were worthy concepts that did not need to be rejected but could be reclaimed and properly defined. Where it was wrong, the social gospel should be rejected. Where it was right, those particular elements should be affirmed. Where it was ambiguous, the questions should be clarified in biblical terms that affirmed the "pure, unadulterated Gospel," on the one hand, and the social obligations of the gospel (broadly considered), on the other.

Fourth, Francis Grimké recognized that the double standard evidenced by fundamentalist avoidance of select social issues represented a depar-

---

[32] Ferry, "Francis James Grimké," 116–19.

ture from biblical Christianity.[33] For Grimké, biblical Christianity certainly privileges the eternal and spiritual, but it also enjoins upon Christians not only the temporal obligations of God's law but also the enjoyment of God's good creation. Sacred matters are ultimate, but the souls of Christians are inseparable from the bodies of Christians. These bodies are to be used to enjoy God through love of neighbor and love of God's world.

Obviously, these four themes (the distinction between sacred and secular, the appreciation for the secular accompanied by a privileging of the sacred, the rejection of the social gospel's loss of the sacred, and the rejection of fundamentalism's loss of the secular) are complex and worthy of deeper exploration. The following chapters seek to provide just that, focusing in turn upon Francis Grimké's treatment of the individual, the family, the church, and society.

[33] George Marsden, *Fundamentalism and American Culture*, 2nd ed. (New York: Oxford University Press: 2006), 124–40, 199–257; Mark Sidwell, "Francis Grimké and the Value and Limits of Carter Woodson's Model of the Progressive Black Pastor," *Fides et Historia* 32, no. 1 (2000): 99–117.

PART I

THE INDIVIDUAL

Christian Character and Piety

CHAPTER 3

PERSONAL IDENTITY, PROPER RESPECT, AND RIGHTEOUS DISCONTENT

Francis Grimké's understanding of personal identity drew deeply from his conviction that all human beings are created in the image of God and therefore worthy of equal honor and respect. The beauty of God's image in all humanity was one of the most frequent themes in both his public writings and his personal reflections. At the same time, he also saw the benefits of familial and ethnic ties. Such relationships, he argued, also could contribute positively to a personal sense of self.

In fact, Grimké taught that the formation of a healthy self-concept demands that people hold on simultaneously to both the universal and the particular aspects of their identity. Self-respect and contentment depend upon a strong sense of self shaped by a commitment to the human race as a whole and also working for the good of one's ethnic and familial community. The two must go together. While Grimké believed that particular obligations to family and community hold a special place, especially for the oppressed, he also refused to place these obligations in tension with more universal obligations. Throughout his life and ministry, he remained committed even to the nation that oppressed him and the denomination that marginalized him. Yet these same commitments crucially enabled the kind of righteous discontentment that could fuel the perseverance necessary to

effect long-term social change in the face of otherwise discouraging circumstances. As this part of the book considers Grimké's understanding of
the individual Christian's identity and growth, this chapter focuses on how
Grimké developed a vigorous notion of personal identity that embraced
both universal and communal relationships, which, in turn, enabled him
to pursue a healthy form of social protest.

God's Image

The year 1899 in many ways marked the beginning of a period of unprec-
edented prosperity and influence for the United States on the global stage.
The US Senate ratified the Treaty of Paris in February of that year, which
brought a formal end to the Spanish-American War. Yet, just as the Black
soldiers were clipped out of photographs in the press stories depicting
Teddy Roosevelt's victory, Grimké worried that the "strained relations" between the races in the South reflected unacceptable attitudes on the part of
White people toward Black people.[1] In June of that year he gave an address
in which he appealed to the image of God as the foundation for understanding human identity.[2]

In that address, Grimké lamented that southerners viewed Black people as their inferiors, and he called upon people to bring their views in line
with the teaching of Scripture. As he put it, "According to this book, which
we receive as the word of God, the only infallible rule of faith and practice,
God 'hath made of one blood all nations of men' [Acts 17:26]." All people
share the same blood, and this reality reflects the teaching of Genesis that
God created all human beings in his image. Therefore, there "isn't a hint or
suggestion" of, or even anything that could be "twisted" into an argument
for, the superiority of one race over another. Grimké rejected the attempt
of southern Whites to make such an argument in "dealing with the race
question."[3]

After laying this foundation, he proceeded to connect the image of God
to both the law and the gospel. If all people were created in God's image,
then the same "moral standard" applies to all races. The Ten Command-

---

[1] Amy Kaplan, "Black and Blue on San Juan Hill," in *Cultures of United States Imperialism*, ed. Amy Kaplan
and Donald E. Pease (Durham, NC: Duke University Press, 1994), 219–36. For the history of the "Buffalo
Soldiers," see Bruce A. Galsrud, ed., *Brothers to the Buffalo Soldiers: Perspectives on the African American
Militia and Volunteers, 1865–1917* (Columbia, MO: University of Missouri Press, 2011).
[2] Francis J. Grimké, "The Remedy for the Present Strained Relations between the Races in the South"
(1899), in *Works*, 1:317–33.
[3] Grimké, "The Remedy for the Present Strained Relations," 319, 320.

ments, the Sermon on the Mount, and Paul's teaching on the centrality of love in 1 Corinthians 13 apply equally to all. Even more importantly, the gospel "plan of salvation" is the same for all of God's people. People of "all races stand upon precisely the same footing." All are "invited," and, similarly, all are "equally welcomed." The apostles were directed to disciple all nations. Citing Galatians 3:28, Grimké drew the obvious conclusion that "the same gospel is to be preached to all." Drawing from the parable of the good Samaritan, he pointed out that if both the same moral standards and the same gospel message are for all people, then it is not enough for "white men to treat white men as they would like to be treated" or "black men to treat black men as they would like to be treated." As those created in God's image, all people stand in relation to all other people by the same rules, and all people stand in desperate need of the same grace.[4]

Grimké applied this twofold biblical affirmation of the equality of all people with reference to law and gospel to both temporal governance and evangelism. Regarding temporal concerns, he pointed out that the Declaration of Independence of the United States mirrored the biblical teaching that all people "are created equal" and therefore "are endowed by their Creator with certain inalienable rights [*sic*]." The US Constitution also reflected these same principles in guaranteeing to all its citizens the right to vote. These documents echoed the biblical teaching, as Grimké put it, that "civil and political rights" should be shared equally by members of all races. The failures of the United States and of White southerners were "contrary to the Word of God" and contrary to the "expressed provisions and declarations of the Constitution."[5]

This multifaceted temporal failure required multifaceted solutions, and one of the most important remedies involved education that needed to be "social, political, moral, and religious."[6] Here it is important to emphasize that this temporal concern needed to be addressed both politically and religiously. Grimké carefully distinguished these facets, but he also refused to separate them. He observed that though editors and teachers certainly had a role to play, "ministers especially" possessed a crucial role as they proclaimed God's moral law. Ministers, of all people, were aware that racial failures in society and the mistreatment of Black people in the South were "not in harmony with the letter or spirit" of God's word. Therefore, Grimké

---

4 Grimké, "The Remedy for the Present Strained Relations," 320–22.
5 Grimké, "The Remedy for the Present Strained Relations," 322–23.
6 Grimké, "The Remedy for the Present Strained Relations," 324.

wrote, "It is their duty to bring the teaching of that Word to bear upon present conditions, however unpopular it may be to do so." Having treated the roles of ministers, he then went on to describe the roles of teachers and editors, observing the needed effect of these three forces working together.[7]

It also is important to emphasize that the role belonged to all Christians as members of the church and not just to Christian ministers. In addition to "ministers, and elders, and deacons," "members" also possessed a duty to model these principles as an example for others. The "Ten Commandments" and the "Sermon on the Mount" may be solutions for the "race problem," but they "must have in back of them a living church—a church made up of men and women who are willing to take them up, and put them on their hearts, and live them out."[8] The duty belonged to all the members of the church in their various roles, and therefore Grimké could say that if the situation in the South failed to improve, the failure would largely belong to the church.[9]

In addition to these temporal concerns, which belonged to believers and to unbelievers alike, and which should be addressed through the preaching of God's moral law by church leaders and through the living example of church members, Grimké also applied the doctrine of God's image to more properly spiritual concerns, including evangelism. In 1916, he gave a provocative address, subsequently printed and distributed in the form of a tract, sensitive to the fact that "it is now almost impossible to get a matter like this into the [mainstream] religious press."[10] Proper evangelism required the whole preaching of the law and the gospel. It also needed direction—namely, the renewal of the person evangelized. Those created in God's image needed the salvation of Jesus to be "renewed after the image of Him that created" them.[11]

The failure to see all people as God's image bearers and the failure to pursue the renewal of all people in God's image through evangelism were nothing less than fatal to work of evangelism in general and the ministry of the Institute for Evangelism in particular. Such failures contributed to

[7] Grimké, "The Remedy for the Present Strained Relations," 328.
[8] Grimké, "The Remedy for the Present Strained Relations," 328. Grimké's explicit inclusion of women with men is notable, especially because this talk came twenty years prior to the passing of the Nineteenth Amendment to the Constitution of the United States, which gave women the right to vote.
[9] Grimké, "The Remedy for the Present Strained Relations," 331.
[10] Francis J. Grimké, "Evangelism and the Institutes of Evangelism" (1916), in Works, 1:523–28; his reasons for printing the address as a tract appear on p. 527. For more on the context of this address, see chap. 2.
[11] Grimké, "Evangelism and the Institutes of Evangelism," 524.

a form of evangelism that was not just flawed but a hypocritical reproduction of false religion. As Grimké preached against such false evangelism, the doctrine of the image of God shaped his conception of the relationship between law and the gospel and its application to both temporal and spiritual concerns.

Narrowing the picture, Grimké also focused his doctrine of the image of God more particularly on other important implications. In his well-known 1910 address "Christianity and Race Prejudice," he emphasized the universally shared identity of all human beings. God created all humans in his image, and in that sense all people were created by the same Father. So also, in that same sense, all human beings are siblings. Though he carefully taught the unique relationship of brothers and sisters in Christ, Grimké was comfortable affirming the language of the universal "Fatherhood of God" (as the Creator of all) and the correlated "brotherhood of man." He put it quite bluntly, in fact, stating, "Literally this is true—men are brothers—the human race is one." Furthermore, this is not merely an abstract principle but one for daily life. Not only should all people *believe* that they are blood brothers, but they should also "feel toward each other as brothers" and "treat each other as brothers." In this regard, Grimké freely admitted his own shortcomings: "I used to speak of the cracker element of the South" as "poor white trash," he admitted, "but I never do it any more."[12]

In addition to the universal, natural bonds that all human beings should recognize, considering their creation in the image of God, Grimké emphasized another sense in which Christians of all races constitute one family. Referring to Ephesians 4:4–6, Colossians 3:11, and 1 Corinthians 12:12–13, he stressed that Christians have been baptized into one Lord, one faith, and one baptism. These realities mean that unity in the family of Christ supersedes other national, ethnic, and class distinctions. The family of Christ shares the same Holy Spirit and therefore constitutes one united body. As a result, Christians share a twofold unity. First, as human beings

---

12 Francis J. Grimké, "Christianity and Race Prejudice" (1910), in *Works*, 1:448. The use of the word "cracker" by Black people as a racial epithet to describe White people began in the 1800s and was common by the end of the century, certainly well before Grimké delivered this address in 1910. The word also carried class connotations as a reference to poor White people, though the racial connotation gradually became more predominant. It is not clear to what extent Grimké had in mind poverty in addition to race. But his awareness that the term carried negative, racialized connotations is clear, as is his regret for using the word. For the developing sense of the word, see Dana Ste. Claire, *The Cracker Culture in Florida History* (Gainsville: University Press of Florida, 2006), and especially John Solomon Otto, "Cracker: The History of a Southeastern, Ethnic, Economic, and Racial Epithet," *Names: A Journal of Onomastics* 35, no. 1 (1987): 28–39.

their family includes all other human beings. Second, as believers in Christ their family includes all other Christians.

It is crucial to pay close attention to Grimké's twofold understanding of "the Fatherhood of God" and the "brotherhood of man." Whereas some other proponents of the social aspects of the gospel collapsed these two senses, Grimké's approach differed sharply from such modernist approaches. For Grimké, unlike the modernists, the image of God shared by all humanity and the special relation shared by Christians are both important and yet always distinguishable. While all human beings are one family according to the first principle, Christians possess an even greater unity with their fellow believers resulting from union with Christ and their shared possession of the Holy Spirit. Therefore, the failure of self-professing White Christians to embrace their Black brothers and sisters was a double failure, and because of this it was even more lamentable.[13]

Grimké also notably relied on the "organic" language so popular in that era, and he connected it with biblical teaching to reject race prejudice and separation. Unity in Christ and the shared possession of the Holy Spirit constitute believers as "one organism."[14] Relying on the imagery of the vine and the branches in John 15, he emphasized that believers in Christ "are all branches of the true vine," which therefore share the "same life-force." In other words, "unity with Christ" is inseparable from "unity with one another." As a result, the American tendency to allow race to lead to "separate churches and separate pews, and separate presbyteries, and separate conferences, and separate cemeteries, and separate every thing" was an affront to the unifying work of Christ and the shared possession of the Holy Spirit. Christian unity included "all races and colors and nationalities," and Grimké was adamant that this organic unity ought to be expressed in the regular institutional life of the body of Christ.[15]

Francis Grimké made the biblical teaching of the shared possession of the image of God central to his teaching on personal identity. All human beings created in God's image are worthy of dignity and respect. Believers in Christ not only share this image with all human beings, but as those redeemed in Christ they possess an additional unity that demands respect. The failure of the American church, and White Christians in particular, to

13 Grimké, "Christianity and Race Prejudice," 450.
14 Grimké, "Christianity and Race Prejudice," 452.
15 Grimké, "Christianity and Race Prejudice," 452–53.

celebrate and pursue the unity clearly taught by Jesus and all the Scriptures was legitimate grounds for righteous discontent.

Communal Identity

At the same time, Grimké's emphasis on the implications of the universal human possession of God's image did not lead him to ignore the special bonds of families and other communities. In fact, he deemed it appropriate to have a special concern for one's family and a special pride in one's communal identity. Such bonds were crucial, and especially so for minority groups seeking resilience in the face of persecution and oppression. As Grimké responded to the racially motivated violence of the early twentieth century, he encouraged a strong sense of cultural identity and community, and he frequently looked to honorable examples of prominent figures, especially Frederick Douglass, to make his case.

The racial violence in America in the early years of the twentieth century was one of the motivating factors that led Grimké to develop a positive understanding of communal racial identity. As racially motivated riots broke out in American urban centers during these years, Grimké frequently addressed his congregation, took opportunities to speak, and published addresses that helped Black Christians to process and respond to these events. The events of the "Red Summer" of 1919, and especially the violence in Washington, DC, in July of that year, brought the pain close to home. That summer a Black man was held for questioning regarding the sexual assault of a White woman. Later that night, a White mob roamed the streets of Washington assaulting and beating Black passersby at random. The lack of police response to this violence allowed it to escalate, and over four days nearly forty people were killed or sustained wounds that led to their deaths in the days that followed.[16]

This tragedy in the nation's capital sadly reflected a long-developing trend. The violence rose to a crescendo during that summer of 1919, but Grimké addressed similar circumstances regularly over the years of his ministry. The riots in Atlanta in September 1906 motivated one of his most poignant addresses. His emotional appeal lamented the tendency of White

---

[16] David F. Krugler, *1919: The Year of Racial Violence: How African Americans Fought Back* (New York: Cambridge University Press, 2015), 66–98; Gregory Mixon, *The Atlanta Riot: Race, Class, and Violence in a New South City* (Gainesville: University Press of Florida, 2004); David Fort Godshalk, *Veiled Visions: The 1906 Atlanta Race Riot and the Reshaping of American Race Relations* (Chapel Hill: University of North Carolina Press, 2006).

people to stereotype the Black community by associating all Black people with the criminal activity of isolated individuals. Not only was this tendency racist; it contributed to the violence. It also was hypocritical. White people did not associate the actions of White criminals with all Whites, but they did generalize the actions of their racial "others." Grimké pointed out that all people have the right to be judged on the basis of their own actions rather than the actions of others.[17] Racial stereotyping was both a symptom and a cause of race prejudice. This race prejudice, in turn, led to feelings of hostility, bad judgments, the prideful pursuit of self-superiority, and insensitivity to the needs of others. Left unchecked, these negative attitudes toward other communities led to discrimination, the restriction of rights, bitterness, and hatred.[18]

And so it was that Grimké emphasized the importance of a healthy and positive sense of communal identity, pointing to Frederick Douglass as a model and source of such community pride. As Grimké put it, "When we remember that he was identified with us, that he was a member of our race, our hearts should swell with pride as we think of him." Grimké also appealed to Douglass's example as a tireless advocate and servant of his people. He both was "one of us," said Grimké, and "loved us with a most passionate devotion." Out of this devotion Douglass "consecrated himself with all of his splendid powers to the work of uplifting us, and of creating a public sentiment in favour of justice and humanity in dealing with us." Therefore, Douglass was not only an inspiration but also worthy of admiration and appreciation.[19]

Grimké appreciated Douglass for his character as well as his commitment to advancing the interests of Black people. He embodied and exemplified communal pride. Clearly the celebration of a common humanity did not preclude the celebration of individuals or communities. Therefore Grimké encouraged Black children growing up to remember Douglass and his legacy, and to emulate him.[20]

In fact, it was in part because Douglass modeled a vigorous understanding of the doctrine of the image of God that Grimké celebrated his legacy in such glowing terms. Douglass "carried about with him the consciousness that he was made in the image of God."[21] He possessed a strong

---

17 Francis J. Grimké, "The Atlanta Riot" (1906), in *Works*, 1:414.
18 Grimké, "Christianity and Race Prejudice," 443–46.
19 Francis J. Grimké, "Frederick Douglass" (1908), in *Works*, 1:64.
20 Grimké, "Frederick Douglass," 64–65.
21 Grimké, "Frederick Douglass," 68.

sense of personal dignity, conducted himself in a way that commanded respect, lived honestly, and maintained a wholesome personal character. Douglass lived above reproach, and it was an honor to associate with him and to be associated with him.

Francis Grimké was proud of the Black community and of figures like Frederick Douglass who represented it well. Grimké's profound doctrine of the image of God led him to a strong respect for all human beings, a particular love for fellow Christians, and a special sense of obligation to his race. These commitments were not in tension with one another but, rather, mutually reinforcing. They served as a life-giving source of identity in the face of despair for the racial violence plaguing his country, and they provided a sense of duty and purpose.

Proper Self-Respect

As Grimké developed and applied the biblical notion of the image of God, he affirmed a thoroughgoing respect for self and others. His understanding of this "respectability" was fundamentally different from the type described by Evelyn Brooks Higginbotham in her important and frequently cited *Righteous Discontent*. There Higgenbotham narrates an engaging and compelling account of the importance of women in the Black church at the turn of the twentieth century. Her work convincingly demonstrates the significant role of women in contributing to the development of the Black church as an institution and, even more significantly, as a public sphere in which Black identity was shaped and given a voice. At the same time, her study traces the ways in which the growing institutional influence was realized in part by adopting the dominant values of White society through a "politics of respectability." Higgenbotham illustrates a complex picture in which Black women were influential in resisting both racism and gender subordination, and yet their influence also contributed to the assimilation of Black identity to the dominant culture.[22]

---

[22] Evelyn Brooks Higginbotham, *Righteous Discontent: The Women's Movement in the Black Baptist Church, 1880–1920* (Cambridge, MA: Harvard University Press, 1994), 14, 18. In her depiction of the women of the "Talented Tenth," Higginbotham shows how these women successfully undermined the racism and paternalism of their benefactors and that their assimilation of "respectable" values did not preclude genuine achievement (chap. 2). Furthermore, women were clearly significant in making the Black church an "ideological and social space for articulating group needs and implementing programs for their fulfillment," thus serving as a representative and authoritative voice of the race (chap. 3; quote on 47). Higginbotham helpfully demonstrates that while White women were often chauvinistically motivated, their partnership with Black women at times led to a genuine understanding of Black culture on its own terms (chap. 4). Her depiction of a nascent feminist theology in the Black church certainly calls into question any generalizing tendency to dismiss it as an "insipid, anti-theological" tradition (chap. 5). In fact, the

By contrast, Grimké self-consciously rejected such a "politics of re-spectability" and excoriated Black leaders who pursued it. In his medita-tions, he wrote, "I have always made it a principle in life, not to allow what others may think of what I am about to do or say, to influence my conduct." His understanding of respectability was grounded not in the approval of White society but, rather, in moral principles. In no uncertain terms he de-clared: "If following my convictions meets the approbation of others, well; but if not, it is a matter of no special importance to me. It is a bad business to try to act in a way that will keep us in favor with others. It is a great deal better to do what is right."[23]

This very issue contributed to his discontent with the social approach of another prominent Black leader of his day, Booker T. Washington. In his private meditations, Grimké accused Washington of replacing the fight against segregation with the pursuit of White approval. Worse, Grimké ac-cused him of garnering White favor to raise money more effectively. For Grimké, Washington's respectability politics lacked self-respect and was a shameful pursuit of material gain and a failure to stand up for human rights. Grimké accused Washington of being more interested in material possessions than doing the right thing.[24]

According to Grimké, such "politics of respectability" were an affront to God wherever they were found. In another place, he contrasted the ap-proach of presidents Woodrow Wilson and Theodore Roosevelt. He accused Wilson of standing in the way of progress and of seeking to keep Black people in a "condition of inferiority." By contrast, Grimké perceived that President Roosevelt's openness to equality was more in line with basic

women's convention of the Black church not only gave Black women a national voice within the denomi-nation but also offered them a trajectory of influence on the broader arena of American social reform. Black women made significant contributions to concerns of the social gospel and pursued those concerns through interdependent secular and religious avenues (chap. 6). In each of these cited chapters, Higgin-botham powerfully demonstrates the role played by Black women in creating a public space in which they contributed to the shape of Black identity and the texture of its public discourse. Higginbotham's work, especially in the final chapter, is suggestive of the ways in which a particular community can reinterpret the reigning values of a society according to its own purposes.

At the same time, while Higginbotham explicitly distinguishes between "dialogic" and "dialectic" approaches, affirming the former method for its ability to describe the "multivalent" factors shaping any particular social setting and values, her book frequently resorts to two-dimensional polarities, whether regarding race ("white" vs. other), region ("Yankee" vs. other), period ("Victorian" vs. other), religion ("Puritan" vs. other), class ("bourgeoise" vs. other), etc. At times the book even slips into the terminology of dialectic, for example on pp. 28 and 40. As a result, the study at times frames the narrative according to essentialized binaries, juxtaposing, for example, "white" vs. "black" values, in spite of its claim to understand its figures and ideas according to a "multiplicity of meanings and intentions that interact and condition each other" (16). That description of purpose—namely, the pursuit of a "multiplicity of meanings and intentions"—is a compelling one, and it is the one attempted here.

23 *Works*, 3:58–59.
24 *Works*, 3:7–8.

principles of justice. Here again, Grimké appealed to the moral implications of the doctrine of God's image as the basis of proper respect. God is "no respecter of persons"; each human being should be seen and treated as a "child of God, created in his image"; and this image transcends all "color and race variety."[25]

As usual, Grimké was careful to affirm universal principles without losing the distinctive nature of the Christian faith; he clearly distinguished the equality of all "before God" from the equality of those "in the church of God."[26] Grimké's understanding of respect was grounded in what he took to be transcendent principles of right and wrong. He contrasted White leaders who shared his principles from those who did not, and he criticized Black leaders who pursued White respectability for merely material reasons. When Booker T. Washington died, Grimké acknowledged in his meditations that "his location in the South made it necessary, of course, for him to be cautious, to think well before speaking," but Grimké also lamented that "there was no good reason why he should have so conducted himself." So Grimké drew a sharp contrast between the legacy of Frederick Douglass, who championed the image of God and proper respect, and whose death he saw as a great loss to the cause of justice, and the legacy of Booker T. Washington, who pursued material gain through the politics of respectability, and whose death Grimké predicted would be a "loss to Tuskegee, but will not be to the race."[27]

Two related sets of principles built upon the doctrine of God's image enabled Grimké to develop his concept of proper respect in this way. The first set of principles gave him the ability to differentiate and order distinct aspects of personal identity. Humanity, nationality, race, and religion are all crucial components of a personal identity, and yet these components need proper order, each with its level of rights and respect. Grimké observed that racial identity, important as it might be, is not the proper basis for grounding human rights. Rather, basic human rights belong to all human beings. Therefore, proper self-respect refuses any restriction of such basic human rights.

National citizenship grants additional political rights that also transcended race. For Grimké, these rights of citizenship, like human rights, were "colorless" and "classless," or else they were "nothing." Yet these

---

[25] *Works*, 3:65.
[26] *Works*, 3:66.
[27] *Works*, 3:15–16.

human rights and rights of citizenship were not enough to make a person happy. True happiness and proper respect depend upon the possession of "true religion." Only the person "who has been awakened to a sense of the importance of religion, is bound to give a good account of himself, to make a place for himself in the confidence, respect, and esteem" of others.[28] Thus, Grimké's carefully ordered conception of personal identity shaped his understanding of proper respect.

A second set of principles dealt with the ends or purposes of human life. Reflecting on eternal life, Grimké wrote in his meditations, "When the earthly pilgrimage is over, how sad it will be, if we have been living a self-centered life." He connected a self-centered life with an existence lived for "creature comforts" and for "perishable things." A person concerned with life in this present world only is a person living a self-centered and ultimately unsatisfying life. By contrast, the person who prioritizes "life eternal" is someone ultimately capable of living for things "worthwhile," worth being "remembered by," and worthy of both love and respect. Here again, it is the person whose life is oriented to God and the things of God, rather than the person whose life is oriented to material comfort or assimilation, who is worthy of respect.[29]

A major theme running through all these principles relates to the importance of moral character. For Grimké, Christian moral principles were inherently worthy of respect. Respect was not based on whether a person was "white or black," "rich or poor," "educated or uneducated," or "high or low." Rather, "character alone is the one sure test of superiority."[30] A common refrain in Grimké's meditations concerned the misplaced trust and respect given to immoral spiritual and political leaders. Toward the end of his life, Grimké recounted a trip to the barbershop where his barber referred to a politician who was "of education and ability" but "utterly bankrupt morally." Grimké bemoaned the perspective of his barber that this politician was "one of the great men of our race," a perspective sadly all too common.[31] Later in his ministry, Grimké recorded a similar sentiment regarding a newspaper article about another politician of similarly "debased" character.[32] Grimké's expectations for spiritual leaders were even higher. Pastors should be characterized by many qualities and skills, including

---

[28] *Works*, 3:202–3.
[29] *Works*, 3:341.
[30] *Works*, 3:116.
[31] *Works*, 3:130.
[32] *Works*, 3:210.

intelligence, education, piety, and executive ability, but the highest priority is moral character. "No immoral man has any business in the ministry." A candidate found to be lacking in moral character or reputation should be "shut out" from the ministry by denominational and local church leaders. Indeed, "every pulpit should be shut against him, and he should be deposed from the ministry."[33]

In this way, Grimké set forth a pattern of respectability that differed dramatically from prevalent social and cultural norms of his day. The ultimate goal was not merely the admiration of other people, especially the dominant culture. As he put it memorably in his meditations: "Jesus cared nothing about popularity. He was not afraid of public sentiment nor did he court it." Grimké acknowledged that contrary to the example of Jesus, "We love the praises of men. We are not willing to suffer for the sake of principle. We would rather be popular than to be right. Most of us are moral cowards, weaklings, afraid of our own shadows, deficient in strength of moral purpose. It is a shameful confession to make, but it is true."[34] Instead of focusing on a "politics of respectability" centered on popular sentiment, Grimké advocated concern for divine approval: "It isn't what men think of you, though it is well to live [so] as to be worthy of their respect, but what God thinks of you is the important thing. If he thinks well of you, if you are living in a way to merit his approbation, you need not be disturbed by what others may think of you."[35]

Grimké explicitly opposed the cultural pressures of assimilation associated with the "politics of respectability." He believed that respect was inherent rather than earned, and he frequently framed his notion of respectability in contradistinction to the social norms and practices of White society. For example, in 1926 one of the hotels associated with a "General Presbyterian Rally" in Washington, DC, for the purposes of fundraising and recruitment objected to the inclusion of people of color. As a result, the committee in charge of the rally notified the Black Presbyterian churches that none of their members would be permitted to attend. When one of the officers of the organization contacted the leadership of Grimké's church to request a meeting to explain their reasoning, Grimké declined to attend the meeting and instead wrote a brief, scathing letter to be read

---

[33] *Works*, 3:214–16.
[34] *Works*, 3:282.
[35] *Works*, 3:583.

in his absence. The text of the letter laid out Grimké's understanding of proper respect in detail:

> To the elders and Trustees of the Fifteenth St. Presbyterian Church:
>> Brethren:
>> As a church, we may never have another such opportunity as this, of showing our self-respect, and of entering our protest against the cowardly surrender of Christian principles to the utterly ignoble sentiment of race prejudice which is more and more manifesting itself not only here but all over the country. We owe it to ourselves; we owe it to the cause of Christ, to sever our connection with this movement unless we are received on terms of perfect equality. We ought not to countenance for a moment, the cowardly, and as it seems to me, shameful attitude of the men having it in charge, and claiming to be followers of the Lord Jesus Christ. I should be ashamed of myself, and ashamed of this church over which I have presided for more than forty years if we should submit to this insult. There is nothing for us to do but to sever our connection with the movement, if we are to retain our own self-respect, and respect even of the men who are trying to force this humiliation upon us. We must stand up squarely, uncompromisingly for Christian ideals and principles. No amount of material advantage, even if such was offered, could compensate for the injury which such a surrender of principle, would inflict upon our souls.
>> I felt that I wanted to say this to you, the officers of the church. If there is any one thing that I have sought to beget in you, during my long ministry among you, it has been a manly, self-respecting spirit. And I feel that my labors have not been in vain.[36]

Remarkably, the presbytery heeded Grimké's call and repudiated the decision of the organizing committee to exclude people of color from the banquet. Recording the outcome in his meditations, Grimké reflected: "Never be ashamed of the fact that you are identified with the colored race. And never let the colored race be ashamed of the fact that you are a part of it. Be upright, straightforward, honorable in all your dealings. Only by so living can you be a credit to yourself or to your race."[37]

At the end of his life, Grimké explicitly expressed his opposition to social assimilation on the terms of White society. For Grimké, social contact with White people was "not a thing to be forced" and, in fact, was "not

---

[36] *Works*, 3:156–57.
[37] *Works*, 3:157.

a thing that is desirable except on the terms of perfect equality." Frankly, social interaction should not be sought when there is a hierarchical expectation of assimilation of one group to another. Social relations across races are acceptable only when they are between equals. "Until the white man gets rid of his race prejudice," Grimké wrote, people of color "who respect themselves" have "no desire for social contact" with White people, "and they will accept it only where they can conserve their self-respect." It was this mentality that led Grimké to look back on his long ministry and to record with integrity: "I have lived in Washington City, for example, for fifty years, and during all that time have been a member of the Washington City Presbytery, in good and regular standing: and yet I have never had a social call from a white member of it, [n]or have I ever made a call on any of them." He concluded bluntly, "I have gone on the even tenor of my way, finding all my social relations with my own people, and have been perfectly content with their society." In Grimké's eyes, the expectation of assimilation was a violation of proper respect and precluded the possibility of shared society.[38]

On Thanksgiving of 1918, reflecting on the Allied victory of World War I, Francis Grimké gave an address that well summarized his view of proper respect. In a city with "scores of churches" of various denominations where the Bible was taught, where nearly all federal officials were members—the "President of the United States and his Cabinet, the members of the Senate and the House of Representatives, and the Judges of the Supreme Court"— one would expect the basic principles of Christian teaching to shape social and political norms and practices. The belief that all people were created in God's image, worthy of dignity and respect, and deserving of equal treatment under the law should be reflected in society. Instead, Grimké pointedly observed, people of color were not even allowed into restaurants and restrooms. Society was ruled by Jim Crow rather than Jesus Christ. In a city "where Christianity has back of it so much respectability," laws and life were characterized by anything but proper respect.[39] Grimké looked forward to a time when, contrary to this sad reality, "the super-man of the future is not to be of the German type, nor of the contemptible little type that we find here in America, assuming and acting upon the theory that under a white skin only is to be found anything worthy of respect; but of the

---

[38] *Works*, 3:343–44.
[39] Francis J. Grimké, "Victory for the Allies and the United States a Ground of Rejoicing, of Thanksgiving" (1918), in *Works*, 1:574.

Christ-type."[40] True Christianity was respectable and a source of respectability. The false Christianity practiced by White Christians alongside or in support of race prejudice "can never be made respectable" or a source of proper respect.[41]

For Francis Grimké, the inherently good and true deserved respect. Whether people chose to give respect where respect was due was of secondary concern. Therefore, his teaching and practice of the Christian life centered on moral laws grounded in the image of God and the importance of living in keeping with the preaching of Jesus and his gospel. Preaching without a corresponding manner of living had "no value." As he put it, "We must live what we preach if we hope to influence others; if we hope to command the respect of others."[42] Respect for Christ was of greater importance than receiving respect from others.[43] Those who lived their lives for the sake of Christ were worthy of respect and emulation, and they stood out from those who served their own interests in gaining comfort and acceptance.[44] In the context of yet another discussion of respect, he put it bluntly, "I have come to see that it isn't the white man's religion that counts for anything; but only the religion of the Lord Jesus Christ."[45]

Righteous Discontent

His commitment to rooting his identity in his creation and redemption in the image of God gave Francis Grimké great confidence and hope. The consistent failures of American people and churches to promote proper respect did not lead him to despair. On the contrary, his belief in God's faithfulness enabled him to face injustice and disrespect with faithful conviction and resiliency. To rest in Christ meant a refusal to adopt a spirit of discontentment, but, at the same time, Grimké's commitment to God's moral law and recognition of the implications of the image of Christ led him to maintain a healthy and proper discontent with the injustices of his day. His righteous discontent was a source of hope and moral strength.

Grimké expressed this hope in December 1900 in a sermon series on one of his favorite texts, Psalm 27. Though his congregation faced many

---

[40] Grimké, "Victory for the Allies and the United States," 576.
[41] Works, 3:352.
[42] Works, 3:101.
[43] Works, 3:142, 192.
[44] In addition to the examples above, see Grimké's celebration of the example of Wendell Phillips in Works, 3:58.
[45] Works, 3:244.

discouraging circumstances, the words of Psalm 27:14 were a source of great hope: "Wait on the LORD; be of good courage, and he shall strengthen thine heart."[46] His people had to suffer growing racism, hostile media, negligent and even false preachers, increasing violence, and political apathy and opposition, yet Grimké encouraged them to trust in the Lord and to find strength in him. In his sermon, he referenced the recent massacre in Wilmington, North Carolina, where a White mob set fire to the building of the Black-owned *Wilmington Daily Record*, killed at least fourteen Black citizens, and carried out a political coup, forcing the lawfully elected mayor and Republican members of the city council to resign.[47] Even communities where Black people made progress toward political representation during the Reconstruction era faced discouraging and violent reversals in those years. It is easy to see why Grimké turned to the Psalms to find encouragement to share with his congregation.

As he often did, Grimké reflected on a variety of sources of hope concerning both material and spiritual matters. The Christian faith and the justice of God ultimately would prevail, he reminded his congregants, and these deep sources of hope should enable them to wait on the Lord. And yet he also encouraged them to reflect on the growing consciousness of God's faithfulness to provide for the material needs of Black people in America, and a corresponding willingness of Black people to stand up in defense of their rights. He recounted numerous stories of God strengthening the hearts of those who placed their trust in him. God thereby enabled them not only to persevere in the face of dire circumstances but also to boldly advocate for change. "Thank God for these myriad voices that I hear everywhere protesting; for this discontent with present conditions which I see everywhere manifesting itself."[48] God's people were waiting on the Lord, and Grimké observed the providential signs of the growing power of their voices.

God's faithfulness to his image bearers and to his own just character led Grimké to reflect frequently on the nature of this "righteous discontent." In his sermons and addresses, he regularly observed that such discontent was growing and that it was an effective engine of social change. The week of the inauguration of President William Howard Taft, Grimké

---

[46] Francis J. Grimké, "Signs of a Brighter Future" (1900), in *Works*, 1:260–73.

[47] For more on the Wilmington Massacre of 1898, see the collection of essays gathered in David S. Cecelski and Timothy B. Tyson, eds., *Democracy Betrayed: The Wilmington Race Riot of 1898 and Its Legacy* (Chapel Hill: University of North Carolina Press, 1998).

[48] Grimké, "Signs of a Brighter Future," 261.

gave an address, as was his custom on inauguration week, in which he
reflected on the state of racial justice in the United States.[49] He encouraged his listeners to persevere in their fight for racial justice. He reminded
them that change would not come without suffering. He challenged them
to endure the suffering, but not to do so quietly. "We are not sitting down
in sweet content," he observed. "I thank God from the bottom of my heart,"
he continued, "for these mutterings of discontent that are heard in all parts
of the land. The fact that we are dissatisfied with present conditions, and
that we are become more and more so, shows that we are growing . . . in the
qualities that will enable us to win in the end."[50] As he neared his conclusion, he encouraged his audience to continue to agitate and to do so loudly.
Such expressions of righteous discontent were an effective way to pursue
just treatment.

The theme of growing righteous discontent continued to be a major
theme of his sermons and addresses throughout the remainder of his ministry. A decade later, in the midst of the racial violence of 1919, he delivered
an address entitled "The Race Problem—Two Suggestions as to Its Solution."
Grimké's two suggestions included White people, first, recognizing that
racial injustice was not accidental and, second, adopting new attitudes of
"justice and kindness" toward the circumstances of Black people.[51] He held
out hope that Whites would indeed come to this realization and change in
this way, and he argued that the growing discontent of Black people "is one
of the hopeful signs that a better day is coming—must come."[52] Grimké saw
this growing discontent as an indication that Black Americans were beginning to see themselves as truly human and worthy of equal treatment. He
believed in the necessity of Black self-belief before White people would
come to share in that belief.

Grimké communicated the exact same message in the summer of 1919
in a letter to the editor of Philadelphia's *Evening Bulletin*. He thanked the editor for continuing to draw attention to the race riots besetting the nation.
"It is encouraging," he wrote, "to know that there are some white people
among us who see clearly what the real cause of these occasional mani-

[49] Francis J. Grimké, "Equality of Rights for All Citizens, Black and White Alike" (1909), in *Works*, 1:418–
40. Though the inauguration of President Taft took place on March 4 of that year, Carter Woodson gives
the date for the address on March 27. The text of the address, however, states that it was delivered the
week of the presidential inauguration (418–19).
[50] Grimké, "Equality of Rights for All Citizens," 438.
[51] Francis J. Grimké, "The Race Problem—Two Suggestions as to Its Solution" (1919), in *Works*, 1:597.
[52] Grimké, "The Race Problem," 592.

festations of discontent is." Once again, he brought together the themes of this chapter: personal identity, proper respect, and righteous discontent:

> The colored people, to say the least, are human beings, and are entitled to be treated just as other human beings are treated. They have made in the last fifty years wonderful progress; and the more they develop, the more dissatisfied they will become with the manner in which they are at present treated. It shows that they are growing in self-respect.[53]

Human beings, created in God's image, should be treated as such. The disrespect shown to Black people in America was treatment unworthy of God's image bearers. Their dissatisfaction was a righteous display of discontent and a sign of hope.

Toward the end of his life, in 1930, Grimké offered some provocative reflections on the Gold Star mother and widow pilgrimages. That year, the United States government funded a program to send nearly 6,700 women to Europe to visit the graves of their husbands and sons who died in the First World War. Newspapers reported that "Negro gold-star mothers" would not be allowed to sail together with the "white gold-star mothers." Instead, the government placed the Black women on a "second class vessel." Just as the media erased the valor of Black Americans from pictures of victorious troops after the Spanish-American war, now the government refused to show the same honor to the mothers of Black American patriots who sacrificed their lives in World War I.[54] For Grimké, such actions, in the language of his day, were "an insult to the entire Negro race." In fact, the decision was a denial of equality, which "every self-respecting Negro resents, and will continue to resent." Therefore, "the Negro will never cease to protest against it, and to do everything in his power to show his discontent." Black soldiers gave their lives to fight for a country that still would not recognize them or even their grieving family members as citizens with equal standing and deserving of equal treatment. But, as Grimké pointed

---

53 Francis J. Grimké to the editor of the *Evening Bulletin*, July 29, 1919, in *Works*, 4:242–43.
54 Rebecca Jo Plant and Frances M. Clarke, "'The Crowning Insult': Federal Segregation and the Gold Star Mother and Widow Pilgrimages of the Early 1930s," *Journal of American History* 102, no. 2 (2015): 406–32. See also John W. Graham, *The Gold Star Mother Pilgrimages of the 1930s: Overseas Grave Visitations by Mothers and Widows of Fallen U.S. World War I Soldiers* (Jefferson, NC: McFarland, 2005); G. Kurt Piehler, "The War Dead and the Gold Star: American Commemoration of the First World War," in *Commemorations: The Politics of National Identity*, ed. John R. Gillis (Princeton, NJ: Princeton University Press, 1994), 168–85; Rebecca Jo Plant, "The Gold Star Mother Pilgrimages: Patriotic Maternalists and Their Critics in Interwar America," in *Maternalism Reconsidered: Motherhood, Welfare, and Social Policy in the Twentieth Century*, ed. Marian van der Klein et al. (New York: Oxford, 2012), 127–47.

out, "Patriotism is not a matter of color, or to be measured according to the color of one's skin. The Negro's patriotism cannot be discounted."

The memory of such stories pricked more and more consciences as the years passed, and Grimké's words proved to be prophetic. The righteous discontent of Black Americans demanded a reckoning. Human beings, created in God's image, demanded to be reckoned as such. They were worthy of proper respect, "to say the least." Francis Grimké believed that God cared for all his image bearers, and he believed that a reckoning was coming for those who refused to listen. He championed a cause he believed was just. He did not desire a mere White "respectability." He demanded proper respect as God's image bearer. His righteous discontent, grounded in the law of God, was morally just, and it was rhetorically effective. As one newspaper, discussing the Gold Star mothers and widows' pilgrimages, discerningly put it, "Beware of just discontentment: its power is great."[55]

---

[55] *Works*, 3:473–74.

CHAPTER 4

PERSONAL SANCTIFICATION

Francis Grimké believed that God is good and powerful, and that the justice of God will prevail. As a result, his righteous discontent at unjust circumstances led him to trust God's promises and follow God's commands, and it strengthened him against despair and cynicism. These convictions required him to hold on simultaneously to the whole spectrum of the Christian faith. By contrast, historians observe a persistent temptation in American Protestantism, and particularly within the Reformed tradition, for individual churches and theologians to choose between "doctrinalist," "pietist," and "culturalist" emphases. Doctrinalist churches tend to emphasize correct teaching about God. Pietist churches tend to focus on genuine devotion to God. Culturalist churches tend to advocate for justice on behalf of God.[1] In his life and ministry, Grimké consistently refused to choose between these impulses, and as he taught and practiced the Christian faith, he held all three firmly together.

Grimké's ministry also held closely together the individual and the corporate dimensions of the Christian life. In descriptions of present-day religious belief and practice, many sociologists observe a divide in the ways American Christians think about the intersection of faith and social issues. Whereas White Christians tend to think about social issues in terms of individual responsibility, Black Christians in America are more likely to think about social issues as matters of corporate

---

[1] George M. Marsden, introduction, "Reformed and American," in *Reformed Theology in America: A History of Its Modern Development*, ed. David F. Wells (Grand Rapids, MI: Baker, 1997), 3.

responsibility.[2] These observations raise a host of important questions
about the nature of current Christian belief and practice, as well as how
they developed. Notions of a social gospel are frequently invoked to
elucidate answers to such questions, and parts 3 and 4 will explore in
greater detail the social gospel traditions and Grimké's relationship to
them. The present chapter takes up Francis Grimké's understanding of
Christian sanctification, particularly how his understanding of dependence on God for growth in personal holiness helped him to hold together the individual and the corporate dimensions of the faith, as well
as doctrine, worship, and ethics.

Moral Character

The righteous discontent that drove Grimké's prophetic critique of American Christianity grew in part out of his pastoral emphasis on moral character in the Christian life. The importance of moral character was a favorite
theme of his preaching and teaching in the pulpit, in the press, and in his
occasional lectures. This theme shaped his reflections on the ministries of
prominent individuals, it was a test of genuine Christianity, it was crucial
for healthy citizenship, and it was essential to addressing social problems.
Perhaps most importantly, Grimké almost always connected the individual
and the communal aspects of moral character.

Possibly his most programmatic treatment of the subject was an
address Grimké delivered in 1911, titled "The Paramount Importance
of Christian Character, the True Standard by Which to Estimate Individuals and Races."[3] Coming on the heels of the formation of the NAACP
and delivered in the midst of increasingly frequent race riots and at the
beginning of a decade that would see Jim Crow segregate Washington,
DC, it reminded his listeners that God was not a "respecter of persons"
on the basis of their social status. Grimké appealed to a litany of biblical passages to make his case and then recounted the story of Peter and
Cornelius in Acts 10 to remind his audience that "what makes a man
acceptable to God is not his nationality, is not his race; but his personal
character: it is the man that feareth God, and worketh righteousness,

---

[2] Michael O. Emerson and Christian Smith, *Divided by Faith: Evangelical Religion and the Problem of Race in America* (New York: Oxford University Press, 2001).

[3] Francis J. Grimké, "The Paramount Importance of Christian Character, the True Standard by Which to Estimate Individuals and Races" (1911), in *Works*, 1:473–89.

that is acceptable to him."[4] The address was both a call to repentance and a call to holiness.

The theme of personal holiness and moral character shaped Grimké's reflections on the ministries of prominent individuals. Speaking of Frederick Douglass, he remembered, "Here was a man of genuine courage—a man who dared to do right; who dared to be true to his convictions; who was never afraid to be on the unpopular side; but who lived, and wrought, and suffered, in the sublime faith which expressed itself in the assertion, 'One with God is a majority.'"[5] Of Frederick's wife, Helen Pitts Douglass, he said, "I do not believe, under any circumstances, she would knowingly have swerved a hair's breadth from what she felt to be right."[6] Having officiated at their wedding, Francis knew the Douglasses well and could speak with some authority regarding them.

Grimké offered similar reflections on the moral character of significant figures in American society and in his own church community. Speaking of Theodore Roosevelt, he referred to the former president's own words: "There is need of a sound body, and even more need of a sound mind. But above mind and above body stands character."[7] In his comments on Roosevelt's life and political legacy, Grimké observed various ways in which he lived in accordance with this dictum. When it came to members of his church, Grimké returned to similar themes. Remembering the life of Rosetta Lawson, a longtime member of the congregation, he recalled her involvement in the temperance movement and her concern not only for "individual character" but also its connection to "the future of the race with which she identified."[8] Whether it was prominent leaders of the United States or members of his church who were not famous but nevertheless models of moral character, Grimké emphasized these aspects of their lives. While these figures were not perfect, he edified his audiences by endorsing the positive moral characteristics of exemplary lives.[9]

---

[4] Grimké, "The Paramount Importance of Christian Character," 483. Though he used the masculine language of his day, it is important to note that the very next page records Grimké's declaration that "God doesn't care any more for a man than he does for a woman."

[5] Francis J. Grimké, "Frederick Douglass" (1907), in *Works*, 1:60.

[6] Francis J. Grimké, "Helen Pitts Douglass" (1903), in *Works*, 1:72.

[7] Francis J. Grimké, "Theodore Roosevelt" (1919), in *Works*, 1:183.

[8] Francis J. Grimké, "Mrs. Rosetta Lawson: Remarks of the Rev. Francis J. Grimke before the Adult Bible Class of the Fifteenth Street Presbyterian Church, of Washington, D. C., of Which He Was Teacher, in Connection with a Temperance Lesson May 24, 1936," in *Works*, 1:219.

[9] Much recent historical work emphasizes the changing ways in which late nineteenth- and early twentieth-century Black elites positioned themselves in relation to the Black masses. As Kerri K. Greenidge notes in her study on the Grimké family, Kevin K. Gaines argued that the discourse of racial uplift entailed a political valence as Black elites responded to the racial nadir. Jacqueline M. Moore, by contrast,

These remembrances illustrate not only the emphasis Grimké placed on moral character but also the way he consistently held together individual and corporate morality. On each occasion mentioned above, he identified the respective person as a model of individual character and concern for the moral character of society.[10] In fact, as he described the ideal to which a pastor should strive, he carefully connected personal morality with social moral concern. Ministers were "moral teachers" who should follow the example of the biblical prophets, apostles, and disciples in their concern for what is right, to "lift the individual and the race to the lofty plane of Christian manhood and womanhood."[11] Concern for character applied to both the individual and humanity as a whole. He saw the presence of this holistic moral character as the test of genuine faith.

In fact, Grimké made clear the impossibility of separating individual from corporate moral character, and this connection also informed his understanding of citizenship. In his 1905 address "The Negro and His Citizenship," Grimké applied Paul's appeal to his Roman citizenship in Acts 22:25–29 to a host of contemporary questions. He observed that citizenship carried with it both rights and duties. Paul not only demanded his privileges as a Roman citizen but also recognized his obligation to live as one who appreciated his citizenship. Therefore, Grimké wrote, "We are to remember that we are part of a great whole, and that the whole will be affected by our conduct, either for good or bad." Good citizens must live with the awareness that their personal moral decisions have public moral consequences. "If we live right, if we fear God and keep his commandments, and train our children to do the same, we ennoble our citizenship; we become a part of the great conservative force of society, a positive blessing to the community, the state, the nation."[12] Demanding one's rights meant that one must also remember one's obligations to others. He built his understanding of citizenship and its privileges upon the foundation of his un-

explores the ways in which this was a project of "self-definition." Regardless of the precise emphasis, the point in common is that there was an increasing tendency for elites to distance themselves from the masses. It is notable, however, that Grimké chose to highlight exemplary members of the congregation in addition to more prominent, famous figures. This is not to say that Grimké was unaffected by the cultural tendencies of his community, but it is noteworthy nevertheless. See Gaines, *Uplifting the Race: Black Leadership, Politics, and Culture in the Twentieth Century* (Chapel Hill: University of North Carolina Press, 1996), 1–19; Moore, *Leading the Race: The Transformation of the Black Elite in the Nation's Capital, 1880–1920* (Charlottesville: University of Virginia Press, 1999), 2–4; and especially Greenidge, *The Grimkes: The Legacy of Slavery in an American Family* (New York: Liveright, 2022), 369n28.
[10] See Grimké, "Frederick Douglass," 60; Grimké, "Helen Pitts Douglass," 75; Grimké, "Theodore Roosevelt," 183–84; Grimké, "Mrs. Rosetta Lawson," 219.
[11] Francis J. Grimké, "The Afro-American Pulpit in Relation to Race Elevation" (1892), in *Works*, 1:225.
[12] Francis J. Grimké, "The Negro and His Citizenship" (1905), in *Works*, 1:391–96, 397–98.

derstanding of moral character and its obligations. A well-rounded citizen must embrace and embody a fully orbed moral vision.

This commitment to the importance of moral character was foundational to Grimké's engagement of social problems throughout his ministry. For example, one of his most well-known addresses on race prejudice emphasized that racism in America was an indictment of the moral character of the nation, its churches, and its people. While he regularly preached about the atoning work of Christ and its necessity for the forgiveness of sins and eternal life with God, he was not afraid to preach also of Christ's moral teachings and moral example, and his address titled "Christianity and Race Prejudice" put this emphasis in the center. He preached with confidence, for "real genuine Christianity" was not "powerless in the presence of race prejudice." On the contrary, such real faith had "the mighty power of God" at its back. By contrast, the Christianity "represented in white America" had "failed to do its duty." The steady increase of race prejudice in a society with so many Christians was "a standing indictment of the white Christianity in this land." Grimké was not willing to conclude—yet—that the Christianity of White America was totally "spurious," but its moral corruption was a challenge to the core of its very life.[13]

On the question of how the church could respond to the plague of race prejudice, he began by calling it to return to the moral teaching and example of Jesus Christ. Recalling the contempt for Samaritans, publicans, and sinners in Jesus's time, Grimké highlighted Christ's consistent calling to love others. Jesus challenged the "petty prejudices and meannesses" of his day. His teaching "tended ever to make men broader, more liberal, more humane, more sympathetic, more kind, and more loving." As a result of his teaching, people "knew where he stood on all the great moral issues of his day." Jesus taught love of all others, and he taught such love boldly.[14] In addition to Jesus's teaching, Grimké also emphasized his example. Jesus "sought to improve conditions" not only by his teaching but also by "the life which he lived, by his personal character and conduct." He refused to countenance the "unholy prejudices" surrounding him. He "never allowed himself to be influenced" by such prejudices. He dined with Zacchaeus, he chose a tax collector for a disciple, he directed his path through Samaria, and he shared a drink with the woman at the well. In all these ways, Jesus

---

13 Francis J. Grimké, "Christianity and Race Prejudice" (1910), in *Works*, 1:463–64.
14 Grimké, "Christianity and Race Prejudice," 465.

dignified "all classes," and his very life "was always, and everywhere a living protest against all the evils about him." Jesus's moral character and
moral teaching directly addressed the social problems of his day.[15]

Thus Grimké's vision of righteous discontent was shaped by the ministry of Jesus, and it emphasized moral character. Such moral character was
a test of the genuineness of Christian faith, was essential to the makeup of
true citizens, and directly addressed the social problems of his day, especially race prejudice. In all these ways, Grimké consistently treated moral
character in both individual and communal terms. Character was crucial
not only to individuals but also to social well-being.

Sanctification

Clearly moral character was close to Grimké's pastoral heart. Because his
moral vision was anything but static, he frequently stressed the importance of personal growth and development. This moral formation was a
continual process that involved intentional and persistent effort. In many
ways, Grimké's emphasis on personal moral formation and the development of Black people mirrored other social, religious, and political leaders
of his day. Historical studies of nineteenth- and twentieth-century society
frequently note that discourse surrounding respectability paralleled the
developing collective awareness of the problems of modern societies in
Europe and the Americas.[16] Conversations surrounding the development
of moral character and respectability often went hand in hand.

At the same time, Grimké's emphasis on moral character and its development drew deeply from the well of historic Christian reflection upon
biblical teaching about sanctification or growth in holiness. His understanding of moral character was as much God-centered as it was human-
centered. He utilized the language of holiness in a way that clearly shaped
his teaching about morality, respectability, and social issues. Ultimately,
he was concerned with respectability in God's sight more than in the sight
of other people. In all these ways the vertical dimension of his understanding of moral character was no less important than the horizontal.

Grimké's theology of sanctification was explicitly a traditional Protes-

---

[15] Grimké, "Christianity and Race Prejudice," 465–66.
[16] For example, Woodruff D. Smith, *Respectability as Moral Map and Public Discourse in the Nineteenth Century* (New York: Routledge, 2018), demonstrates that the discourse of respectability during this period was fundamental to the processes of modernization and globalization, and that it was "embedded" within a wide range of public discourses, including the antislavery movement.

tant one. In his meditations he defined sanctification by quoting directly from the Westminster Shorter Catechism: it is "the work of God's grace, whereby we are renewed in the whole man after the image of God, and are enabled more and more to die unto sin, and live unto righteousness."[17] He distinguished sanctification carefully from "deliverance from the guilt of sin," which "required the death upon the cross of the Lord Jesus Christ" and the shedding of his "precious blood." In so doing, he closely followed his theological training at Princeton Theological Seminary by distinguishing justification from sanctification and yet holding them closely together. Just as justification is an act of God, so also sanctification is God's work, for "redemption from the power of sin is no easy task, and will come only as we yield ourselves to the gracious influence of the Holy Spirit."

Though he attributed the work of sanctification to the Holy Spirit, sanctification also calls forth the works of the believer. As Grimké continued, "There will be no getting out from under the power of sin except where we sincerely desire to be delivered, and earnestly cooperate with the Holy Spirit." God promised to justify and to sanctify all his people, and none of his children will fail to demonstrate this effort, because sanctification, like justification, belongs to all of those predestined to eternal life. Quoting from the book of Revelation, Grimké concluded his reflection on sanctification hopefully by grounding it in the doctrine of God's predestination: "It [sanctification] must come, sooner or later, if we hope to make our home with God. For it is written 'And there shall in no wise enter into it anything that defileth, neither whatsoever worketh abomination, or maketh a lie;' but they which are written in the Lamb's book of life."[18] The theological rigor and precision of Grimké's meditations enabled him to hold together the complex richness of biblical teaching on growth in holiness.

It should be evident that Grimké's optimism regarding the possibility of moral growth grew out of his belief that sanctification is a work of God. Because sanctification is first and foremost God's work rather than a merely human work, the Christian can believe with confidence that growth in holiness is not only possible but inevitable. In this way Grimké's confidence was related closely to his dependence upon God, which also is illustrated by the emphasis he placed on prayer in general, and especially in relation to moral growth. He challenged his congregation to pray boldly for growth

---

17 Q. 35, in *Creeds, Confessions, and Catechisms: A Reader's Edition*, ed. Chad Van Dixhoorn (Wheaton, IL: Crossway, 2022), 418.
18 *Works*, 3:636–37.

in holiness, confident that God would grant this prayer to his people; he wrote that those who take "hold of God in the struggle upward" are sure to succeed.

Grimké believed this was true not only for individuals but for humanity broadly. If all human beings were to reach out "after God in earnest prayer for strength to overcome" their "besetting sins," they would be sure to prevail. His hope was that all people would heed the scriptural call to "pray without ceasing," in order that God would magnify the "great and positive elements" in them and enable them to "resist with all the energy of our natures the things which stand in the way of our progress, which tend to drag us down."[19] Grimké clearly was not a universalist, but he did call all people turn to God in prayer.

Grimké's emphasis and reliance on prayer also illustrates his high view of the Holy Spirit's work in the life of the believer. He reflected on the person and the power of the Holy Spirit often in his meditations. One particularly memorable example came toward the end of his ministry as he reflected on a presbytery meeting of churches in Washington in 1920. Apparently, a notable leader of the presbytery gave an address there lamenting the discouraging state of the Presbyterian churches in the nation's capital. The leader stated that circumstances were so bad, he considered his own ministry in the city "almost a failure." Grimké wryly noted in his meditations that if this brother had reason to be discouraged about the state of Presbyterianism in the city, he (Grimké) had even more reason to be discouraged. At that very meeting the presbytery voted to take oversight of a retirement home that excluded Black residents. The question had been raised as to whether Black residents would be admitted under the new arrangement, and the answer was no. Whereas the brother had served for twenty-five years in the city, Grimké noted that he himself had served for forty, and despite his best efforts his very own fellowship of churches continued to carry out racist policies. Of all people, he had reason for discouragement.[20]

Nevertheless, he refused to allow discouragement to overtake him. "The longer I live," he wrote, "the more am I impressed with the blessedness of a true living faith in God." This blessedness includes "a peace which more than compensates for all the ills of life." It enables endurance, "never mind what trials or afflictions may come upon us." True faith not

---

[19] Francis J. Grimké, "God and Prayer as Factors in the Struggle" (1900), in *Works*, 1:286.
[20] *Works*, 3:97.

only "enables us to bear them" but also "interprets them as nothing else does." True faith gives new eyes that see with hope. "To realize that God is with us, that he is round and about us, that we are ever under his sustaining and protecting care, is always to be strong, is always to find comfort, is always to come out, as the apostle expresses it, more than conqueror." Grimké concluded this reflection on hope in the face of discouragement on a note of gratitude for the sanctifying work of the Holy Spirit. "How much we have to be thankful for, how sweet and consoling is the thought that God is our Father, that Jesus Christ is our Saviour, and that that Holy Spirit is our sanctifier, our helper."[21] The faithful Holy Spirit would sanctify his people and sustain and protect them through any circumstances. Francis Grimké took comfort from his belief in the power of the Holy Spirit, and he refused to be discouraged.

In addition to the Holy Spirit, the word of God was also closely tied to the work of God in sanctification, according to Grimké. He lamented that "too many of our ministers, for the sake of a little cheap popularity, pass over the word of God." This lack of scriptural rootedness produced "weak, sickly, namby-pamby" Christians that "can't be depended upon in any moral crisis." Grimké emphasized, "Where the word of God is neglected, and people are fed on other things, leanness of soul always follows." By contrast, when it came to "the development of Christian character," the "most helpful thing" a minister can bring to God's people is the word of God. "A ministry that does not build on the word of God but which depends on other things, will be sure to be a barren one." Citing a litany of scriptural passages in support of his emphasis on God's word in sanctification, Grimké concluded: "These are sufficient to show what place the word of God occupies in the development of Christian character and life. It is the Divinely appointed food upon which the Christian must feed." As a result, the minister who fails to provide a rich diet of Scripture is one whose "ministry is a farce."[22]

The inseparability of the work of the Holy Spirit and God's word helps to explain Grimké's emphasis on divine law in sanctification as well. He unwaveringly rejected a selective use of the Bible, teaching instead the profitability of all Scripture. In his sermon "Religion and Race Elevation," he alluded to Jesus's teaching, declaring that "in proportion as we recognize

---

21 *Works*, 3:98.
22 *Works*, 3:297–98.

this [divine] law, and make it our guiding principle, we are building on the rock; in proportion as we lose sight of it, as we depart from it, we are building on the sand."[23] In his sermon series on the parable of the prodigal son, Grimké emphasized the coherency of natural law and divine law. Just as the natural law is observable "everywhere in creation," he proclaimed, "spiritually it is the same." To be precise, "it is by doing what [God] directs us to do, by keeping His commands and precepts, by recognizing His authority; not by having our own way; not by doing as we please, but by doing what He pleases to have us do." God is the author of all law, divine and natural, "whether that law be formulated and set before us in in the shape of commands and precepts or lie in the nature of thing[s] within us and about us." Grimké taught that as it is fatal to bodily health to ignore the laws of medicine, it is fatal to spiritual health to ignore the commands of God recorded in Scripture. Christian sanctification demands the preaching of all God's law. As God's people hear and submit to his word, the Holy Spirit sanctifies their lives and makes them more like God.[24]

In addition to the Holy Spirit and the word of God, Grimké stressed the role of the church in sanctification and growth in moral character. As he put it, "The Church is also an institution that has in it very great possibilities for good." Whereas other social activists of the day tended to make the church an agency for social change, more than a place of spiritual concern, Grimké navigated carefully between these options with very precisely formulated priorities. The church "is where the people meet for worship, where the Bible is read and expounded." Clearly, it is not merely or primarily a political agent of social change. And yet, the church "gives a splendid opportunity for creating moral and spiritual impressions, for the inculcation of truths of the greatest importance, and for arousing and stimulating the individual and community to what is highest and best." Spiritual truths cannot be separated from moral concerns. Moral concerns are always both individual and communal. The gathered church is the primary location for the spiritual formation of believers. In this very precise chain of logic, Grimké cast a vision for sanctification that closely connected the ministry of the church with the moral formation of believers. Sanctification is fundamentally communal and social. In this way, the corporate worship

---

[23] Francis J. Grimké, "Religion and Race Elevation," in *Works*, 2:585. According to Woodson's footnote, Grimké preached this sermon on numerous occasions up and down the East Coast, beginning in 1906.
[24] Francis J. Grimké, "The Prodigal Son and Kindred Addresses" (1923), in *Works*, 2:291–95.

of God is the primary context of moral development.[25] As he put it in his meditations, "The mission of the Christian Church is to lead men to Jesus, and to build up Christian character."[26]

In his teaching on Christian sanctification, Francis Grimké demonstrated a remarkable ability to connect a traditional theology of holiness to the everyday lives of his congregation, as well as the broader public. His teaching on the importance of personal growth certainly echoed the concerns of his day regarding "respectability," but respectability for its own sake was clearly not the driving engine. Rather, Grimké's vision of personal growth and development exhibited the contours of a traditional Protestant definition of sanctification as a work of God's grace in the life of his people to make them holy. He regularly emphasized the sovereignty of God to accomplish this work, and therefore the role of the Holy Spirit. He closely connected the Spirit's work to the revelation of God's moral will in sacred Scripture. These moral precepts cohere with those revealed in the creation itself. A holy life will prove to be a better life in the end, regardless of present circumstances. Finally, the primary location of individual moral development is the church. The sanctification of the person is inseparable from the corporate worship of God and the sanctification of God's people. In short, Grimké's teaching on moral character led him to a rigorous emphasis on sanctification as the means of moral formation.

Personal Holiness and Social Concern

Just as Francis Grimké connected personal moral character to the character of society, so also he connected sanctification and moral development to both the individual and the community. Personal sanctification and societal change went hand in hand. While he identified many factors contributing to the racial problems of his day, one significant factor was the lack of personal sanctification pursued within the church. In other words, while Grimké avoided making personal sanctification the panacea for societal problems, he did point out that the lack of holiness on the part of professing Christians was a major factor. The ability to love, respect, and treat racial others as equals is one fruit of Christian sanctification, and therefore conformity to God's moral law benefits both individuals and society. In these

---

[25] Francis J. Grimké, "The Things of Paramount Importance in the Development of the Negro Race" (1903), in *Works*, 1:389–90.
[26] *Works*, 3:77.

ways and others, Grimké drew connecting lines between personal holiness and social concerns.

In his famous "Christianity and Race Prejudice," Grimké declared in various ways that freedom from racial prejudice is an aspect of Christian sanctification. He emphasized that actions speak louder than words. Rather than "public declarations" and "resolutions," his concern was "the practice of congregations" and the pastors who led them. A sanctified church would not only affirm equality but welcome people of other races, treat them well, and extend equality "in all the relations of life." As a result, he lamented that racial inequality in American society was growing worse, not better. The racial practices of American churches reflected a growing embrace of sinful hatred rather than holiness. "It is surprising how little influence the religion of Jesus Christ has had in controlling the prejudice of men, in lifting them above the low plane upon which race prejudice places them," he lamented. "The very opposite of this is what we would naturally have expected to find—that with the growth of the Christian church [would come], not an increase, but a decrease of race antipathy."[27] The growth of race prejudice in society illustrated the lack of sanctification in God's people.

In fact, though Grimké regularly appealed to God's natural law and general revelation in creation as sources of wisdom for believers and unbelievers alike, he also argued that the Christian faith represents the apex of moral teaching, and therefore that the application of Christian principles is a benefit to society. "One reason why there are so many moral wrecks in society today," Grimké declared, is the lack of "home training" of Christian children in biblical morality.[28] His emphasis on marriage and the nurture of children is the subject of chapters 5 and 6, but here it is worth pointing out that his concern for these family matters flowed from the connection he drew between personal sanctification and social change. Christian teaching must touch on moral specifics because general sermons addressing sin without specificity cannot bring the conviction of heart so crucial to the process of growth in holiness. Sermons should therefore deal with "evils in the home, evils in society, evils in business, in politics, individual, personal evils."[29] Personal sanctification and societal change are interconnected.

---

[27] Grimké, "Christianity and Race Prejudice," 455–56, 461, 463.
[28] Grimké, "Religion and Race Elevation," 579.
[29] Francis J. Grimké, "Marriage and Kindred Subjects" (first delivered 1897; grew into a series of thirteen sermons, hereafter numbered), in *Works*, 2:184.

One interesting aspect of that connection is the high priority he placed on the role of women, whom he associated with "glory" and "dignity." In fact, he introduced a sermon on the role of women by emphasizing their contribution to every aspect of human society. Speaking of the "dignity of women," he underlined the "serious" nature of the topic and its relevance to "the individual, the family, society, the state, or the race and nation." The dignity of women not only is a blessing to them but also "will make a difference with the home; it will make a difference with society; it will make a difference with the state; it will make a difference with the race and nation." Indeed, Grimké declared, "There isn't a single interest that will not be affected, for better or worse, by the answer that is given" to the question of the dignity of women. Therefore, introducing one sermon, he said, "It is of this question that I want to speak particularly this morning to the girls and the young women."[30]

The topic was so important to Grimké that he could not address it in a single sermon, and so he continued the same thread the following week. Having emphasized in his first sermon that "true womanhood" does not depend upon looks, dress, social skills such as dancing, or the opinions of men, he proceeded to emphasize in the subsequent message a feature of womanhood for those "growing up to occupy the high position to which they have been called." For women to have "influence" over "male friends and acquaintances," they "will have to give attention to the beautifying of their souls." Grimké believed that the sanctification of women, as well as men, contributed to the betterment of society, and he taught the importance of the influence of women in society. In this sermon he went on to affirm a variety of roles for women that were quite traditional, including their roles as wives and mothers, but in yet another sermon the next week he declared that womanly virtue is "strong in body, strong in mind, strong in character, morally strong." Society needed strong women with "power in the moral life of the community."[31] Grimké was aware that he was pushing against many of the social conventions of his own day. He proclaimed:

> All that I have been saying on this subject may seem a little strange to some of us, to most of us, perhaps; we have been in the habit of thinking of women in a little different light,—as yielding, as pliable, as easily moulded, as clay in the hand of man, the potter. We have been in the habit

---

[30] Francis J. Grimké, "Addresses on True Womanhood" (1923), in *Works*, 2:389.
[31] Grimké, "Addresses on True Womanhood," 391–98, 401–2.

of associating the quality of strength with man rather than woman. And there is a passage of scripture that would seem to give some color to that view of the case. The apostle Paul, in his first epistle to the Corinthians says, "Quit you like men, be strong" [1 Cor. 16:13], as if he meant to say that strength was a masculine and not a feminine quality. This is not his meaning, however. Strength belongs to the one as well as to the other, is expected of the one as well as of the other. It is necessary for the woman to be strong as well as the man. . . . What we need are strong women; we need them everywhere. We need them for the home; we need them for the schoolhouse; we need them in our churches; we need them in all of our social organizations. Mothers should understand this and should be strong themselves and should train their daughters to be strong; to stand for what is worthy in character and life, and to make their influence felt in creating a sentiment in favor of such things.[32]

There is no doubt that Grimké operated within the bounds of conventional biblical interpretation in differentiating men and women and assigning distinct roles to them. At the same time, his notion of respectability transcended and even pushed against social conventions. Not only did Christian men need to be sanctified in order that they might work for a better society, but Christian women did as well. As Grimké put it, " 'Be strong,' was as applicable to the women as to the men." The sanctification of Christian women was good for society. It was so important that it led him to preach *yet another* sermon on the topic the following week in which he identified the center of such sanctification, "the fear of the Lord."[33]

While Grimké closely connected Christian sanctification to societal change, he also tempered his expectations with humility and trust in God. He believed that a faithful God would sanctify his people and the world, but he also trusted him to do so in his own timing and by his own means. He exhorted his brothers and sisters to be sanctified in order that the world would become a better place, but he also refused to become bitter at the sorry state of affairs in the Christian church. On the fiftieth anniversary of the Emancipation Proclamation, he gave an address entitled "Fifty Years of Freedom." In that address he celebrated the improvement of circumstances for Black people in America, but he also lamented how bad things

---

[32] Grimké, "Addresses on True Womanhood," 417.
[33] Grimké, "Addresses on True Womanhood," 417, 424.

still seemed to be. Despite the slow pace of change and the obstacles standing in the way of justice, he warned against bitterness, declaring, "If we are to fight successfully, fight in the most effective way, we must be calm, we must not be spurred on by bitterness, by hatred, but by the consciousness that what we are contending for is right and therefore, is best for all." The fight for change should be characterized by self-control. In response to foolishness, "let us possess our souls in patience; let us be calm, self-possessed," he urged his listeners.[34]

The calling of the Christian is to faithfully pursue holiness, trusting that a faithful God will sanctify his people in due time. Similarly, Grimké also believed that God would bring justice in accordance with his plan. God is sovereign over both personal sanctification and social change, and the two are connected. If sin remains in individual Christian lives, believers ought not to be surprised or discouraged when it remains in society. And yet, they also must not be complacent.

Perhaps the most important application of these realities relates to prayer. If God alone can bring final justice, then trust in God leads to prayer. Instead of harboring bitterness toward oppressors, God calls his people to pity them and to pray for them: "The thing that we ought to do, and, that I wish very much that we would do, and do more than we have been in the habit of doing, is to pray for these misguided, unfortunate, greatly to be pitied individuals who are fighting us." Such prayer should be characterized by the firm belief, on the one hand, that "the Spirit of God can open blind eyes, can unstop deaf ears, can soften the hardest hearts." On the other hand, and even more positively, "the Spirit of God can regenerate, can give an entirely new bias or direction to character and life." Grimké observed that prayer gives hope for justice, because "this is what is needed. These people need to be changed, to be set right." Through prayer, change is possible, and the "possibility of such a change, both for their sakes and for ours, should lead us to work and pray earnestly for it."[35]

Francis Grimké believed unwaveringly in the connection between personal sanctification and societal change, and he trusted God to be true to his promises to sanctify and to bring justice. Grimké's faith led him to have confidence in Christian moral teaching, to believe in the power of prayer, to strive hard for moral and social change, and to love his enemies.

---

[34] Francis J. Grimké, "Fifty Years of Freedom" (1913), in *Works*, 1:501.
[35] Grimké, "Fifty Years of Freedom," 502.

Doctrine and Ethics

Grimké refused to separate Christian living from Christian belief just as he refused to separate the individual and the communal aspects of growth in Christian holiness. By refusing to prioritize either Christian doctrine or Christian ethics, he pushed against two significant tendencies of the Christian traditions of his day. On the one hand, advocates of the social gospel tended to emphasize deeds over creeds. On the other hand, fundamentalists tended to defend the historic creedal convictions of the Christian faith while refusing to address the ethical implications of the Christian faith for racial equality and justice.[36] For Francis Grimké, genuine Christianity held historic creeds and the ethics of racial justice together.

Grimké frequently emphasized the importance of deeds in his meditations. He often echoed the language of social gospel advocates, not only by affirming the need for good works and social engagement but also by stressing the common humanity of all. For example, on one occasion he wrote:

> What is most needed today is Christianity,—Christianity in its purity, simplicity and power. Not the Christianity of creeds, but of the living, loving, gracious Christ who looked upon all men as brothers, children of one common Father, and who came not to be ministered unto, but to minister and to give his life for others.[37]

Here he explicitly juxtaposed a "Christianity of creeds" with the sort of Christian faith characterized by "living" and "loving" in accordance with a "gracious Christ."

Apparently, his experiences as a pastor in America during this period regularly led him to reflect on the nature of the Christian faith in this way. On another occasion, he explicitly juxtaposed a Christianity of "dogmas"

---

[36] Daniel R. Bare recently has demonstrated that this tendency of White fundamentalists to separate historic Christian doctrinal commitments from agitation for racial equality and justice was not characteristic of a significant contingent of self-identifying "Black fundamentalists." Francis Grimké is similar to these Black fundamentalists in this regard, yet he does not fit easily into the category of Black fundamentalism as a result of his Presbyterian understanding of the church and his commitment to cooperation with a diversity of theological and political allies. Chaps. 7 and 8 deal with these themes more fully. See Bare, *Black Fundamentalists: Conservative Christianity and Racial Identity in the Segregation Era* (New York: New York University Press, 2021).

[37] *Works*, 3:17. The latter part of this chapter demonstrates that Grimké also clearly affirmed the importance of traditional Christian doctrine and creedal statements. This portion of the chapter demonstrates that he was as comfortable confronting those who might be called "creedalizers" (those defending creeds while denying the clear moral teaching of Scripture) as he was confronting those frequently referred to as "moralizers" (those selectively defending the moral teaching of Scripture while denying the creeds).

with that of "the spirit of Jesus." In his meditations, he wrote: "What the world needs more than anything else is Christianity. And by Christianity I do not mean belief in a creed, in a series of dogmas, but the spirit of Jesus working in the hearts and minds of men in such a way as to control their thinking, and feeling, and willing, as to dominate their lives." Here again he pointed out the hypocrisy of a formal "orthodoxy" disconnected from a "spirit of love." "There are men today in the church," he lamented,

> who are loud in their denunciation of heresy, who are standing up strenu-
> ously for what they call orthodoxy, who in their own character and con-
> duct are guilty of the greatest heresy of all, the heresy that violates the
> spirit of Jesus Christ, that tramples ruthlessly upon the most sacred thing
> in religion—the spirit of love.[38]

Grimké made the irony of such heterodox "orthodoxy" explicit, and he named it as heresy.

In so doing, he again resonated with advocates of the social gospel. He consistently emphasized brotherhood, in addition to love, and he tied them together: "If we haven't love, everything else counts for nothing in the sight of God. The most sacred as well as the most precious thing in religion is love—a true sense of brotherhood." He envisioned a Christian faith characterized by brotherly love and worldly service. According to this vision, true Christian maturity, the fruit of a truly sanctified life, would be a blessing to society.

> The Christianity that the world needs, and that is sufficient to solve all
> of its problems, individual and national, is the Christianity of Jesus—the
> Christianity of love—the Christianity that goes about doing good, and
> that recognizes all men as brothers, children of one common Father—the
> Christianity that is the friend of publicans and sinners, and that becomes
> all things unto all men, if by any means it can be helpful to them.[39]

Grimké consistently held together the individual and the communal aspects of holy living, and he was not afraid to speak of benefits to society of
Christians who followed the way of Jesus.

Yet he also felt the need to differentiate this vision of orthodox Christian sanctification from that of social gospel advocates. His meditations

---

[38] *Works*, 3:487.
[39] *Works*, 3:41.

offer clear evidence that he carefully read and engaged with authors associated with the movement. This will be the subject of chapters 7 and 8, but
one example here particularly illustrates Grimké's engagement with the
theological impulses of the social gospel. In response to the statements of
John Watson, he offered a provocative and nuanced critique:

> In a statement of Dr. John Watson I find these words: "If any one had come
> to Christ at Capernaum or Jerusalem, and said, Master, there is nothing
> I so desire as to keep Thy sayings. Wilt thou have me, weak and ignorant
> though I be, as Thy disciple?" Can you imagine Christ then, or now, or at
> any time interposing with a series of doctrinal tests regarding either the
> being of God or the history of man? No, it may be. And yet doctrinal ques-
> tions, though not asked, would be involved in following him. We follow
> him as the Son of God, as the Saviour of the world; we follow him because
> we are conscious of a need within us, and which we believe he is able to
> supply. Consciously or unconsciously, we cannot follow Jesus without
> carrying along with us certain convictions about him, and the relation
> which he sustains to God. To have no convictions about him, to have no
> convictions in regard to our own needs, will never induce anyone to fol-
> low him, never has, and never will. All this talk about a creedless religion,
> a religion that is not rooted and grounded in convictions of some kind,
> is absurd, may be true of idiots, but not of rational creatures in the full
> possession of their mental powers. A religion that is not rooted in convic-
> tions, will not last, will not take us anywhere. It is religion that is built
> on faith that holds us and out of which comes life, spiritual and eternal.
> There is a great deal of cheap talk that is going the rounds in disparage-
> ment of creeds, out of which no good can come. A man whose religion is
> creedless can be of very little value, is of very little value.[40]

While Grimké provocatively advocated for deeds in addition to creeds, he
deemed the idea that Christianity could operate without creeds idiotic

---

[40] *Works*, 3:244–45. Because Grimké did not cite the reference, it is not clear whether this is a reference to the John Watson associated with the interpretation of Christianity through a Hegelian lens and
the spread of the social gospel in Canada or the John Watson of Scotland, who identified himself as a
theological moderate opposed to what he described as the rigid evangelicalism of the Free Church of
Scotland. The overlap with social gospel ideas and idioms is clear either way. Because Grimké referred to
the latter figure in his meditations on other occasions, he most likely was referring to the John Watson
from Scotland. Concerning him, see the various comments scattered throughout W. Robertson Nicoll,
Ian MacLaren: The Life of John Watson (New York: Dodd, Mead, 1909), esp. 364–66. Grimké refers to this
work in *Works*, 3:192, 357, and Carter Woodson attributes the statement to him via Woodson's index to
the book. In addition to Watson, Grimké regularly cited authors associated more directly with the social
gospel, including White social gospel figures like Josiah Strong in "Fifty Years of Freedom," 515, and Black
theological modernists like William Stuart Nelson in *Works*, 3:191.

"cheap talk." For Grimké, Christianity was more than creeds, but it was not less.

Grimké articulated similar sentiments in support of the Christian creedal tradition at least as often as he spoke of the importance of deeds. He acknowledged that what someone "really believes" will "always be reflected in his character and life" and will "determine his character and conduct." He strenuously objected to the idea that "it doesn't matter what a man believes, it is the life that he lives that counts." He opposed the idea that theological beliefs are unimportant by asking a rhetorical question: "Is there such a thing as life apart from belief in some shape or form?" His answer was unequivocal: "Where there are no convictions, no principles, no ideals, life becomes impossible to a rational creature. . . . Every rational creature, whether he wants to or not, cannot escape convictions of some kind by which his actions will be determined." Grimké was expressly aware that there was increasing "clamor" for a "creedless church." In his view, however,

> a creedless church is no church at all: and will never be able to carry any weight with it, in influencing men to forsake their sins and cleave only to that which is good. There is no getting along without creeds of some kind in building character. It must have something to rest upon. It cannot be built on nothing.[41]

Creeds and moral character go hand in hand. Growth in holiness presumes a moral standard. A moral standard cannot be divorced from a theological system. In this way, the idea of a creedless sanctification is a contradiction in terms. The idea of sanctification depends upon the beliefs of the creed.

In another place, he wrote that to take away the creed would be to destroy the church:

> We hear a great deal now about a creedless church: as if to have a creed is discreditable to it. The simple fact is a church without a creed, without convictions, without fixed principles to which it adheres and by which it is governed, is no church at all. Such a church is unworthy of the name. It can command no respect, and can exert no uplifting and ennobling influence. It can expect no one to follow its lead, because it is leading nowhere. It stands for nothing. It represents nothing. It is nothing.[42]

---

41 *Works*, 3:281.
42 *Works*, 3:487–88.

Grimké fundamentally opposed any separation of deeds from creeds, and he also opposed the prioritization of deeds over creeds. Instead, he believed they went hand in hand. In fact, he expressed deep skepticism regarding so-called creedless Christians. He left no room for ambiguity, and he didn't mince words. "This whole talk about creedless churches and creedless individuals is pure nonsense."[43] Ethics and doctrine are inseparable and mutually dependent.

In sum, Francis Grimké's understanding of Christian sanctification led him to depend on God for growth in personal holiness. As he pastored, taught, and led, he held together the individual and the corporate dimensions of the faith. He refused to choose between doctrine, worship, and ethics and saw them as mutually reinforcing. In fact, his famous sermon "Christianity and Race Prejudice" connected the "Fatherhood of God" to the "fullness of Christ" that belonged to every "child of God," including those of every "race or nationality."[44] Therefore his rich Trinitarian understanding of personal sanctification served as the source of his confidence in the fight against race prejudice and the pursuit of moral character and personal growth. This confidence led him to exhort others to pursue the hard work of discipleship with diligence, but his high moral vision was not moralistic. He viewed growth into the fullness of Christ as ultimately depending upon the work of God's Holy Spirit. As he proclaimed to his congregation on its seventy-fifth anniversary:

> My earnest prayer is, that at the very beginning, as we start out anew, that God may baptize us all with his Holy Spirit; that he may give us all such a vision of Jesus Christ, and of what he wants us to be, and what he wants this church to be and do, that we shall be filled with a Divine enthusiasm that will never die out of our souls, but that will keep us ever pressing on—ever faithful to every duty and every responsibility.[45]

---

[43] Works, 3:487.
[44] Grimké, "Christianity and Race Prejudice," 448.
[45] Francis J. Grimké, "Anniversary Address," delivered on the seventy-fifth anniversary of the Fifteenth Street Presbyterian Church, Washington, DC, November 19, 1916, in Works, 1:553.

PART 2

THE FAMILY

Christian Nurture and Hospitality

CHAPTER 5

CHRISTIAN MARRIAGE AND THE ROLE OF THE FAMILY

Francis Grimké placed considerable emphasis on marriage and family in his preaching and teaching at Fifteenth Street Presbyterian Church. This ministry focused on biblical teaching against the backdrop of his own experiences and the experiences of his close circle of family and friends. His deep love for his wife, Charlotte, known affectionately by the family as "Lottie," and the difficult and sadly brief marriage of his brother Archibald to his wife, Sarah, together formed a well of experiences from which to draw. He also was the officiant of the extremely controversial marriage of Frederick Douglass and his second wife, Helen Pitts. At a time when interracial marriage was socially unacceptable to many, Grimké's public defense of their union revealed important aspects of his thinking related to a range of issues. Living as he did during a time of significant social and cultural upheaval, he also expressed nuanced views regarding the relationship between biblical teaching and changing contemporary understandings of the meaning and purpose of marriage. This chapter explores these contexts, as well as Grimké's teaching on Christian marriage and the role of the family in the Christian life.

The Marriage of Frederick Douglass and Helen Pitts

On January 24, 1884, a carriage brought Frederick Douglass and Helen Pitts to the Grimké home, where they planned to be married, with Francis officiating. Not only were the Douglasses and the Grimkés close friends, but Frederick was also a frequent attender of Fifteenth Street Presbyterian Church. It was an intimate occasion. Francis's wife, Charlotte, and a former senator, Blanche Bruce, and his wife, Josephine, were the only others in attendance. Though Douglass did not share the plans for the wedding even with his own children—who, according to reports, learned of the union from a journalist—the news of his marriage could not be kept hidden for long. The fame of Frederick Douglass and the scandal of an interracial marriage caught the attention of the national press.[1]

Racial animosity clearly drove the public interest in the wedding. Over two years passed between the death of Anna Douglass and Frederick's marriage to Helen. By all accounts Frederick mourned Anna's passing deeply.[2] Yet, over time, Douglass came to love Helen Pitts, and the two, knowing the storm a public relationship would create, nevertheless choose to solemnize their marriage. For over a month after the ceremony, newspaper headlines around the nation expressed outrage at the wedding of a Black man to a White woman. Frederick Douglass's celebrity only amplified the public's indignation. "A Black Man's Bride," "The Venerable Colored Orator Takes a White Wife," and "His Queer Choice," ran the headlines. Newspapers misreported the age of the newlyweds, often exaggerating Douglass's age and lowering Pitts's to make it appear that an older man had married a much younger woman, whom they also often described as lowborn or "common." Though White racism drove the headlines, the marriage offended Black commentators as well. The *Washington Grit* described the marriage as "a national calamity," and the *Weekly News* of Pittsburgh lamented: "We have no further use for him as a leader. His picture hangs in our parlor, we will hang it in the stable."[3]

In retrospect, it is not surprising that the marriage of Frederick and Helen scandalized Americans of that day. As Douglass's biographer, David Blight, observes: "This was the nineteenth century, and there had never been such an open interracial marriage by such a famous and important

---

[1] See David W. Blight, *Frederick Douglass: Prophet of Freedom* (New York: Simon and Schuster, 2018), 649–50; Francis J. Grimké, "The Second Marriage of Frederick Douglass," *Journal of Negro History* 19, no. 3 (1934): 324–29.

[2] Blight, *Frederick Douglass*, 630–31.

[3] See Leigh Fought, *Women in the World of Frederick Douglass* (New York: Oxford University Press, 2017), 229–46; *Washington Star*, January 25, 1884; *National Republican*, January 25, 1884; *Huntsville (AL) Gazette*; *Birmingham (AL) Pilot*; *Petersburg (VA) Southern Tribune*; *Little Rock (AR) Mansion*; *Pittsburgh Weekly News*; *The Grit (Washington, DC)*; all in *New York Globe*, February 9, 1884, Evans Collection, scrapbook 4. Cited in Blight, *Frederick Douglass*, 651.

black man. . . . For some, Douglass's wedding seemed like a collective loss or even disgrace."[4] For his part, Douglass took the position that his marriage was a personal rather than a public matter, and he excoriated the press for evaluating the union between a man and a woman according to their race. In one interview, Douglass alluded to Paul's speech in Acts 17 and said: "God Almighty made but one race. . . . I adopt the theory that in time the variety of races will be blended into one. . . . You may say that Frederick Douglass considers himself a member of the one race that exists." In a public response to another report, Douglass reminded the American people that the predominant reason for the mixing of the races in America was the exploitation of Black women by White men. Douglass did not mince words, concluding that "it would seem that what the American people object to is not the mixture of the races, but honorable marriage between them."[5] Opposition to interracial marriage was racism not so thinly veiled.

Though it was uncommon in his day, racial intermarriage was a subject on which Francis Grimké was well versed. Only a few years earlier, his older brother, Archibald, had married Sarah Stanley, the White daughter of an Episcopal priest named Moses C. Stanley. The marriage led to the estrangement of Sarah from her family owing to her father's disapproval.[6] From his position in more conservative Michigan, Moses Stanley expressed doubts about the progressives in Boston, claiming defensively that their support for equality did not extend to the intermarriage of their own daughters.[7] Whether or not his accusations of progressive hypocrisy were accurate, the rest of the country certainly lagged behind the expressed ideals of progressives in Boston. At any rate, because of Archibald's marriage to Sarah, and perhaps also in view of his own mother's complicated relationship with his father back on the plantation in Charleston, Francis had several years to reflect on the institution prior to Douglass's controversial union. He delivered the fruits of that reflection in a public article defending the marriage.

Originally published in 1934, Grimké's "The Second Marriage of Frederick Douglass" was not only a defense of the marriage but also a strong

4 Blight, *Frederick Douglass*, 651.
5 Interview, *Washington Post*, January 26, 1884, in *Douglass Papers*, ser. 1, 5:145–47; Douglass to J. M. Dalzell, February 1, 1884, in *Washington Star*, February 9, 1884, Evans Collection, scrapbook 4. Cited in Blight, *Frederick Douglass*, 652.
6 Kerri K. Greenidge, *The Grimkes: The Legacy of Slavery in an American Family* (New York: Liveright, 2023), 220–25.
7 M. C. Stanley to Sarah Stanley, February 21, 1879, in Archibald Grimké Papers, box 1, folder 5, Moorland-Springarn Research Center, Howard University, Washington, DC; cited in Dickson D. Bruce, *Archibald Grimké: Portrait of a Black Independent* (Baton Rouge: Louisiana State University Press, 1993), 38.

endorsement of the character of Helen Pitts. Of the marriage, Grimké acknowledged that "the intermarriage of the races may not be a wise thing, in
this country, in view of present conditions." This assessment had nothing
to do with the merits of intermarriage itself, but rather it was a commentary on the sorry state of things in America, for he also wrote: "If he wanted
to marry a white woman, and she wanted to marry him, it was a matter
between them only. It was nobody else's business. . . . The right to marry
if they want is inherent, God given. No one may rightfully forbid it." The
article emphasized Helen's loyalty to her husband, his legacy, and her support of the advancement of Black people in America. In fact, a significant
portion of the article addressed her self-sacrificing efforts to establish a
memorial to Douglass at his home in Cedar Hill, that it might serve as "a
great educational force, a center from which could radiate influences that
would keep the race steadily pressing on." Grimké acknowledged that "she
was poor, in the sense that she had to work as a clerk to earn her living," but
this poverty, rather than a detriment, "was to her credit." Those who spoke
ill of her did so "because they knew nothing of her personally." According
to Grimké, "She was a lady in the best sense of the term."[8] It was important
to him to defend both parties, Frederick and Helen, as well as the validity
and permissibility of interracial marriage itself.

For Grimké, racial intermarriage functioned as a symbol of racial dignity and equality. In "Christianity and Race Prejudice," he equated the rejection of racial intermarriage with Jim Crow and White feelings of race
superiority. Indeed the rejection of interracial marriage was one of the de-
vices of White supremacy intended to make Black people feel inferior. "The
whole aim and purpose is to impress upon this Negro race that it is inferior
to the white race, and that there must be no mingling and intermingling
on terms of equality."[9] In "God and the Race Problem," he declared that
any minister opposed to racial intermarriage was either "infected with the
virus of race prejudice" or "a moral coward." In contrast to such cowardice,
Grimké offered the example of the White minister Byron Sunderland, who
opened the doors of his church in order that Frederick Douglass might have
a place to speak when all other doors in his city were closed, even though
Sunderland "knew that he would be severely criticized" for opening his
pulpit to a Black man. Grimké's mind quickly connected the dots between

---

[8] Grimké, "The Second Marriage of Frederick Douglass," 324–29.
[9] Francis J. Grimké, "Christianity and Race Prejudice" (1910), in Works, 1:444.

racial intermarriage, racial dignity and equality more generally, and the legacy of Frederick Douglass. "Is there anything in the Bible against the intermarriage of the races?" Grimké asked. "No," was the answer. "Is there anything in the religion of Jesus Christ which forbids such a union? No. Why then should a minister of Christ say, 'I would have refused to marry them'?"[10] Grimké did not believe these were hard questions to answer.

Marriage in the Grimké Family

Clearly Francis developed strong views about interracial marriage, and his personal experiences lent urgency to the issue and a well of practical wisdom from which to draw. While he and Archibald had very different experiences, they both developed views of marriage shaped by Christian Scripture and yet formed in the crucible of their own personal trials.

Archibald's marriage was brief and tragic. Despite her feelings for Archibald, Sarah faced a difficult racial situation in Boston. It is hard to know how much the racist views of her family also shaped her actions. There is some evidence that she did not embrace the Black community in Boston, on the one hand, and that her marriage to Archibald alienated her from her previous social circles, on the other. As many of her former acquaintances moved to Boston's South End or to the suburbs in Cambridge and Brookline, she and Archibald prepared to move from the racially mixed neighborhood in the West End to a predominantly White neighborhood in Hyde Park.[11] Before the move, however, Sarah decided to leave Boston with their three-year-old daughter, Angelina, to reunite with her estranged family in Michigan. Over the next year, it became clear that she had no interest in moving back to Boston, and the next five years thereafter were fraught for her and Archibald as they argued over the terms of their separation and parental custody.[12] A few years after their separation, in 1887, Sarah sent Angelina, then seven years old, back to Boston to live with her father. Sarah spent the remaining years of her life traveling and lecturing. Having struggled with a chronic heart condition, she ultimately committed suicide eleven years after Angelina's return to Boston.[13] Archibald never remarried, and he did

10 Francis J. Grimké, "God and the Race Problem" (1903), in *Works*, 1:370.
11 Greenidge, *The Grimkes*, 244–45.
12 Greenidge, *The Grimkes*, 247–48.
13 Greenidge, *The Grimkes*, 297–98.

his best to raise Angelina, who also spent a significant portion of her childhood living with Francis and Charlotte.[14]

Francis's marriage to Charlotte, however, was a different story. They
met in 1865, the day Francis and Archibald arrived in Boston. "Lottie" was
the daughter of the prominent Philadelphia sailmaker and activist, James
Forten. Forten was one of the founders of the American Anti-Slavery Society, and his wife, also named Charlotte, was a founding member of the
society as well, along with her uncle, Robert Purvis, and her aunt, Harriet
Forten Purvis, who were among the most significant antislavery leaders
in Philadelphia.[15] When Francis and Charlotte married in 1878, just a few
months after Archibald and Sarah, their wedding brought together two of
the most prominent abolitionist families in the country. Their marriage
was a momentous occasion, and it proved to be a loving one. Though they
lost their only daughter, Theodora, when she was only six months old, they
took solace in their love for one another.[16] Their home was by all accounts
a happy one, and they enjoyed hosting and entertaining together in their
racially diverse neighborhood on Pierce Place.[17] From the frequent references to Lottie by all of Francis's most prominent ministry partners and
fellow activists in their letters, clearly the two were inseparable in service
and in life.[18]

Francis's record of his grief in his meditations after Charlotte died in
1914 is palpable. He recalled her many wonderful gifts and talents. "She
was one of the rarest spirits that ever lived." Indeed, "there never was a
sweeter, purer, gentler nature." He commented on her "refinement," her

---

[14] In his biography, Bruce notes that one of Sarah's friends wrote a letter that may be interpreted as an
accusation of marital unfaithfulness, and he also notes that the charge was vague and certainly does
not offer any details. There is no other evidence that Archibald was unfaithful, though it is possible
that Sarah accused him of such, because Angelina grew up repeating the claim. Bruce concludes that
whether there was any substance to the accusation "is only a matter for speculation." Bruce, *Archibald
Grimké*, 39. Mark Perry concludes similarly in his narrative of the Grimké family: "There is no evidence
that [Sarah] was right, however, and it is hard to believe, from Archie's own writings, that he would ever
be unfaithful." Mark Perry, *Lift Up Thy Voice: The Grimké Family's Journey from Slaveholders to Civil Rights
Leaders* (New York: Viking, 2001), 265. Greenidge draws a similar conclusion about the charges, writing
that "there was never any evidence this was true." Rather Angelina's belief that her parents "would have
remained together had [Archibald] remained true" was a "myth" that "provided comfort for a little girl
who understood neither her parents' sudden separation nor the whiteness of her early life." Greenidge,
The Grimkes, 248.
[15] Perry, *Lift Up Thy Voice*, 259.
[16] Greenidge, *The Grimkes*, 241.
[17] Greenidge, *The Grimkes*, 238.
[18] Daniel A. Payne to Francis J. Grimké, November 1, 1890, in *Works*, 4:24; Mrs. John C. Wyman to Francis J. Grimké, October 15, 1915, in *Works*, 4:151–52; Lillie Buffum Chace Wyman to Francis J. Grimké,
April 23, 1925, in *Works*, 4:402–3; Mrs. John C. Wyman to Francis J. Grimké, October 20, 1919, in *Works*,
4:253–55; Anna J. Cooper to Francis J. Grimké, December 17, 1930, in *Works*, 4:444–45; Anna J. Cooper
to Francis J. Grimké, March 27, 1932, in *Works*, 4:457; Anna J. Cooper to Francis J. Grimké, September 8,
1936, in *Works*, 4:554–55.

"young and buoyant" spirit in both youth and old age, and her literary and artistic discernment. "I have lived with her for thirty five years," he concluded, "and I can truthfully say: She was a most devoted companion. . . . And yet with all her sweetness, gentleness, and rare delicacy of nature, she was a woman of great strength of character. She could take a stand and hold it against the world." Though he lamented her loss, he acknowledged that his mourning was not without hope. He reflected on her being together with their daughter, Theodora, in the eternal presence of God. Our "earthly ties are very precious," he wrote, but "they are not to end with the grave." On the one hand, he cried, "I shall miss her more than words can tell, and shall continue to miss her till we meet again." And at the same time, he rejoiced, "She is free, and full of life, blessed life, that will never more become eclipsed."[19] He proceeded to record similar loving, yearning, and hopeful entries in his meditations in the months ahead and every year on the anniversary of her death until the end of his life.[20]

Whereas Francis and Charlotte experienced a lifelong marriage filled with love, Archibald and Sarah struggled through a brief few years filled with racially laden friction and a difficult parental partnership. Yet both chose to marry freely. Their diverse marriage experiences, however constricted by societal or familial expectations, were free from the nature of the circumstances experienced by their mother, Nancy Weston, on the plantation in Charleston. Nancy's relationship with Henry Grimké, however "free," was nevertheless that of property to its owner. Though Nancy refused to complain or to speak ill of the boys' father, the fact remains that she resided with them in the slaves' quarters, and not in the plantation residence. When it comes to understanding the context of Francis Grimké's teaching on marriage, the events in his own marriage, those of Archibald's, and the relationship between Nancy Weston and Henry Grimké were all significant. The experience of racial difference, public perception, power disparity, abandonment, love, mutuality, partnership, and duty in marriage all stirred his reflections on the Scriptures and shaped the counsel he gave his congregation. Certainly, these factors were important in Archibald's life as well. After so many years in Boston, his transition to the Washington, DC, chapter of the NAACP involved his role in arguing against the attempt

---

[19] *Works*, 3:5–6.
[20] *Works*, 3:8, 10, 12, 34, 50, 69, 80, 93, 100, 107, 114, 115, 126, 165, 220, 267, 330, 474, 543, 610. There is no evidence for Greenidge's claim that Francis's motivation in marrying Charlotte was predominantly or even significantly his "increasingly status-conscious" mentality. See Greenidge, *The Grimkes*, 231. Indeed, the evidence in his meditations is overwhelmingly to the contrary.

to prohibit interracial marriage in the District of Columbia, though that is another story.[21] The experience of his own marriage, as well as that of his brother and mother, profoundly informed his preaching and teaching on the subject.

The "Companionate Marriage" Controversy

Francis Grimké preached at least two major sermon series on marriage. The first was in 1887, the year Archibald sent seven-year-old Angelina to live with him and Charlotte in Washington. He preached a version of the same series again in 1917, just a few years after the failed federal legislation that would have banned interracial marriage in the District of Columbia, bringing the nation's capital into conformity with the law of all the southern states.[22] The second series came just before a nationwide controversy over what became known as "companionate marriage." In 1927, newspapers across the country reported the marriage of an eighteen-year-old high school student to her twenty-year-old boyfriend, a college student. The marriage took place without traditional vows, permitting their divorce without alimony if they remained without children after two years. The couple planned to live separately (he in college; she with her parents) while they completed their education. Their marriage was an illustration of what historians have characterized as a transition during this period from a view of marriage oriented around lifelong commitment and procreation to a notion that emphasized mutual sexual desire and emotional fulfillment.[23]

One of the better-known popularizers of the idea of companionate marriage in the early twentieth century was Judge Ben Lindsey. His articles and radio messages in the mid-1920s laid the groundwork for a book on the topic coauthored with Wainwright Evans in 1927.[24] The series of Lindsey's articles published in the *Redbook* magazine between October 1926 and

---

[21] Perry, *Lift Up Thy Voice*, 334.

[22] In 1912, there was an attempt to pass a federal law to ban interracial marriage. At the time, it was legal in the District of Columbia, though twenty-nine of the forty-eight states already had anti-miscegenation laws, and eleven other state legislatures were considering them. See Peggy Pascoe, *What Comes Naturally: Miscegenation Law and the Making of Race in America* (New York: Oxford, 2009), 168. After the attempt at a federal ban failed, 1913 saw a more modest attempt to make interracial marriage illegal in the District of Columbia. The bill passed without debate in the House but failed in the Senate. A similar bill also failed in 1915, when it again passed the House, only to die in a Senate committee. As mentioned above, Archibald Grimké played a role in helping to defeat the legislation, distinguishing the District of Columbia from all the southern states on the issue.

[23] See Rebecca L. Davis, "'Not Marriage at All, but Simple Harlotry': The Companionate Marriage Controversy," *Journal of American History* 94, no. 4 (2008): 1137–63.

[24] Benjamin Barr Lindsey and Wainwright Evans, *Companionate Marriage* (North Stratford, NH: Ayer, 1927). See Davis, "'Not Marriage at All,'" 1142.

April 1927 caught the attention of Grimké and his close associates. Bolton Smith, the Memphis attorney who worked to form the National Committee on Inter-Racial Activities for the Boy Scouts of America, which in turn created the African American Scout troops, was a friend of the Grimkés and sympathetic with aspects of Lindsey's thoughts. In a series of letters, he expressed his interest in Lindsey's works and asked Francis to share his own view. Having read Lindsey's book *Companionate Marriage*, Smith wrote, "I have come to the conclusion the old morality has been far too rigid." He indicated a highly complex rationale, one too complex to unfold in the space of a short letter—namely, that "some things which I have thought of as wrong and beyond forgiveness in plantation field hands may present another aspect." Exactly what aspect, he neglected to say, declaring that "the subject is too big to take up here nor is it really one for argument— rather for silent weighing in the mind wishing only to see the true road for human happiness." He concluded his letter with an appeal that Francis read Judge Lindsey's *Redbook* articles.[25]

Either Grimké did not reply to Lindsey's arguments promptly, or the two may have had a rather pointed conversation on aspects of the book and Smith wanted Grimké to explore its themes more deeply, for he wrote him a few months later recommending that he read a new work of social science entitled *Races, Nations and Classes*, by Herbert Adolphus Miller.[26] Miller was an associate of W. E. B. Du Bois, taught sociology at Oberlin College and then at Ohio State University, and generally was critical of the idea of racial assimilation to "American" values. Smith's tone in this follow-up letter was conciliatory: "After so much emotional talk on the subjects it is good to read something coldly scientific—The cause in which you used to believe loses nothing through such a presentation." His postscript again recommended Lindsey's writings and invited Grimké to return his opinion on Lindsey's most recent *Redbook* article.[27] The most likely explanation for the letter is that Smith knew Judge Lindsey's position was incendiary, that Grimké was slow to reply, and that he desired to press his engagement with the matter.

Apparently, Grimké responded by sending Smith copies of his sermons on marriage. Smith's reply indicates that Grimké's understanding of divine revelation represented a key difference with Smith's thoughts on the

---

[25] Bolton Smith to Francis J. Grimké, November 16, 1926, in *Works*, 4:408.

[26] Herbert Adolphus Miller, *Races, Nations and Classes* (Philadelphia: Lipincott, 1924).

[27] Bolton Smith to Francis J. Grimké, March 19, 1927, in *Works*, 4:415.

matter. "I feel that divine revelation continues now as in the past," Smith replied, and furthermore that "men put into the mouth of God many of their own views then as now." On the one hand, Smith minimized the authority of the text of Scripture itself, and on the other hand, he suggested that traditional doctrinal commitments based on the text were unwarranted interpretations. Whereas Grimké held a traditional view of scriptural authority, which emphasized the trustworthiness of Scripture's words, Smith endorsed a modernist view that located inspiration not in the "forms" of Scripture but rather in "profound *principles* of right." Smith concluded, "We cannot be expected, all of us, to look at these things alike."[28] Grimké probably would have agreed with the premise that views on marriage reflected potentially irreconcilable differences resulting from different views of divine revelation, scriptural inspiration, and scriptural authority. He was less sympathetic with Smith's confidence in his personal ability to identify "principles of right" that contradicted scriptural teaching.

Along with his sermons on the subject, explored below, Grimké's letter to Smith underlines his high view of Scripture and its application to practical matters in the Christian life. He was willing to grant that Lindsey's ideas on companionate marriage were worthy of reflection. Even if his conclusions were unsound, Lindsey raised important questions. Referring to his April *Redbook* article, Grimké conceded, "There is much in it that should give us serious thought." Nevertheless, Grimké's doctrine of scriptural inspiration and authority led him to reject the core of Lindsey's argument. "I fail to see that anything which he has suggested is an improvement on the great law laid down by God in his holy Word governing the relation between the sexes," he wrote. Regarding the seventh commandment and biblical teaching on marriage and sexuality, "it is to be presumed that Moses under divine guidance, knew quite as much about all the matter, in all its bearings, as Judge Lindsey does." Having identified his reliance on scriptural teaching, Grimké identified two principles drawn from Scripture. First, "adultery" refers to "all carnal sexual intercourse between the sexes out of lawful wedlock, or its equivalent." Second, the biblical reason for this principle is that the "life-generating power" is to be "exercised only within the family circle." Scripture links procreation with marriage. The bearing and raising of children, and not only the mutual enjoyment of husband and wife, is central to the biblical concept of marriage. Grimké's trust in scrip-

---

28 Bolton Smith to Francis J. Grimké, April 5, 1927, in *Works*, 4:415, emphasis original.

tural revelation led him to trust the biblical connection between marriage and procreation. Childbearing should not be separated from marriage, and marriage should not be (willfully) separated from childbearing.

Thus, Grimké rooted his opposition to contemporary notions of companionate marriage in his doctrine of Scripture. He observed that "many attempts have been made to override, to set aside the code of morals in the Bible; but in vain. It still stands, and will stand to the end of time, as the only true, the only wise, the only safe course to pursue." Therefore, "it is a bad policy to be playing hide and seek with morals" by teaching young people that sexual relations may be pursued outside of marriage, or that the permanence of marriage may be questioned. Biblical teaching is clear, Grimké reasoned, and therefore, "we are safe as individuals, as families, as communities, only so long as we hold to the lofty standard of morals laid down in the word of God." He emphasized to Smith that the clarity of biblical teaching meant that no amount of articles or books by Lindsey would change his mind. "Those are my views on the matter, and nothing that Judge Lindsey may say, or a thousand Judge Lindseys may have to say will change in the least my views." Referring to the teaching of Jesus in the Sermon on the Mount, he concluded:

> Only as we build on the Word of God: only as we are following the line marked out there are we building on rock foundations. If we build on anything else, sooner or later, the structure is bound to go down. The more I study the Word of God, the more am I impressed with its superlative value, its transcendent importance to the human race.[29]

Francis Grimké's Sermons on Marriage

Grimké's teaching on marriage clearly reflected his commitment to the trustworthy nature of scriptural truth. To understand his sermons, it is important to keep in mind the contexts considered above—namely, his defense of interracial marriage on biblical grounds and his nuanced critique of the companionate marriage movement's minimization of marital duties, especially the shared task of raising of children. After establishing a

---

[29] Francis J. Grimké to Bolton Smith, undated, in *Works*, 4:485–86. Though undated, the letter must have followed Smith's March letter, to which Grimké makes explicit reference. Grimké wrote, "Since writing you, I have read Judge Lindsey's article in the April number of Red Book," and Smith's April letter expresses, "Many thanks for your letters and for the sermons." Smith to Grimké, April 5, 1927. Therefore, Grimké's undated letter either accompanied the sermons Smith mentioned or, more likely, was a follow-up letter composed soon after sending them.

biblical foundation for the nature and purpose of marriage in an introductory sermon, Grimké proceeded to preach a series of sermons on the qualifications, blessings, and duties of marriage. These sermons in turn set the stage for extended reflections on marital happiness. The series concluded with an honest treatment of the biblical grounds for divorce and the respective roles of civil and spiritual authorities. In general, the sermons reflect Grimké's principled application of scriptural teaching to the practical and daily aspects of the Christian life.

When it came to the nature of marriage, it is interesting that Grimké chose as his text Genesis 2:18, "And God said, it is not good for man to be alone; I will make him a helpmeet for him."[30] From the beginning, he emphasized the blessing and the relational aspects of marriage. At the same time, he emphasized that "like every other relation in life," marriage entails both "requirements" and "conditions." Therefore, the "laws governing this relation can no more be disregarded with impunity than the laws governing any other relation." Grimké characterized marriage as a relationship framed by rules. He also explicitly named his primary purposes in preaching the series: first, "to help those who have not yet entered into the marriage relation . . . to avoid the errors and mistakes of those who entered it blindly" and, second, "to help those already [married] . . . to a partial solution, at least, of some of their difficulties."[31] He took a realistic approach to marriage, assuming that his congregation needed guidance for present difficulties as well as preparation to minimize future ones in order to enjoy its relational blessings.

With these purposes in mind, he then offered a three-part definition of marriage. First, it is "a union instituted by God" in the garden of Eden. As a result, "it is a part of the Divine plan for humanity that men and women should be so united." Second, "it is a union between one man and one woman." Grimké grounded this principle in Genesis 2:24 and 1 Corinthians 7:2, which, he noted, command husbands to have one wife rather than many. In addition to these biblical foundations, he also based his arguments on natural law (equal birth rates of men and women) and the law of nations (reflecting the general agreement of "Christian lands"). Third, marriage "is a union of the affections." Here he emphasized the importance

---

[30] Though most of the sermons in the series are dated to both 1897 and 1913, Woodson gives only the former date for this sermon. The rising temperature of the companionate marriage controversy may have led Grimké to frame the series from another angle when he preached through it a second time. See the note on Francis J. Grimké, "Marriage and Kindred Subjects" (sermon 1 of 13), in *Works*, 2:121.

[31] Grimké, "Marriage and Kindred Subjects" (sermon 1), 121–22.

of "a strong, pure love" in marriage, but he carefully distinguished this love from "sentimentality" or mere "elation of feeling." Turning to Paul's teaching in Ephesians 5 and appealing to the example of Christ's love for the church, Grimké emphasized that love within marriage is more than "care" for one another, being "agreeable to each other," being "close friends," or finding "pleasure" in each other. If Christ's love for the church is the model for marital love, Grimké observed that "the Bible idea of this relation, you will perceive, is a very exalted one" and therefore "makes it clear that it should be entered into only by those who are bound together by the strongest affection." He acknowledged that his definition of marriage set a high bar for entering it, and consequently that the acceptance of this three-part definition of marriage would lead to fewer marriages, but he did not see this as a problem at all. "Better, infinitely better it is to have fewer marriages, than such marriages as we see, in so many instances now-a-days," he observed wryly.[32]

In addition to deep and genuine love, Grimké considered "respect" and "mutual confidence" essential to a true "union of the affections." He believed that self-respect and respect for others are both rooted in character and, therefore, that partners with strong character will tend to respect each other.[33] Conversely, "the marriage between people who are not self-respecting, and who have no real, true respect for each other, is sure to be a failure." He articulated the principle of mutual confidence in terms of "mutual trust" and "implicit faith." By emphasizing respect and mutual confidence alongside love, Grimké presented a picture of affection that affirmed the importance of feelings but also emphasized that feelings must be grounded in concrete characteristics, which, unsurprisingly for him, were ethical in nature. Practically speaking, this emphasis on character meant that "marriage should never be hastily contracted," for it took time to ensure that such assessments were not made superficially. He characterized the marriage of recent acquaintances "unwise," and he discouraged marriages based on looks or finances or status. This last point is especially worthy of attention. Grimké acknowledged the realities of wealth and status. Wealth is not "a thing to be despised," for it "may be made a great blessing" and a source of "comfort" and "happiness." Yet "people drawn together from such considerations cannot, in the nature of the case, be happy." Similarly,

---

[32] Grimké, "Marriage and Kindred Subjects" (sermon 1), 123–25.
[33] For more on Grimké's understanding of self-respect, see chap. 3.

on the topic of social standing, he granted, "There can be no objection to aspiring to ally ourselves in marriage with people of distinction in order to get into what we call good families." But "if that is the sole reason or the princip[al] reason for desiring a union, it will not be likely to be a happy one." In fact, "it is better to marry a woman in the humblest walks of life, if we love her and she commands our respect and confidence, than to marry a princess simply because she is a princess." Wealth and social status are real factors of life, but they are trumped by respect and mutual confidence based on shared principles of moral conduct and, related to this, by love grounded in mutual admiration and commitment.[34] "To sum up," Grimké declared, "marriage is not a union based on external beauty, wealth or position. It is a heart-union from first to last."[35]

After setting forth a vision of marriage as a "divinely established relation" between "one man and one woman" and as a "union of the affections" only to be entered into by couples assured of their mutual respect and trust, Grimké proceeded to preach on the qualifications, blessings, and duties of marriage. The qualifications included being of the proper age, being satisfactorily distant in relation, and the husband being able to support a family. Here again, Grimké relied upon both Scripture and natural law, along with the law of nations, in supporting these positions.[36] He also emphasized the importance of a shared Christian faith, drawing from 2 Corinthians 6:14 and 1 Corinthians 7:39 to emphasize that Christians should not be "unequally yoked" and should marry "in the Lord." He pointed out that the importance of a shared faith not only relates to the Christian faith in general but also extends to traditions within Christianity. For example, he noted the significant differences between Protestants and Catholics on the canon of Scripture, the role of tradition, the authority of the church, the nature of the priesthood, the sacraments, and the very

---

[34] Grimké's private meditations on his own marriage attest to the fact that he practiced what he preached. The claim that his marriage was motivated by insatiable social climbing not only lacks historical evidence but is contradicted both by his stated principles and by the record of his private reflections. Cf. Greenidge, The Grimkes, 231.

[35] Grimké, "Marriage and Kindred Subjects" (sermon 1), 125–30.

[36] Grimké, "Marriage and Kindred Subjects" (sermon 2), 132–41. Whereas he frequently utilized general revelation to illustrate or strengthen his arguments from special revelation, at times his reliance upon cultural conventions went well beyond the application of scriptural teaching. His arguments from Scripture typically reflected standard interpretations and placed him in the mainstream of the Reformed tradition on these topics. For example, his teaching on marital age and consanguinity reflected statements in the Westminster Standards. And yet his arguments from the law of nations at times leaned heavily upon the cultural assumptions of his day. For example, he taught that women who worked as teachers should cease to teach after marrying in order that their husband might support them financially, and he taught that women should not marry men working in the alcoholic beverage industry (139, 140).

definition of grace. Because it is "impossible ever to harmonize" such irreconcilable beliefs, parents would inevitably have to choose one or the other set of beliefs for their children. Therefore, he held that it is "unwise" for Catholics and Protestants to marry. In regard to the Protestant denominations, though they shared "the great essentials" and therefore he would not "say it is unwise" to marry a member of another Protestant denomination, still "it would be better" to "find a partner of your own distinctive faith if possible." For Grimké, it was good to be a "zealous" practitioner of the Christian faith, and therefore it was important to find an equal partner in marriage.[37]

Having discussed the qualifications for marriage, he then preached several sermons on the blessings and duties of matrimony. It is interesting that he placed heavy emphasis on the blessing of companionship, on the one hand, and the duties of love, on the other. The biblical teaching that love is more than a feeling and must be expressed in lifelong honor, support, and faithfulness pushed against the contractual nature and lack of commitment endorsed by the companionate marriage movement. At the same time, Grimké readily acknowledged the many good elements of the movement's emphasis on mutuality and companionship. The primary problem with the movement was not its emphasis on companionship but its evacuation of commitment, its contractual view of sexual relationships, and its redefinition of love in purely emotional terms.[38] The companionship of marriage is a beautiful thing, for "it is the companionship, the delightful fellowship with the one who is nearer and dearer to us than all others on earth, that makes home so attractive to us, and so hard for us to tear ourselves away from it, even for a little while." Such companionship, Grimké pointed out, demands a promise to "live together till death us do part," for Scripture reveals that "God intended" for the marriage relation to "permanently" bring "together two lives."[39]

This understanding of the close relationship between blessings and duty in turn informed Grimké's teaching on marital happiness, a subject on which he dwelt for three sermons. He encouraged his congregation poetically:

---

[37] Grimké, "Marriage and Kindred Subjects" (sermon 3), 141–46.

[38] On the positive aspects of companionship and the blessings of marriage, see Grimké, "Marriage and Kindred Subjects" (sermon 4), 153–63, esp. 156. On the duties of marriage, see Grimké, "Marriage and Kindred Subjects" (sermons 5 and 6), 167–73 and 173–85. On honor, see 177–78; on support, see 179–80; on faithfulness, see 182–83.

[39] Grimké, "Marriage and Kindred Subjects" (sermon 4), 157.

There is still another thing about this delicate and beautiful plant we call love that it would be well for us also to remember. While it may be diminished, it may also be increased; while it may be weakened, it may also be strengthened, invigorated. It is capable of expansion, of growth, of development.[40]

In this way, he acknowledged the reality of marital difficulties and unhappiness but also emphasized the possibility of cultivating happiness through mutual devotion. His goal was to paint a picture of marriage worth pursuing, and the widely known happiness of his own marriage lent credibility to his words. While Grimké never hesitated to give strenuous exhortations, his preaching often emphasized the blessings of following God's commands.

Though the sermon series ended on a positive note with the theme of happiness in marriage, on other occasions Grimké preached on the biblical teaching regarding divorce.[41] Following the summary of biblical teaching in the Westminster Confession of Faith, he identified adultery and willful desertion as the two grounds permitting the dissolution of a marriage. Citing Matthew 19:3ff. and 1 Corinthians 7:12–15 he declared, "According to the Bible, then, marriage is a union for life, to be dissolved only by death, or for the cause of adultery or willful desertion."[42] He acknowledged that other difficulties, including habitual drunkenness, persistent cruelty, life imprisonment, a bad temper, and cases of insanity might make a separation necessary, but that none of these circumstances warrants a divorce.[43] "Sad as these conditions are, do they, after all, justify the severance of the marriage bond—the setting of people free to marry again? The answer which the Bible gives to this question is, no, emphatically, no."[44] Indeed, "it follows that all persons who are divorced on other than scriptural grounds and marry again are guilty of the sin of adultery." In fact, he continued,

---

[40] Grimké, "Marriage and Kindred Subjects" (sermon 8), 205.

[41] Though Carter Woodson included the sermons on divorce in the same numbered series in Grimké's collected works, the dates of these sermons are noticeably disconnected from the other sermons. The second preaching series on marriage took place in the summer of 1917, and he gave the sermons on divorce on December 2, 1917, and June 29, 1919. See Grimké, "Marriage and Kindred Subjects" (sermon 12), 238, and Grimké, "Marriage and Kindred Subjects" (sermon 13), 249, for the dates.

[42] Grimké, "Marriage and Kindred Subjects" (sermon 12), 240, 242–43, 245. He explicitly cited the order of "the Presbyterian Church" on p. 246: "I want to say also, in this connection, this is not only the teaching of the Word of God: it is also the law of the Presbyterian Church, the great body of believers bearing that name throughout the world. And, so far as I know, is the law of all Evangelical Christian churches. The twenty-fourth chapter of our Confession of faith deals with the subject of marriage."

[43] Grimké, "Marriage and Kindred Subjects" (sermon 13), 250–56.

[44] Grimké, "Marriage and Kindred Subjects" (sermon 13), 252.

"They are just as much adulterers, in the sight of God, as two single people would be who simply took up with each other and lived together without any marriage ceremony."[45] Throughout both sermons, he acknowledged the distance between biblical teaching on the subject and societal norms, even civil law, and he repeatedly lifted up the superiority and the trustworthiness of biblical teaching in spite of this distance. He concluded the first sermon on the topic, "Nothing is clearer, from what is taking place about us today, than the folly of man's attempting to improve on God's law in regard to the matter."[46]

Francis Grimké's teaching on marriage applied biblical revelation to practical concerns. In fact, in preaching on marriage he explicitly criticized sermons that avoided such application. Such sermons were of "no practical value." As he put it, "Not less, but more sermons that deal with practical every day problems of life [are] what is needed in all of our pulpits." Regarding such problems, the "truth is what is needed, and one reason why some people are no better than they are is because they have been all their lives running away from the truth."[47]

Grimké's reliance on biblical truth allowed him to cut through the cultural confusion of his own day. He was a champion of interracial marriage in a time when it was illegal in most of the country: he officiated the marriage of Frederick Douglass, defended the marriage of his own brother, and offered a strong biblical rationale for the "right" to marry across racial lines. On the other hand, biblical revelation enabled him to offer a nuanced critique of the companionate marriage movement. He declared that the emphasis on companionship was right and good, and he affirmed it poetically. His own reputation and marriage to Charlotte lent credibility to his words. But he relentlessly took issue with the movement's rejection of lifelong commitment. He also criticized the emphasis on feelings and personal fulfillment at the expense of duty and self-sacrifice. He claimed, with a sense of irony, that advocates of companionate marriage delivered the opposite of the happiness they sought and promised. Jesus taught that happiness in marriage comes through commitment and self-sacrifice, and

---

[45] Grimké, "Marriage and Kindred Subjects" (sermon 13), 245.
[46] Grimké, "Marriage and Kindred Subjects" (sermon 13), 248.
[47] Grimké, "Marriage and Kindred Subjects" (sermon 6), 184.

the rejection of these aspects of biblical marriage undermined not only the institution but the very good people longed for in their misguided pursuit of other paths.

Some recent treatments of Grimké's teaching on marriage and social issues more broadly have characterized it as "Victorian," captivated by a conservative nineteenth-century moral vision.[48] This claim is worthy of serious consideration. Some aspects of Grimké's teaching on social issues were indeed driven as much by the culture of his day as by biblical revelation. The temperance movement's advocacy of total abstinence from alcohol could not claim the practice or teaching of Jesus in its favor. Grimké's view that women should not work outside the home after marriage is hard to square with various passages of Scripture, including Proverbs 31. These certainly are examples of aspects of Grimké's teaching fueled as much by cultural assumption as by biblical teaching.

On the other hand, there are two significant problems with the characterization of Grimké's ministry as Victorian and conservative. First, this characterization anachronistically conflates "Victorian" with "conservative" upper-middle-class striving. On the contrary, Leslie Butler demonstrates compellingly that the Victorian conception of personal cultivation had its roots "not in class-bound terms of etiquette but in liberal Protestantism." It was Unitarians like William Ellery Channing who "championed self-improvement as the development of those moral, religious, intellectual, social, and imaginative faculties that all humans possessed." It was "Victorian liberals" who saw "cultivation" as "a continual process." If Butler is correct, the identification of Victorian with conservative class striving makes it impossible to understand Grimké in his own time and place. As she notes:

> Victorian cultivation might seem to lend itself to twenty-first-century scorn as the exclusive concern of snobbish and posturing elites. But to collapse a set of rich and compelling meanings into a reflection on social refinement or the display of polished manners would impoverish our understanding of a concept that continues to animate American life.[49]

---

[48] For example, Kerri Greenidge says that Grimké "cultivated a conservative culture of racial respectability that reinforced the lessons of his enslaved youth for a new generation of Black leaders and tastemakers." For Greenidge, "the result was a pastorate that reenacted rather than challenged the intraracial fissures and personal injuries" of slavery and its legacy. Greenidge, *The Grimkes*, 240.

[49] Leslie Butler, *Critical Americans: Victorian Intellectuals and Transatlantic Liberal Reform* (Chapel Hill: University of North Carolina Press, 2007), 7.

In some ways Grimké reflected mainstream Victorian values. In other ways he pushed against them. It is as simplistic to identify Grimké with Victorian values as it is to identify Victorian values with conservatism.

The second problem with referring to Grimké's social teaching as Victorian conservatism is that categories like "liberal" and "conservative" are moving targets. The temperance movement of Grimké's day manifestly was not conservative. Progressive advocates for abolition and women's suffrage were a significant driving force of the temperance movement. This demonstrates that the identification of the elements of Grimké's teaching that were "conservative" or "liberal" requires that we consider them according to his own historical context. Grimké's advocacy for interracial marriage was not conservative either. On this basis and others explored in parts 3 and 4, this book will continue to challenge the simplistic identification of Grimké's teaching on racial issues with conservative notions of racial uplift. On the other hand, while Grimké was progressive on the temperance issue and had a complicated relationship with the racial discourse of his day, his advocacy for a traditional conception of marriage was distinctly conservative. In short, relative to his own day, on these three issues Grimké's teaching could be described respectively as "liberal," "moderate," and "conservative."

Rather than describing Grimké as Victorian or conservative or liberal, it is more accurate to acknowledge his willingness to allow the Bible to challenge a variety of cultural assumptions. His uncritical embrace of the temperance movement and some of his views on women's roles reveal that he was not always consistent in his stated goal. Some of his views reflected his cultural environment more than the Bible. Nevertheless, according to his own words and also in the eyes of his contemporaries, his social vision was characterized by the attempt, however imperfect, to be faithful to scriptural teaching. Looking back, present-day critics may be justified in referring to some of his views as Victorian. But Francis Grimké's willingness to push against both conservatives and liberals in his own day gives credence to his expressed intention to submit to God's word regardless of cultural approval.

CHAPTER 6

THE NURTURE OF CHILDREN

In 1934, W. W. McCary wrote to Francis Grimké to thank him for sending a pamphlet entitled "Our Young People! How to Deal with Them."[1] In the letter he acknowledged a variety of social factors making it difficult for young people to follow the Christian faith, including "'companionate marriages' of indefinite length without the formality of written agreements." In his mind, the cultural pressures of the day related to marriage were closely tied to the pressures experienced by young people more generally. Though he later moved to New York, he developed a relationship with Grimké when McCary pastored in Fairmont Heights, one of the first planned communities for African Americans in the Washington, DC, area. It housed the county's first public school for African Americans, built in 1912.[2] McCary's concern for the well-being of young people was a consistent theme of his letters to Grimké, and surely his years of ministry to the families of Fairmont Heights played a significant role in that concern.[3]

It is not surprising that McCary appreciated Grimké's teaching regarding children, for, like marriage, the nurture and education of children was a prominent theme in Grimké's teaching ministry. The earliest date given for the sermons in Grimké's collected works was the summer of 1888, and

---

[1] W. W. McCary to Francis J. Grimké, November 27, 1934, in *Works*, 4:519–20.
[2] McCary's letters, addressed from New York, are dated 1934. See Betty Bird, "Building Community: Housing for Middle-Class African Americans in Washington, DC, and Prince George's County, Maryland, 1900–1955," in *Housing Washington: Two Centuries of Residential Development and Planning in the National Capital Area*, ed. Richard Longstreth (Chicago: Center for American Places at Columbia College, 2010), 61–84.
[3] See also W. W. McCary to Francis J. Grimké, December 10, 1934, in *Works*, 4:522–23.

he also preached the bulk of them again in 1901 in a series coinciding with the end of the school year. He also preached many of the same sermons again at the beginning of each school year in the early 1920s and on other occasions. In addition to his sermons, Grimké frequently recorded his reflections on the role of the home in the Christian life. This chapter will trace the central themes of Grimké's reflections on the home as well as his teaching on the education of children in the Christian home.

The Role of the Home in the Christian Life

Throughout their lives together, Francis and Charlotte Grimké shared a loving home. On the third anniversary of his beloved Lottie's death, Francis recorded in his meditations a reflection that revealed his deep love for her and his longing to be with her. "It seems strange to be off on a vacation without her," he wrote. "I always take her picture with me and put it in my room just where I can see it, and no day passes but that I am reminded of her." His memory of her was still vivid. In fact, he wrote, "The old time still exists, and the old bond still holds, and will ever hold." The passage of time could not diminish, he said, the "kindly sentiment that bound us together, and that still binds us together."[4] Their love and commitment to one another bound their household together, and during their many years of marriage, it made it a home.

That same anniversary week, he also reflected on his visit with a dear friend from his seminary days at Princeton, Matthew Anderson. They sat together on Anderson's porch in Philadelphia, watching the busy passersby in the street. It led him to wonder what the streets of heaven would be like, and whether they would be similarly busy. Thus, as he spent time in the earthly home of one of his dearest spiritual brothers, it turned his attention to his eternal home. And as he passed through this earthly world, he contemplated his spiritual destiny: "Wherever I go, or however long I may be away, that spot is my home, and it is there that I finally turn my steps." He remembered Jesus's words in John 14:2: "In my Fathers [sic] house there are many mansions, or abiding places. I go to prepare a place for you." Ruminating on those words, he wrote: "It is certainly a happy thought. We are not to be wandering everywhere [in the next life] without a local habitation. We have homes here; and we shall have them on the other side." What

4 *Works*, 3:34–35.

will these homes be like, and what will relationships be like there? "We do not know definitely. . . . One thing we are assured of, 'It will be the abode of peace and happiness.' Beyond this, we need not be concerned."[5] These reflections reveal the deep affection he felt for his earthly home and household, and the even higher priority he placed on his eternal home. One of the primary purposes of his earthly home was to be a place of preparation for eternal life, and he looked forward to life in that eternal home with great hope.

As Grimké held on to this hope of an eternal home, he emphasized the importance of the earthly home throughout his life and ministry. The section below will explore this emphasis in detail by reviewing his sermon series on the education of children, and he made clear that a strong home provides the context for effectiveness in that education. In 1917 he gave an address before the Presbyterian Council in Rochester, New York, titled "The Home as a Training School." There he put it memorably: "The question therefore is, not as to whether the home shall have a part in this mighty moulding process which is to shape the future (It is bound to have) but what part?" The influence of the home can be positive or negative, either "in the direction of making good men and women" or "men and women of the opposite type." He concluded, "As a matter of fact every home is working in one or the other of these directions."[6]

Grimké related his focus on the home to his characteristic emphases on Scripture and the kingdom of God. Regarding Scripture, he wrote in his meditations that the Bible is the source not only of "the great principles and ideals" for building "individual character and life" and social mores but also of the "life and character of the family." Therefore, it should be read widely by families just as by individuals and societies, for it contains "more real wisdom for the guidance of humanity" than any other book.[7] Just as the family must depend on the Scriptures for wisdom, so also the family must rely on the work of God in bringing his kingdom. "The welfare of the individual, family, the community, will depend upon the extent to which [the kingdom] comes." While the coming kingdom correlates with the acceptance of and obedience to the "ideals and principles" of Scripture, the ability to embrace and follow those ideals can only come from God. "A change is necessary, and it can come only under the regenerating power

---

[5] *Works*, 3:35–36.
[6] Francis J. Grimké, "The Home as a Training School" (1917), in *Works*, 2:461.
[7] *Works*, 3:563.

of the Holy Spirit, under the reign of Jesus Christ."[8] The family, just as the individual, must depend on God to bring his kingdom and must look to God's word as the guide for kingdom living.

Toward the end of his life, Grimké moved in with the Gray family. They lived near Fifteenth Street Presbyterian Church, on Rhode Island Avenue, and were "dear friends" of the Grimkés. Francis recorded in his meditations that he had been close with their parents as well, and he spoke of their home in glowing terms. "The atmosphere that pervades the home is full of sunshine." Their home was "full of the milk of human kindness," "peaceful," and "full of thought for others," including "people who are sick, sorrowing, suffering" and "the poor and the needy."[9] According to Grimké, the joy in the Gray household grew out of their commitment to following God's command to love and serve others. On another occasion, he described the Grays' commitment to serving the sick in their community, writing that "they never seem to be weary of doing something to help make things pleasanter for others. And the result is, they are always themselves full of sunshine, of good cheer. It is a glorious way to live. It is the way to make life worth living."[10] Thus, in forming his views of the importance of the home, Grimké not only drew on his own household experiences and the teaching of Scripture but also drew from the example of others in his spiritual community.

Several themes characterize Grimké's emphasis on the role of the home in the Christian life. First, he consistently taught on the importance of the home environment for the nurture of children. For example, in his meditations he reflected on a young child sent to spend some time with her aunt. The child, according to Grimké, was "unusually bright" and had great potential, but she also possessed a very strong will. The aunt with whom she was staying was very fond of her and continually gave in to the child when she demanded her way. In Grimké's view, "the sooner that child, beautifully situated as she was, is taken out of that environment and sent back into the environment of her home where she will be under proper discipline, the better it will be for her."[11] The child needed an environment of consistent discipline, and the indulgent environment of her present circumstances did her harm.

8 Works, 3:572.
9 Works, 3:499.
10 Works, 3:603.
11 Works, 3:347.

In his teaching, Grimké defined a home environment as "the sum total of all the influences at work within it." He noted that some homes only emphasize the importance of material concerns like "furniture . . . eating and drinking and dressing, about money-making and having a good time." Others emphasize intellectual matters: "They keep in touch with the world of thought." Yet others have a significant moral atmosphere in which "the chief emphasis is laid upon character, upon truthfulness and honesty and purity and sobriety." Finally, some homes set a strong "religious or spiritual tone." For Grimké, "religion, where it is real, genuine, gives a distinct tone to the atmosphere of the home where it exists. You can't mistake it. It always makes itself felt." The home environment "is the mightiest in determining the character of our children." In fact, children "are not only affected by the home life, but are more powerfully affected by it than by anything else."[12] The context of the home environment is even more influential than the content of formal teaching. Therefore, the home environment as a whole is the most important factor in the nurture of Christian children.

After the family environment, Grimké emphasized the closely related role of hospitality in his reflections on the home. In addition to his time with the Gray family, Grimké lived temporarily with other families at the end of his life as a widower. In some cases, he rented a room. He recorded reflections on his time in 1928 with one such unnamed family in his meditations:[13] "There are some things that you can't pay for. I boarded in a family last summer. The physical surroundings were beautiful; the house was well furnished, well cared for, and the food was good, good in quality and well prepared and served. I paid the board, paid in full what was charged." He went on to note that such surroundings had a price, but nevertheless his experience there went beyond what any price could pay, for "there was one thing which I did not pay for, could not pay for, and that was the kindly spirit that pervaded it. You can pay for food, you can pay for lodging, but you can't pay for kindness. There [are] no financial estimates that can be placed upon it. It is beyond price."[14] The hospitality of the home, expressed not only in furnishings, food, and service, but more importantly in kindness, left its mark.

A third theme of Grimké's teaching on the home relates to "goodness,"

12 Francis J. Grimké, "Marriage and Kindred Subjects" (sermon 2), in *Works*, 2:23–24.
13 Though the reflection is undated, it is situated just before a meditation on the death of Rev. Oscar L. Mitchell, a pastor of St. Mary's Protestant Episcopal Church in Washington, DC, who died on October 17, 1928, and just after reflections on sermons on August 5 and 12, which were Sundays in 1928.
14 *Works*, 3:285.

particularly the ultimate desirability of a positive moral influence. He
sounded this theme prominently in his preaching on the story of the prodigal son. The parable resonated strongly with Grimké, for he preached on
it repeatedly throughout his ministry.[15] In doing so, Grimké devoted significant attention to the character of the home. He acknowledged that the
prodigal's home possessed material comforts, evidenced by its description
in the gospel text and also by the fact that the father possessed significant wealth. In addition to these things, however, he placed considerable
emphasis on the home as a "place of love," and even more so as a place of
"good moral influences." One the one hand, it was the moral character of
the home that pushed the son out, for his desire for a "profligate life" led
him to "get as far away as possible." It was also the moral character of the
home that led to his sense of guilt upon return, expressed in his confession
to his father, "I have sinned against thee." On the other hand, it was the balance of love and moral goodness that ultimately drew him back. Although
pursuing his selfish and sinful desires appeared superficially attractive,
the moral influence of his home ultimately served to convict him of sin,
and the love of his home assured him of grace upon his return.[16] These
meditations on the home characterized the conclusion of the sermons as
well. Grimké concluded the series by emphasizing that, "away from home,
in the paths of sin, the prodigal was poor, naked, hungry, friendless, mis-
erable; at home, listening to the voice of Wisdom, of his better self, he was
richly attired, had all his wants abundantly supplied and was surrounded
by those who loved him most tenderly."[17] The goodness of the father expressed itself in the character of his home, and Grimké understood the
parable to be not only a picture of grace and forgiveness but also a pattern
for the Christian home.

Francis Grimké believed that the earthly home was to be a place of
preparation for eternal life, and he looked forward to life in that eternal
home with great hope. He drew from the experiences of his own home,
scriptural teaching, and the homes of others to cast a vision for the importance of the home environment for Christian nurture. For Grimké, the
Christian faith could and should be taught, but it also must be formed by
the home experience. Therefore, that environment should be characterized

---

[15] See the twelve sermons collected in Francis J. Grimké, "The Prodigal Son and Kindred Addresses," in
Works, 2:260–386.
[16] Grimké, "The Prodigal Son and Kindred Addresses" (sermon 3, 1923), 281–83.
[17] Grimké, "The Prodigal Son and Kindred Addresses" (sermon 12, 1923), 384.

by spiritual concern, kind hospitality, and positive moral influence. Such an environment can raise up saints and call prodigals home.

The Education of Children in the Christian Home

While the role of the home and the home environment generally figured largely in Francis Grimké's teaching and reflections, he devoted much of his teaching ministry to the education of children more specifically. He emphasized training for young people in his ministry at Fifteenth Street Presbyterian Church and in his public service outside the church. He was active as a trustee of the schools for African American children in Washington. He also was a member of the Board of Trustees of Howard University. He frequently accepted invitations to speak to children. Some of the sermons published in his collected works were preached at his church, and he also delivered many of them to the instructors and students of various schools and colleges. In addition to Howard University, he also gave lectures at Hampton University and at the Tuskegee Institute. His legacy of teaching young people continued well after his death, as his will provided funds dedicated to scholarships at his alma mater, Lincoln University, in the name of his mother, Nancy.[18] Education was one of his top priorities in his vocational ministry.

The series of sermons Grimké preached on the nurture of children communicated a philosophy of Christian education that prioritized children, focused on the intersection of nature and nurture, and stressed attributes of personal character. He rooted the sermons in Proverbs 22:6, "Train up a child in the way he should go, and when he is old, he will not depart from it." Though the series was more topical than expository, engagement with Scripture, especially the Ten Commandments, contributed significantly to the sermons. He also drew insights from contemporary psychology and the social sciences. Many of the sermons drew connections between Christian formation and racial uplift, but Grimké consistently prioritized the former. In his mind, faithful Christian practice pleasing to God was the most important thing. Racial uplift was close to his heart, but ultimately it was of secondary importance. As he put it, "Race pride, disassociated from high character, from a straightforward, upright moral life is of no value as an asset in the development of the race."[19] Racial uplift was not an end

18 See Carter Woodson's introduction in *Works*, 2:ix.
19 Francis J. Grimké, "The Training of Children and Kindred Subjects" (sermon 12 of twelve), in *Works*, 2:120.

itself. Instead, he conceived it as a by-product of moral character. As seen in his treatment of sanctification in chapter 3, true moral character was, for him, a product of the Christian faith. Along these lines, his sermons on the nurture of children were sermons on Christian catechesis, the training of followers of Christ.

In the introductory message of the series, Grimké sought to impress upon his congregation the primacy of the nurture of children by underlining both the joy and the solemnity of raising children and by highlighting the spiritual nature of their souls. Raising children is one of the central tasks of the Christian life. Grimké characterized it as "second to none in point of interest and importance." In fact, "properly directing or superintending the development of a human soul" is "perhaps, the greatest of all problems."[20] In the Christian life nothing surpasses the task of nurturing a human soul.

For Grimké, the nurture of young souls was both a joyful and a solemn task. He opened the sermon by waxing poetic on the joy of bearing and raising children: "The coming of a child into the home is a great event." It is such a great event that the joy is hard to communicate except to those who have experienced it. "Only those who have felt the thrill that comes from the consciousness of parenthood can appreciate the greatness of the event." Becoming a new parent "opens up new springs of joy." Citing the poem "My Bird," by Emily C. Judson, he acknowledged the beauty, mystery, and awe that comes into a parent's life upon the birth of a child. Like the mother in the poem, all parents can "in a measure" enter into these feelings. "We have all felt the joy—the great, glad, strange new joy that comes into the heart when for the first time the voice of infancy is heard in the home."[21]

And yet, Grimké also pointed out that the joy of children brings with it solemn duties. In "that same glad hour" of joy, parents recognize "the no less important, yea, the vastly more important fact, of the solemn duties and responsibilities" that come with a new child. He made explicit his rhetorical purpose in highlighting the joy of birth: "There is in this thought of parenthood much to make us glad; but there is in it also that which should solemnize the heart and put a seriousness into life such as scarcely anything else is fitted to do." Indeed, he wrote, "This is the thought

---

[20] Grimké, "The Training of Children and Kindred Subjects" (sermon 1), 1.
[21] Grimké, "The Training of Children and Kindred Subjects" (sermon 1), 1–2.

which I desire particularly to emphasize this morning, to help us feel the seriousness, the deep solemnity, the awful weight of solemn responsibilities which rest upon us as parents."[22]

Having highlighted the joy and solemnity of nurturing children, Grimké underlined, in the sermon's main points, the spiritual nature of the human soul. Children possess eternal souls, and they are eternally accountable before God. In other words, human beings are "immortal" and given the "power of moral accountability." Considering these two spiritual realities, Grimké pressed the urgency of the spiritual task of raising such souls. This emphasis in no way minimized the material nature of the human life, for human beings possess bodies as well. The bodies of children must be "fed, clothed, sheltered, [and their] health looked after," for a child's "very existence depends upon these things." Yet Grimké felt no need to emphasize the bodily nature of human existence, for it "is everywhere recognized." Certainly, some parents failed to care for the bodily needs of their children, but such failures were more the exception than the rule. The failure to recognize and care for the souls of children was a much more common problem.[23]

Grimké's emphatic affirmation of the spiritual nature of the soul in his introductory sermon highlighted the spiritual aspect of the nurture of children. "The child . . . is more than a body. It has also a soul which thinks, and feels and wills." Speaking hyperbolically, he went on,

> The body is the smallest, the least important part of it, in a sense, it is no part of it at all. That in which the personality resides, and which constitutes the real self or ego, is the immortal essence, the soul. It is the soul that distinguishes it from the brute creation. It is the soul that links it with the life beyond; it is the soul that enables it to apprehend the Infinite, and to hold communion with God. In a word, it is in the soul that we must look for all that is most characteristic and glorious in man. So that while it is our duty to look after the physical welfare of our children, a very much higher duty confronts us on the threshold of the new life—the duty of caring for their soul-wants.[24]

Given that his sermon affirmed the material nature of the body, Grimké clearly intended his statement—i.e., that the body is "in a sense" no part

---

[22] Grimké, "The Training of Children and Kindred Subjects" (sermon 1), 2.
[23] Grimké, "The Training of Children and Kindred Subjects" (sermon 1), 5–7.
[24] Grimké, "The Training of Children and Kindred Subjects" (sermon 1), 7.

of the child—to be read rhetorically. His sense was that his contemporary culture erred in the direction of overemphasizing the body at the expense of the soul, and his comments were intended to bring balance. "Unfortunately," he lamented, "we are all, more or less, under the influence consciously or unconsciously, of a gross materialistic philosophy which seeks to exalt the body at the expense of the soul—to treat man merely or chiefly as an animal instead of as a rational spirit." He found examples of this materialism all around him. He offered many illustrations, including the greedy pursuit of material wealth; the lack of emphasis on moral character; its replacement by obsession with dress, furnishings, desire for rich foods; and the obsession with "high living."[25] In short, Grimké's diagnosis of the ills of society was that "the physical man" has "overshadowed everything else." He wanted to recover the spiritual nature of the human person by emphasizing the spiritual nature of the human soul.

Having established the spiritual nature of children to highlight the importance of spiritual formation, he proceeded to preach a series of sermons related to the intersection of nature and nurture. The first one focused on the role of heredity, articulating its physical, mental, and moral nature. Though parents typically demonstrated awareness of the physical aspects of heredity, Grimké sought to make them more aware of the mental and especially the moral aspects. Relying on a host of sources from the social sciences, Grimké sought to impress upon his congregation the ways in which the consequences of their moral decisions would be passed on to their children. "The faults of our children, in the great majority of cases, are simply our own faults coming to life again in them," he soberly reminded them.[26] Citing the popular work of the temperance advocate Alex Gustafson, Grimké invoked his authority to argue that far from being "insulated in our individualities," human beings are "interdependent." Every person's actions affect the lives of other people, for "in nothing can we act without producing an endless consecution of effect touching the lives and rights of others."[27] Especially in the case of children, parents should be mindful of the interconnected moral implications of their own lives.

Already, Grimké's treatment of nature anticipated the importance of

[25] Grimké, "The Training of Children and Kindred Subjects" (sermon 1), 7.
[26] Grimké, "The Training of Children and Kindred Subjects" (sermon 2), 20.
[27] Grimké, "The Training of Children and Kindred Subjects" (sermon 2), 20. The quotation is from Axel Gustafson, *The Foundation of Death: A Study of the Drink Question* (London: Kegan, Paul, Trench, 1884). Many of the sermon's references to recent studies in the physical and social sciences were from Gustafson's work.

nurture, and in his next two sermons he focused on the influence of the home environment, as well as influences outside the home. Here again, he defined the home environment as the "sum total of all the influences" that together make up the "atmosphere of the home."[28] Generally speaking, he highlighted the physical, intellectual, moral, social, and spiritual aspects of this atmosphere. More concretely, he asked parents to consider whether they used the profound influence they had over their children for their good or ill. "Nothing is so powerful as the contagion of example; and there is no example that will be so quickly imitated and that will be so lasting in its influence as the example of father and mother."[29] Thus, Grimké's teaching here echoed the frequent emphasis on the home environment considered above.

In this connection, he reminded his congregation of the importance of a strong home environment to prepare children for the many powerful social influences outside the home. Among those influences, he included friendships, the neighborhood, the community at large, and media in print, as well as the increasingly prominent movies.[30] In each case he warned against the dangers of negative moral influences and the benefits of positive ones. His strong doctrine of original sin made him aware of the tendency in every human heart tugging it toward "evil rather than good." The result of original sin is that children "will be sure . . . to pick up that which is evil quicker than that which is good."[31] Therefore, he called parents to be mindful of the social influences in their children's lives.

Two features of this social commentary are especially worthy of note. First, he explicitly referred to the work of the well-known Unitarian William Ellery Channing. Grimké endorsed Channing's advocacy of great books in his famous work *Self-Culture*. As Channing put it:

> No matter how poor I am; no matter though the prosperous of my own time will not enter my obscure dwelling,—if the sacred writers will enter and take up their abode under my roof; if Milton will cross my threshold and sing to me of Paradise; and Shakespeare open to me the worlds of imagination, and the working of the human heart; and Franklin to enrich me with his practical wisdom, I shall not pine for the want of intellectual

---

28 Grimké, "The Training of Children and Kindred Subjects" (sermon 3), 23.
29 Grimké, "The Training of Children and Kindred Subjects" (sermon 3), 29.
30 Grimké, "The Training of Children and Kindred Subjects" (sermon 4), 32–42. See also the similar nature of the more extended treatment in Grimké, "The Training of Children and Kindred Subjects" (sermon 6), 58–62.
31 Grimké, "The Training of Children and Kindred Subjects" (sermon 4), 35.

companionship, and I may become a cultivated man, though excluded from what is called the best society in the place where I live.[32]

Clearly Grimké's strong affirmations of the doctrines of the Trinity, biblical inspiration and authority, and the exclusivity of the Christian faith set him apart from Channing's Unitarian theological liberalism. Yet he still found aspects of Channing's vision of personal cultivation compelling—namely, his advocacy of "the best books" as cultural "levellers." While Grimké was keen to warn his congregation of the pervasive moral dangers of the culture of his day, it would be inaccurate to refer to this impulse as purely conservative. Concern for moral erosion was shared by Protestant liberals and conservatives alike.[33]

Second, he applied his doctrine of original sin and his concern for positive social influences to his analysis of the public school system, a system he was well positioned to know intimately. He served on the board of trustees for the African American public schools in Washington, DC.[34] The school system in the nation's capital was notable for being the first in the country with a public high school for African American students. This school, which eventually became known as Dunbar High School, held its first classes in 1870 in the basement of Fifteenth Street Presbyterian Church.[35] The school's faculty and administration included a host of prominent Black leaders and close associates of Grimké, not least of which was his niece, Angelina Weld Grimké, who took up a teaching position there in 1907.[36] He was enthusiastic about the school's classical curriculum, and Dunbar High served as a pipeline for African Americans to elite universities.[37]

---

[32] William Ellery Channing, *Self-Culture* (Boston: James Munroe, 1843), 65, quoted in Grimké, "The Training of Children and Kindred Subjects" (sermon 4), 39.

[33] For more on the liberalism of Victorian intellectuals, see Leslie Butler, *Critical Americans: Victorian Intellectuals and Transatlantic Liberal Reform* (Chapel Hill: University of North Carolina Press, 2007).

[34] Whereas White public schools in Washington were overseen by the city council in coordination with the board of education, a superintendent, and a board of trustees, the system for the African American public schools was coordinated solely by this board of trustees. See Alison Stewart, *First Class: The Legacy of Dunbar, America's First Black Public High School* (Chicago: Lawrence Hill, 2013), 26.

[35] Stewart, *First Class*, 32.

[36] Kerri K. Greenidge, *The Grimkes: The Legacy of Slavery in an American Family* (New York: Liveright, 2022), 308. Grimké corresponded regularly with Anna Cooper—among others—the influential principal who played a significant role in establishing the classical curriculum at the school, and with Alice Dunbar, the wife of Paul Laurence Dunbar, the school's namesake. Of the many letters from Cooper to Francis Grimké in his correspondence, see especially Anna Cooper to Francis J. Grimké, December 29, 1926, in *Works*, 4:411, where Cooper thanks Grimké for his sermon on the relationship between parents and children. See also Alice M. Dunbar to Francis J. Grimké, February 14, 1916, in *Works*, 4:159, where Dunbar thanks Grimké for his sermons and promises to have them delivered to the whole school.

[37] Matthew Alexander Randolph, "Remembering Dunbar: Amherst College and African American Education in Washington, DC," in *Amherst in the World*, ed. Martha Saxton (Amherst, MA: Amherst College

Despite his role as a trustee and advocate for the school, he also expressed significant reservations regarding the public school system. He acknowledged that his reservations might "seem heresy to those who believe that the great essential to the perpetuity of republican institutions is intelligence in the masses," and he also couched his comments in caveats that he did "not wish, of course, to be understood as saying one word against the importance of intelligence in the masses, or as undervaluing these schools so far as they contribute to this result." In fact, he acknowledged, "They have done good; are still doing good; and will continue to do good in this line." His concern was based on his view, however, that "intelligence is by no means the most important thing in the equation of life." "Character stands higher, is a very much more important asset." He did not find the education on offer wanting but lamented instead over the school system's record when it came to moral formation: "It is just here . . . that these schools are often more of a curse than a blessing."

Again, Grimké carefully specified the nature of his critique. He explicitly stated that his concern was not the irreligious nature of the curriculum. "I do not, in making this statement, have reference to the fact that our public school system is, to a very large extent, a godless system, that it is mainly concerned with the physical and mental development of the children." Nor was he motivated by its "shutting the Bible out of these schools." Considering his active role in the public school system and his lack of concern for religious instruction in the public school setting, it does not appear that the inclusion of biblical or doctrinal content in the public school curriculum was a high priority. Instead, his primary concern related to the moral character of the students. Grimké's language did point to the correlation between class difference and moral commitments. He expressed apprehension that "children come from every grade of society, and represent all classes and conditions." The center of his uneasiness, however, was explicitly not class but character. His primary interest was the influence of children "foul in speech, coarse in manners, rough in behavior." His reasoning had to do with the intersection of developmental psychology and spiritual maturity. Speaking of Christian children, he argued that "at the age at which they enter, they are not sufficiently developed in moral character" to possess the ability "to reject evil."[38] Grimké's concerns with the

---

Press, 2020), 147–62; Mary Church Terrell, "History of the High School for Negroes in Washington," *Journal of Negro History* 2, no. 3 (1917): 252–66.
[38] Grimké, "The Training of Children and Kindred Subjects" (sermon 4), 35–36.

public school were not curricular, were only secondarily related to class, and were first and foremost about character.

In his subsequent sermon, Grimké further distinguished his moral concern from social concern, and he expressed awareness of the potential danger of sinful self-righteousness in making such moral judgments. He affirmed that parents should protect their children from "bad associates," but he clarified, "I do not mean by this, that we should stop to inquire as to whether they belong to what is called the best society or not, as to whether they are rich or poor, as to the occupation of their parents, or, as to whether they live in fine houses or pretentious ones." He summarized his point in a similar way: "If, in character, they are good, if their parents are upright, respectable people, it doesn't make any difference how poor they are, we may safely allow our children to associate with them."[39] Though he utilized the language of respectability, and though he acknowledged a correlation between class and moral perspective, these statements reflect his consistent effort to distinguish Christian respectability from forms of respectability motivated purely or even primarily by race or class.

He communicated that parents ought to be self-critical in evaluating their own motivations for protecting their children, and he acknowledged that even the best motivations might be misunderstood. He called parents to reflect on whether their educational choices were motivated by a proper concern for the protection of their children or, instead, by self-righteousness or other forms of self-centeredness. He also called parents to concern themselves with the impact of their educational decisions upon their neighbors. Thoughtfulness in these matters might not prevent misunderstanding, but parents who carefully evaluated their motivations and accounted for the needs of the community as well as those of their own children needed not worry if their motivations were misunderstood. Along these lines, he acknowledged that people may characterize parents who placed a primary emphasis on the safety of their children as "stuck up," or they might even accuse such parents of pretentiously feeling "above them." Yet, he countered, "No fear of offending, or of being misunderstood" should mitigate the priority of keeping children safe.

At the same time, Grimké challenged parents to honestly consider whether their pursuit of safety for their children was balanced by a proper concern for the children of others. He acknowledged the tendency of par-

---

[39] Grimké, "The Training of Children and Kindred Subjects" (sermon 5), 44.

ents to prioritize their own comfort and vocational pursuits. He challenged parents to place a higher priority on the moral development of their children than the pursuit of professional or economic advancement.[40] His teaching in his church reveals a concerted effort to identify the particular struggles of his congregation—in this case, an elevated concern with reputation and comfort—and to confront those struggles directly. He called his congregation to consider their obligations to their own children in relation to their biblical calling to love and serve their neighbors. In addition to the duty to care for the moral development and safety of children, he offered extended reflections on "our duty, as parents, to take an active interest in everything that will help to improve the general character of the community in which we live." In these reflections, he encouraged parents to engage both in the church and in other community organizations, including the YMCA and YWCA.[41] For Grimké, parental duties toward children were part of the bigger biblical matrix of duties toward God and neighbor.

Having established the importance of the home environment in relation to the nature and nurture of children, Grimké focused, in the second half of his sermons on caring for children, on the specific attributes of personal character that parents should inculcate. These traits included truthfulness, a desire for justice, purity, industriousness, generosity, respectfulness, punctuality, unselfishness, a strong work ethic, regard for the home, wisdom in personal finance, self-reliance, and conscientiousness.[42] One especially striking feature of these sermons relates to the balance of spiritual and temporal concerns. He carefully constructed his sermons to maintain this balance.

For example, after an introductory sermon on truthfulness, his second sermon was on attributes of personal character and emphasized both personal purity and the pursuit of justice. He refused to choose between advocacy for personal righteousness and social righteousness. His teaching on purity reflected a traditional Christian commitment to the exposition of the seventh commandment. "This commandment," Grimké noted, "as expounded by Jesus, is made to include not only our acts, but also our thoughts, our desires." Referring to the summary in the Westminster Shorter Catechism, he pointed out that the seventh commandment therefore prohibited "all unchaste thoughts, words and acts." Though the subject

[40] Grimké, "The Training of Children and Kindred Subjects" (sermon 5), 47–49.
[41] Grimké, "The Training of Children and Kindred Subjects" (sermon 5), 50–52.
[42] See Grimké, "The Training of Children and Kindred Subjects" (sermons 7–12), 52–120.

was "a delicate one," this delicacy "is no reason why it should be passed over in silence." The biblical teaching on purity "needs to be preached to children as well as to grown people."[43]

Grimké tied his teaching on sexual purity closely to his teaching on justice advocacy. In fact, this very same sermon opened with an extended exhortation for parents to help their children to develop a "strong sense of justice." For Grimké a strong sense of justice was "a most important element of character, and one that is called into almost constant exercise." While this sense of justice is "natural to the human heart," because it is "implanted in us" by God, it nevertheless must be "strengthened and developed" and "carefully trained" so that it might not be "weakened" or "impaired." According to Grimké, the failure of such a sense of justice was the root of both religious persecution and the source of Jim Crow. Having identified these aspects of social justice, he addressed more specifically the problem of violations of the eighth commandment. The biblical prohibition of stealing points to the importance of respect for property rights.[44] In this way, Grimké carefully composed his sermon to address personal morality and social justice. He framed his subjects to help his congregation see how their righteous anger at societal evil should enable them to avoid similar evils in their personal lives.

Another example of the close tie between personal morality and social concern came in Grimké's very next sermon, in which he treated both generosity and respect. Here also he began by focusing on a matter of social advocacy, the importance of a spirit of "sympathy, of generosity, of benevolence." Of all people, Christians should develop an interest in "all who are suffering, who are in need of help and sympathy." Adults must model this spirit of generosity for young people. "Let the children know that we are interested in the poor and suffering: let them know what we are doing for them," he exhorted his listeners. Such an example would lead to acts of mercy that should then be carefully cultivated. His exhortation continued, "And when, under our fostering care, the divine life begins to stir within them, and their little feet are ready to run on errands of mercy, or their little hands to minister to the suffering, let us encourage them to do so."[45] For Grimké, social concern for the poor was of one piece with a more general respect for others. Concern for others is not only the source of generosity

---

[43] Grimké, "The Training of Children and Kindred Subjects" (sermon 8), 76–78.
[44] Grimké, "The Training of Children and Kindred Subjects" (sermon 8), 73–86.
[45] Grimké, "The Training of Children and Kindred Subjects" (sermon 9), 84–86.

but also the source of respect. In turn, respect for others leads to refinement in taste, rules of etiquette, and care for elders.[46] Christians desirous of respect must show it to others, and they must see the close relationship between interpersonal respect and social concern more broadly. Respect is not only about rising to a better social position but also about enabling others to do the same. Grimké framed his sermon on purity and justice to correct societal evils, and he framed his sermon on generosity and respect to encourage the pursuit of societal virtues.

———

Francis Grimké's teaching on the nurture of children sounded many of the same themes as his teaching on marriage. He made these practical topics central to his teaching and ministry on the Christian life, and they were also prominent themes in the personal reflections he recorded in his *Stray Thoughts and Meditations*. Drawing from Scripture as well as his personal experiences, he communicated a vision of the earthly home as a place of preparation for eternal life. Because parents and the home environment were so influential, he made sure his congregation understood how important they were in the lives of children. The Christian home should be a hospitable place of spiritual mindedness and positive moral influence to restore the outcasts and to raise up future saints.

His teaching on the nurture of children also echoed similar notes from his teaching on sanctification. In both cases, the pattern of Christlike character was crucial, and the moral attributes entailed were the same. For children to grow in moral character, parents should recognize and embrace their God-given role as the primary teachers of their children, they must attend to both nature and nurture, and they must embrace the goal of helping their children to grow in the moral teachings of the Scriptures so that they might become more like Christ. Grimké called his congregation to hang on to the proverb "Train up a child in the way he should go: and when he is old, he will not depart from it" (Prov. 22:6). He called his whole congregation, and especially parents, to embrace this vision of Christian catechesis in order to train up young followers of Christ.

---

[46] Grimké, "The Training of Children and Kindred Subjects" (sermon 9), 86–90.

PART 3

THE CHURCH

Christians Gathered and Scattered

CHAPTER 7

THE KINGDOM OF GOD AND THE MISSION OF CHRIST

Francis Grimké maintained that the individual believer's participation in the corporate ministry of the church is a vital part of the Christian life. He also believed that the faithfulness of the church in dependence on the work of the Holy Spirit is crucial to the fruitfulness of its ministry. These convictions contributed to his desire to serve the church as a pastor for fifty years. Indeed, his commitment to this ministry made him willing to continue serving long after he reached retirement age. In fact, when he first attempted to retire, his congregation petitioned him to reconsider, and his love for his people led him to concede and continue serving in a part-time role for several more years despite his declining health and energy. Even after his retirement, he continued to speak and write as long as his health allowed.[1] His firm belief in the beauty and necessity of the church's mission drove his commitment to pastoring and shepherding God's people.

Grimké's understanding of the mission of the church not only fueled his dedication to the ministry but also placed him in a sometimes lonely position in the landscape of American Christianity of his day. On the one hand, his traditional theological commitments to the authority of Scripture, the Trinitarian nature of God, and the divinity of Jesus distanced him from many theologically liberal advocates of racial equality. On the other hand, his observation that communicating the whole counsel of God

---

[1] See chap. 1.

necessitated teaching and advocating for racial justice alienated him from White fundamentalists who typically downplayed those issues and frequently embraced and taught racist views that contradicted the Scriptures.[2] In Grimké's view, the pastoral impulses of theological liberals failed to do justice to the centrality of Scripture and the importance of creedal commitments, whereas fundamentalists failed to adhere to the Scriptures they claimed to defend and drove an unwarranted wedge between theological commitments and holy living. By contrast, his own teaching on the mission of the church explicitly and programmatically emphasized both the proclamation of the gospel and the sanctification of God's people in accordance with the whole counsel of God. In his meditations, he communicated these sensibilities in one of his clearest and most direct statements of the church's mission:

> The true mission of a church in the community where it is located is to preach the Gospel, with the double purpose, first, of winning men to an acceptance of Jesus Christ; and, second, of building them up in faith and holiness. In other words, its value to the community will be in proportion as it is helping to make its members, after they are brought in, better men and women, better Christians, getting them, in character and life, more conformed to the character and teachings of the Lord Jesus Christ. Its value to the community does not depend upon the size of its membership, but upon the quality of the men and women that make up its membership. It is through the individual members, in their personal character and life, in their contact with others, that it is to do its most effective work. I have very little sympathy with the craze that is now taking hold of so many churches, merely to increase in numbers. Numbers count for nothing unless the constituent elements are of the right character. It is quality, not quantity that tells in the work of the Lord.
>
> The main business of the church, therefore, is not only to win men to Christ, but particularly, to make them such in spirit, in temper, in life, as to make them powers for good, centres of life-giving and ennobling influences. The church lacks power, because so few, or comparatively few in it are of the right stamp. It needs to bend its efforts

---

[2] For an account of the prevalence of racist attitudes among White fundamentalists, see the literature cited in Daniel R. Bare, *Black Fundamentalism: Conservative Christianity and Racial Identity in the Segregation Era* (New York: New York University Press, 2021), 1–24. Bare does not argue that all White fundamentalists made racist statements or acted according to explicitly racist principles, but the literature cited does indicate that racist attitudes and actions were common, if not predominant, among White fundamentalists.

towards making more of its members of the right stamp. The basis of all outward expansion must be first inward.[3]

In this way, Grimké closely connected the church's mission to both teaching and building up the community of God's people.

This chapter navigates the historical and theological context of this dual emphasis, focusing on how Grimké framed the biblical teaching on the nature of God's kingdom in relation to the mission of Christ. The following chapter will explore how Grimké connected the mission of Christ to the mission of Christ's people, as well as his emphasis on the church as both a gathered institution and a scattered organism. The Great Commission of Matthew 28 was the linchpin connecting these themes in Grimké's ministry. His teaching on the role of the church in the Christian life emphasized that Jesus commanded his disciples not only to teach the whole counsel of Scripture but also to form a community of faithful believers to be salt and light in the world.

Neither Fundamentalism nor Liberalism

Grimké framed his teaching on the ministry of the church in the context of the developing modernist-fundamentalist controversy.[4] In his teaching ministry, he consistently set himself apart from fundamentalists by teaching that racism in the church fundamentally compromised the spiritual mission of God's people. On the other hand, he regularly confronted both White and Black theological modernists in his personal correspondence, and he frequently recorded similar notions in his private reflections. By simultaneously pushing in both directions, he identified a narrow path for corporate Christian faithfulness in a challenging American theological setting.

Though historians of American Christianity often portray fundamentalism as a movement among White Christians in America, recent studies have challenged this picture.[5] In particular, Daniel Bare has shown that a significant number of Black Baptists also self-identified as

---

[3] *Works*, 3:149.
[4] On the context of the controversy, see Bradley J. Longfield, *The Presbyterian Controversy: Fundamentalists, Modernists, and Moderates* (New York: Oxford University Press, 1991).
[5] Bare, *Black Fundamentalism*. The tendency to describe fundamentalism in narrow terms grew out of a desire to avoid using the term "fundamentalism" in an overly general way that lumped together disparate groups with their own stories and sensibilities. See Joel A. Carpenter, *Revive Us Again: The Reawakening of American Fundamentalism* (New York: Oxford University Press, 1997); George M. Marsden, *Fundamentalism and American Culture* (New York: Oxford University Press, 1980); and Ernest R. Sandeen,

"fundamentalists." Bare's study demonstrates that many influential leaders and institutions among Black Baptists not only affirmed the theological
commitments of the Fundamentals (such as the inspiration and authority
of Scripture, the supernatural nature of the Christian faith, the possibility of miracles, and other related commitments) but also were happy to
utilize the language of fundamentalism and to identify with its key texts
and advocates. At the same time, these "Black Fundamentalists" affirmed
other traditional Christian commitments, such as the equality of all persons before God and, by direct implication, the obligation for Christian
churches to be open to people of all races and ethnicities. They therefore
rejected the explicitly racist views of many prominent White fundamentalists. As a result, though they self-identified as fundamentalists and their
theology overlapped in "fundamental" ways, these Black Christians were
often excluded from the institutions and networks of White fundamentalists. Bare's groundbreaking work indicates that there is promising room
for future studies that seek to bring nuance to the historical picture. The
popular narratives tend to characterize all American Christians during this
period as belonging to one of two traditions, either fundamentalism or
modernism. Similar narratives tend to characterize fundamentalism as a
movement exclusive to White Christianity. Both accounts need updates.
These stories stand downstream from older historical work and warrant
revision in light of more recent findings.

To build on these observations, Grimké's ministry indicates that other
movements within the Christian circles of his day, in addition to Black fundamentalists, should figure more prominently in the popularly received
narratives. The racism of White fundamentalists placed him outside their
networks, and his firm Reformed theological and liturgical commitments
distanced him from the Black fundamentalists, who tended to inhabit Baptist settings. For these and other reasons, it does not make sense to describe
him as a Black fundamentalist. Nonetheless, he steadfastly opposed theological modernism, which often correlated with more socially progressive
positions. So Grimké was not a fundamentalist, and he clearly was not a
modernist either.

Grimké expressed many of his disagreements with theological modernism in the context of discussions of the church's mission. According

---

The Roots of Fundamentalism: British and American Millenarianism, 1800–1930 (Chicago: University of
Chicago Press, 2008).

to Grimké, neither the beliefs nor the methods of the church needed to change fundamentally with the times. One excellent illustration of his willingness to confront theological modernism and the reaction that willingness sparked from prominent figures was an article he published in Baltimore's *Afro-American* in 1930. The occasion was the fourteenth convocation of Howard University's School of Religion. The title of the convocation address was "The Church Faces the College Generation." Grimké took exception to the address, which he characterized as arguing that the church needed to revisit its mission due to increased exposure to the findings of modern science resulting from growing numbers of students attending college. In reply, he asked, "What . . . has the Church to do with facing this College Generation any different from what it has to do in facing any generation?" According to Grimké, the primary problem for the church was the same in every generation, "the problem of saving men, of turning them from their evil ways to God." There was only one way to address this problem, he continued, and that was "by the plain, simple preaching of the Word, backed by the presence and power of the Holy Spirit." Against those desiring to update the church's mission, he did not mince words: "Sometimes we get the foolish notion into our heads that because young people are being educated that they must be saved in some other way. It is all nonsense; and it is vain to attempt to save them in any other way." Citing the example of the apostle Paul, Grimké pointed out that Paul "had but one gospel for all alike, rich and poor, high and low, bond and free, ignorant or educated, wise or foolish." Therefore, he concluded by quoting Jesus, "It is still true, even in this College Generation, 'Except a man be born again, born of the Spirit, he cannot enter the kingdom of heaven.' And nothing that this College Generation can do will ever alter that fact."[6]

Unsurprisingly, modernist supporters of the convocation address objected to Grimké's public criticism of the Howard University religion department. John G. Jackson, just twenty-three years old at the time, would go on to become the prominent author of *Was Jesus Christ a Negro?* and *The African Origin of the Myths and Legends of the Garden of Eden.* He wrote a scathing letter to Grimké in response to his article, declaring that "the term 'foolishness' might be more appropriately applied to your own opinions on the subject." Jackson's criticisms went straight to the heart of the

---

[6] Rev. Francis J. Grimké, "Dr. Grimke Calls the Howard School of Religion's Subject 'Foolishness,'" *Afro-American,* December 6, 1930, https://news.google.com/newspapers.

church itself. As he put it: "The mission of the Church has nothing to do with Jesus Christ. The Christian Church was conceived by Paul and established by Constantine." Therefore, he continued, "Your brand of theology is far too barbarous for this enlightened age."[7]

Though Jackson's modernism inclined him toward atheism, Grimké's article provoked counterarguments from self-identifying Christians as well. J. W. Haywood, dean of Morgan College in Baltimore, wrote a letter to Grimké in which he agreed with his "definition of terms" and the importance of the subject. He even agreed with Grimké's argument that the mission of the church had not changed. His difference related to the method of the church, which he claimed "no one would deny" must be altered. Haywood was not merely arguing for the contextualization of the message of Paul and Jesus, however. He replied to Grimké with a question of his own: "Does the gospel message like other things that human beings have to learn and accept, need to be adapted to the people for whom it is intended, or is there some magic in ancient, dogmatic formulas that makes them effective without regard to the laws of the human mind?" Haywood denied that the essential message of Christianity was "simple, unvarnished truth." Pointing to the theological differences between "Methodists, Baptists, Presbyterians, Catholics, Holy Rollers and all the rest of them," he asked further, "They all have a message; who has THE message?" For Haywood, it was not merely the form of the message that needed an update in accordance with "the experiences that men live thru," "psychology," and "empirical common sense." The very message itself must change.[8] After serving as the dean of Morgan College for seventeen years, Haywood went on to become president of Gammon Theological Seminary in Atlanta. His response to Grimké illustrates that skepticism regarding the biblical message was not limited to atheist opponents but was prominent in mainstream Christian circles as well. Grimké's confidence in the unchanging mission and method of the church, centered on the proclamation of the person and work of Jesus Christ, challenged them all.

Evidence of Grimké's opposition to the theological modernism associated with the social gospel appears in his meditations as well. One of the

---

[7] John G. Jackson to Francis J. Grimké, December 6, 1930, in *Works*, 4:441–43.
[8] J. W. Haywood to Francis J. Grimké, undated, in *Works*, 4:579–81. It is notable that Carter Woodson chose to conclude the volume of letters in Grimké's collected works with Haywood's correspondence. Though Woodson was a supporter of the social aspects of Grimké's ministry, it is likely that he also sympathized with Haywood's assessment of Grimké's notion of the church, and that these sympathies shaped his selection of materials to include in his collection of Grimké's works.

more prominent examples was his biting critique of William Stuart Nelson. Nelson joined the Howard University theology faculty in 1925 after studying at Yale. He went on to serve as the president of Shaw University and Dillard University before returning to Howard in 1940 to succeed Benjamin Mays as dean of the School of Religion. He also founded Howard's *Journal of Religious Thought* and exercised considerable influence at the university more generally through a variety of administrative roles, especially as vice president of special projects.[9] In his meditations, Grimké reflected on a 1927 article in the *Afro-American* where Nelson wrote that "religion must be readjusted to fit an irreverent world," and "religion must change its method of approach it if is to survive." Grimké recorded his disagreement in stark terms, writing that he did not "take any stock whatever in that kind of teaching." According to Grimké, "the survival of Christianity is not dependent upon the attitude of the world towards it" because it has "the abiding presence of Jesus Christ and the indwelling Spirit of God." Therefore, he continued, "There is no power anywhere, no world conditions however bad that can prevent it from surviving." He went on to express his distaste for Nelson's expression "if it [Christianity] is to survive." "I confess I do not like that expression," he wrote, "especially coming from a theological professor. There is no if about it. Of course it is going to survive. If the gates of hell cannot prevail against it what need is there of ever even thinking of its extinction?"[10]

Thus, Grimké explicitly critiqued theological modernism and contrasted its lack of confidence with that of traditional Christianity. Whereas theological modernists fretted about the survival of Christianity in the modern world, traditional Christianity found confidence in God, Scripture, and prayer. Where he had little confidence in theological professors like Nelson, Grimké expressed total confidence in the ordinary "men and women who have been nurtured" in the "old faith in Jesus and his love," and "the Bible as the word of God, a lamp to the feet and a light to the path, the all-sufficient rule of faith and practice." Whereas these ordinary saints gave him confidence, when he turned to "think of what is being done by the Higher Critics, and Modernists to destroy men's faith in the Bible, in the old, old gospel," he said, "I cannot help asking myself the question what

---

[9] Gary Dorrien, *Breaking White Supremacy: Martin Luther King Jr. and the Black Social Gospel* (New Haven, CT: Yale University Press, 2018), 89.
[10] *Works*, 3:191. The article that Grimké references appears in the April 16, 1927, edition of the *Afro-American*.

have they to show that it is comparable with the mighty achievements of
the old gospel and the old faith in the Bible as the word of God, given by
holy men as they were moved by the Holy Spirit." In Grimké's mind, the
"New faith" of the modernists was no match for the "Old." Grimké characterized modernism as a different, erroneous, weak, and ineffective form
of religion. Compared with the truth and strength of historic Christianity,
Grimké concluded rhetorically, "Where can Modernism match it?"[11]

Grimké did not limit his opposition to influential Black leaders associated with Howard University and other colleges and seminaries. He also
criticized White modernists, and when he did, he again located his critiques in discussions of the church's mission. For example, he stridently
disagreed with the famous radio preacher Ralph Sockman, who influen-
tially argued that "churches like colleges must aim to teach their members
how to think rather than what to think." Grimké characterized Sockman's
advocacy of a form of Christian spirituality divorced from specific creedal
claims and scriptural moral teachings as fundamentally misguided. According to Grimké, Sockman's statement flatly was "not true." Grimké in
return affirmed the precise opposite of Sockman's argument. "The mission
of the church is mainly not to teach men how to think but what to think."
Alluding to the Westminster Shorter Catechism's summary of scriptural
teaching, Grimké continued, "By what to think, I understand, what they
are to believe concerning God, and what duty God requireth of man." According to Grimké it was precisely this that "was uppermost in the mind of
Christ" when he communicated the Great Commission to his disciples. Citing 2 Timothy 4:1–4, Grimké attributed the influence of Sockman's denial
of scriptural truth, regarding Jesus and his moral teaching, to the apostle's
predicted "itching ears" (v. 3) of later generations that would "not endure
sound doctrine" and would, instead, "heap to themselves teachers" who
would tell them what they wanted to hear.[12]

Grimké's conception of the church's mission clearly distinguished him
from both fundamentalists and modernists. Most importantly, fundamentalists downplayed or denied the ethical imperatives of the Scriptures
regarding racial equality. Secondarily, fundamentalists also possessed
an impoverished notion of the church's mission and worship. However,
Grimké appealed to the mission of the church most explicitly in his cri-

[11] Works, 3:501–2.
[12] Works, 3:520–21.

tique of theological modernists, whose lack of confidence in the revelation of Scripture, the divinity of Christ, and the presence and power of the Holy Spirit led them to revise the church's mission. In contrast to both movements, Grimké affirmed that the mission of the church taught in the Scriptures was sufficient and that the church needed to look to the whole counsel of God to understand that mission properly.

The Kingdom of God

The kingdom of God was the linchpin that connected the mission of Christ to the mission of God's people in Grimké's doctrine of the church, and it also informed the distinction he drew between the church's mission as a *gathered body* and its mission as a *scattered people*. By drawing these connections, Grimké's understanding of the kingdom of God underlined the importance of church unity, and it served as a source of hope for racial equality. In order to understand the connection he drew between the kingdom of God and these goals of unity and equality, it is essential first to understand his principles regarding the church as the visible kingdom of God and the spiritual nature of God's kingdom.

Grimké followed the Reformed protestant tendency to identify the church with the visible kingdom of God.[13] He made this identification explicitly in his meditations, writing that "we, who are Christians, are members of a great organization, the kingdom of God, an organization that is governed by certain rules and regulations which we are under obligation to respect, to recognize, to see that we conform to them, that our character and conduct are in harmony with them." Here he attached his characteristic emphasis on the importance of Christian holiness to a notion of the church as the "organization" of the kingdom of God. For this reason, the strength of the church's ministry depended on the corporate holiness of its people. In fact, as he put it:

> One reason why the church, which is the visible representative of the kingdom of God on earth, is weak is because there are so many in it who have no proper sense of what is involved in being in it, and even where there is some appreciation of what is involved, there is no very great effort on the part of many to live up to their obligations.[14]

---

[13] For a good example of this Reformed Protestant tendency, see, e.g., the Westminster Confession of Faith, 25.2.
[14] *Works*, 3:233.

Grimké held that the church is the visible representation of the kingdom of God, and therefore its calling is to live in accordance with this lofty vocation.

This identification of the kingdom of God with the visible church helps to explain many of Grimké's statements regarding the church's role in advancing the kingdom. Put simply, the "one purpose" of the church "is to extend the kingdom God, is to draw men out of the world into it, and to make them over after the image and likeness of Jesus Christ." Given this purpose of extending God's kingdom, evangelism and the ethical formation of the church's members are its means for doing so. Similarly, the power given to do this kingdom work is a "spiritual power."[15] On other occasions, Grimké added the church's worship to evangelism and ethical formation as a third means of kingdom advancement. "Every service in the church should be a step in the direction of pushing forward the kingdom of God." Therefore, the "arranging and conducting" of every service must be considered carefully. "We do not meet merely for the purpose of passing the time pleasantly together; we meet for spiritual development." The edification of believers in the church's worship prepares them to "influence others in the right direction."[16] In this way, the church's worship serves to advance the kingdom of God.

Because Grimké emphasized the role of the gathered church in advancing God's kingdom, he also taught that it is essential for individual Christians to be part of its corporate body. In one place he reiterated that the great mission of the Christian church is to see that the prayer "Thy kingdom come" is answered. This "glorious enterprise" means that "all who are Christians should throw themselves heart, soul, mind and strength" into its corporate work.[17] Accordingly, he tied the failure to advance God's kingdom to the fact that "so many are standing aloof" from the church, "content to remain outside the Christian church." Though the failure to join the church was a problem, the primary problem was the failure of existing church members to follow God's commandments. The "flagrant" violations of the "noble and beautiful spirit" of God and God's precepts pushed people

---

[15] *Works*, 3:467–68.
[16] *Works*, 3:492. The link between the church's worship and the advancement of God's kingdom was strong enough in his mind that he later recorded a very similar sentiment: "Everything about a church service should be so arranged, ordered as to advance the kingdom of God, as to benefit the hearers, as to build them up in faith and holiness,—as to make better men and women of them. Whether this result is realized or not, that should be the conscious aim back of every service." *Works*, 3:583.
[17] *Works*, 3:376.

away from God's kingdom rather than drawing them toward it. As a result, he diagnosed a "need of a great awakening throughout the whole Christian church."[18] While he highlighted the church as the visible representation of the kingdom of God and consequently held a highly elevated view of its mission, this high sense of calling lead him not to arrogance or Christian pride but rather to self-examination and to proclaiming the need for the church's reform.

Two further clarifications regarding Grimké's teaching on the church's role in advancing God's kingdom are important. First, though he identified the visible church with the kingdom of God, he was careful to specify that he meant the people and not the building. While he expressed gratitude and even pride for Fifteenth Street Presbyterian Church's "beautiful church building," he emphasized that "however attractive," it "counts for nothing unless the spirit that pervades it, the things that go on in it, are for the glory of God and the good of those who worship in it." He appreciated the importance of the beauty of physical spaces and affirmed this explicitly by stating, "A beautiful building is all right, we cannot make it too beautiful." Nevertheless, this beauty of the physical space is subordinate to the mission of the place, for he added that "we must never lose sight of the fact that unless it is furthering the purpose for which the kingdom of God stands, it is of no value as a spiritual force." What is that purpose? The church's purpose as an expression of God's kingdom is to serve as "a soul-saving agency, an uplifting and ennobling influence in the lives of those who attend its services, and to the community." Grimké consistently placed the emphasis on the church's purpose as a visible expression of the kingdom of God and the duty "to get into" the kingdom and "get others into" the kingdom as well.[19]

Second, it should now be clear that one of the primary applications of this doctrine related to the personal holiness of his congregation, and that this purpose intersected not only with God's glory but also with good service. One of Grimké's chief goals in preaching the kingdom of God was to impress upon his people their high calling as followers of Christ the King. As noted above, this high calling was a source of humility rather than pride, and an exhortation to service rather than selfishness. In another place in his meditations, he made his typical observation that the "church

---

[18] *Works*, 3:248.
[19] *Works*, 3:572.

stands in the world for the kingdom of God; and in all its services and activities, it should help to push it forward." He then tied this articulation of the church's purpose to his predictable exhortation regarding the "character of its members and of its officials." Such leadership was bound to produce fruit; but, he warned, the "reverse is also true. If the men in official positions are not such in character and conduct as to command respect in the church and in the community, progress, in any true sense, will be impossible." If the church wants to be of use to the community, it must choose between serving "God and the world." To be of use in the world, it must not be of the world. Grimké's central point was that the church's calling is not to build itself up for its own sake but, rather, to be "the light of the glory of God as it shines on the face of Jesus Christ" (see 2 Cor. 4:6) and as it reflects God to the world around it. Grimké's position was that the purpose of the church's holiness is not only the glory of God but, in keeping with that, to be of good service in the world.[20] The church is the visible expression of God's kingdom, and its advancement of that kingdom depends on the work of God by the Spirit through the church's evangelism and discipleship in worship and service.

In addition to this emphasis on the church as the visible expression of God's kingdom, Grimké's other key kingdom teaching concerned the spiritual nature of the kingdom. The passages cited above regularly referred to the kingdom of Jesus Christ "being set up in this world."[21] Yet Grimké frequently specified that the precise epicenter of the establishment of the kingdom is "in the hearts" of people. While this establishment of God's kingdom certainly moves beyond the heart to "the community, the state, the nation, the world," the fundamental location of the kingdom is the heart. "The great business in the world is that which has been committed to the Christian Church. . . . In other words, the setting up of the kingdom of God in the hearts of men everywhere." How is the kingdom to be set up in people's hearts? The establishment of God's kingdom in the human heart means "casting down imaginations, and every high thing that exalteth itself against the knowledge of God, and bringing into captivity every thought to the obedience of Christ" (2 Cor. 10:5). The establishment of the kingdom of God could not be separated from material effects, but Grimké explicitly affirmed that these material effects were secondary con-

---

[20] *Works*, 3:539–40.
[21] See, e.g., *Works*, 3:572.

sequences of the establishment of God's kingdom in the hearts of human beings. For Grimké, "the other great enterprises, that have to do with material interest, with the amassing of wealth, are as nothing compared to the task which the Church has in hand." Therefore, the church must devote itself to its spiritual mission and "not waste its time, energy and resources on side issues, on matters of little or no importance in their bearing on the ultimate result." According to Grimké, "God's kingdom can come on earth, and we can all help to hasten its coming." But he made this statement in the context of his affirmation of the precise location of the establishment of God's kingdom in the present age: the human heart.[22]

Grimké also highlighted the spiritual nature of the kingdom by placing the eternal salvation of souls in the center of kingdom work. In fact, he identified the pursuit of God's kingdom with the pursuit of personal salvation. "The kingdom of God, in seeking the salvation of men, must be first . . . and must be kept first, high above every other interest." This centrality of eternal salvation entails direct implications for the nature of the Christian ministry. "The Christian ministry is no place for one who does not see that his supreme mission is to call men to repentance and faith, and who is not fully determined to make everything else in his life subservient to that end." Therefore, ministers of the gospel should "be all the time thinking and planning" to win people to Christ and to point them toward Christian faithfulness. According to Grimké, those who do not share in this calling of winning people to Christ and building them up in Christian character should "get out of the ministry," for they "are out of place in the pulpit." Such evangelism and discipleship is "really our only business," he put it bluntly.[23] Because he equated the kingdom of God with salvation, Grimké consistently taught that the supreme ministry of the church is calling people to faith and repentance in order that they might enter this eternal spiritual kingdom.

By observing Grimké's frequent statements regarding the spiritual nature of the kingdom of God and the church's identity as the visible expression of that spiritual kingdom, one can begin to understand his vision for the church as an engine of kingdom unity and racial equality. Whereas the theological modernists of his day made social unity and racial equality the center of the church's kingdom mission, Grimké affirmed these ideals but

---

22 *Works*, 3:76.
23 *Works*, 3:420.

taught that they were natural consequences and not the mission itself. This also distinguished him from the fundamentalists of his day who failed to appreciate the connection between these social derivatives and spiritual kingdom work. If the church is the visible expression of the kingdom of God, it must include people of all races. If the church is a spiritual kingdom, the proclamation of the gospel and Christian discipleship are its central, indeed "only," endeavors. Grimké traced a narrow path to balance and order these priorities.

The spiritual unity of believers entails direct implications for the unity of the church. Though there "are many folds," there is "but one flock, and one shepherd of all." Therefore, all Christ's sheep must "hear the voice of the same shepherd" and "obey his voice." Hearing and obeying imply spiritual oneness. "They are one in their love to Christ and purpose to follow him, and him only." According to Grimké, this exclusive allegiance to Christ "is the only kind of church unity that counts for anything, that is of any value." Allegiance to Christ implies acknowledgment of all one's fellow citizens in the kingdom, for Christ is a "common Lord of all" and the source of the unity "that we should all be striving for." If "all believers" were "thus united," they "would become a tremendous power for good in the world. Grimké held that church unity is the key to confronting the "kingdom of darkness." Before a unified church, "the kingdom of darkness would soon go down, the strongholds of wickedness would soon be overthrown."[24]

In turn, the unity of the church points to the solution to the "race problem" in the world. Grimké noted the prophet Isaiah's assertion that "the government of Christ . . . is to continue, and is to go on increasing." Speaking of Jesus's rule and authority, Grimké continued, "He is to get more and more the controlling influence in the world, and over the hearts of men." Therefore, Grimké believed that the problems of the present age will not always be with us. "The lion and the lamb will ultimately, under his beneficent reign, lie down together." As a result, there will be a day when "men of all races will find no difficulty in living together in peace and harmony." It was this vision that enabled Grimké to pursue the hard work of ministry and social advocacy. The certainty of Jesus's promise to set up the kingdom of God on earth" is not "a groundless hope."[25]

---

24 *Works*, 3:478.
25 *Works*, 3:328.

Despite present circumstances, Grimké expressed confidence in the real-ization of God's kingdom on earth, the ending of conflict, and the inevitabil-ity of racial unity and equality. "What the Bible says about the reign of Jesus Christ has in it the solution of all the dark problems of earth." Therefore, "all we have got to do is to go on working in faith; working in the confident assur-ance that [t]here are brighter days ahead." Dark times should not be a source of discouragement, for "the Triumph of the Messiah's kingdom is assured."[26]

Grimké's identification of the church and the kingdom of God and his related affirmation of the church's spiritual mission filled him with hope and oriented his ministry. He called the church to devote itself to evange-lism, discipleship, the worship of God, and a life of service flowing out of these priorities. He believed that these spiritual priorities would lead to worldly good, but he saw such material and temporal goods as the con-sequences of the church's mission and not the mission itself. He trusted that God's kingdom would prevail, and this confidence gave him hope for spiritual unity and racial equality in a dark world absent of those condi-tions. As he cast this vision of the kingdom of God, he simultaneously cast a vision for the church's mission.

The Mission of Christ

In addition, Grimké linked the mission of the church to the mission of Christ. Grimké characterized Jesus's mission as a joyful one accomplished through the establishment of his kingdom. The primary aspects of his kingdom mission included saving sinners, teaching his people, and bring-ing peace on earth. This work was not merely moral or exemplary but a supernatural mission accomplished through Jesus's own life, death, and resurrection. After the kingdom of God, the mission of Christ to usher in that kingdom was the next most crucial underpinning of Grimké's under-standing of the mission of the church.

Francis Grimké's teaching ministry regularly emphasized the joy, beauty, and hope of the gospel of Jesus Christ. He invited people to know

---

26 *Works*, 3:331. Grimké expressed this confidence in the immediate context of pessimism regarding the current trajectory of racial equality in America. Contrary to a then-recent article in *Harper's* magazine by Oswald Garrison Villard, Grimké cited Scott Nearing's *Black America* and R. R. Moton's *What the Negro Thinks* to argue that "the color line may be crumbling, but if it is it is barely perceptible." Grimké explicitly placed his hope in the final outcome of God's kingdom rather than present circumstances: "There is a bright side to the problem, and the thing that makes it bright is not so much these little gleams of light that come to us from time to time, in what Mr. Villard directs attention to, but in the certainty of the fact that God is on the throne." *Works*, 3:330.

and enjoy God and the benefits of a life devoted to following God. He exemplified this general characteristic of his teaching ministry particularly in his presentation of the ministry of Jesus. The mission of Christ is a joyful ministry. Isaiah 61:3 was Grimké's bedrock text from which he drew this joy. "Isaiah speaks, in describing the mission of the Messiah, of his giving 'beauty for ashes, the oil of joy for mourning, and the garment of praise for the spirit of heaviness.'" Confident in the mission of Christ, the believer may find happiness "in spite of outward circumstances however dark and forbidding." Amid his own health struggles later in life, he wrote that "somehow God can keep the joy bells ringing in the soul in spite of ill-health and all the other ills that flesh is heir to." He referred to this reality as one of the "miracles of grace."[27] The mission of Christ is a joyful one that sustains body and soul through life's trials.

For Grimké, the first element of the joyful ministry of Christ was the saving of sinners. Grimké stressed the importance of the salvation of sinners throughout his teaching ministry, and he made it a particular focus of his sermon series on the prodigal son. "What nobler mission can anyone set before him than the work of saving men, of rehabilitating those who have lost out, who have gone down under the power of sin," he stated rhetorically. He also noted the beauty and hope of salvation as an attractive aspect of Jesus's mission. Whereas the scribes and Pharisees looked down on Jesus because of his attitude toward publicans and sinners, what they considered a discredit Grimké deemed an apologetic strength of the Christian faith. God took on flesh to draw close to sinners, and "we now think of [this] as one of the very finest things about him." It is "one of the things that most commends him to us."[28] The scribes and Pharisees "maligned" and "misinterpreted" Jesus's motives, but a proper understanding of Christ's mission places the salvation of sinners in the foreground.

Second, the mission of Christ entails the teaching of his people. The following chapter will focus on the importance of the teaching ministry of the church and the Christian minister's role in relation to that ministry. Here it is important to observe that Grimké grounded this teaching ministry of the church and its ministers in the teaching ministry of Christ. This mission of teaching was "the idea of the Old Testament prophet," "the idea of the New Testament ministry," "the direction given to the apostles,"

---

[27] *Works*, 3:331.
[28] Francis J. Grimké, "The Prodigal Son and Kindred Addresses" (sermon 1, 1923), in *Works*, 2:266.

and, most importantly, "largely the mission of Christ." "Much of His time was given to instruction," Grimké observed. The Sermon on the Mount was characteristic of his ministry. The Scripture accounts "again and again" emphasize the centrality of teaching to his mission.[29] The mission of Christ was not only to save sinners but also to teach them how to follow him faithfully.

Third, the mission of Christ is to bring peace on earth. In December of 1918, just weeks after Germany signed the armistice that marked the end of the First World War, Grimké preached a sermon on the incarnation of Christ focused on Luke 2:14, "Glory to God in the highest, and on earth peace, good will toward men." While he expressed gratitude for the victory of the Allies over the Central Powers in the conflict, he also lamented the lack of peace for Black people in America. Though President Wilson spoke of the importance of "justice and fair dealings" abroad, Grimké pointed out the "flagrant" disregard for justice by Wilson's administration. Grimké warned, "If the representatives of the Allied governments have no better idea of 'justice' and 'fair dealings' than President Wilson has, there is no hope whatever that the foundation that will be laid will be lasting." Despite the antipathy of the nation's leaders, Grimké nevertheless held out hope to his congregation based on the mission of Christ. This mission, declared the angels in heaven, was to bring "glory to God in the highest, and on earth." Grimké noted this declaration, to which he responded, with an exultant "What? Peace, peace on earth, that is what He came to bring about, peace on earth." According to Grimké, bringing this peace was "what His mission was."[30] God's faithful people could know with certainty that the mission of Christ included the ultimate accomplishment of peace on earth.

Together these three aspects of Christ's mission pointed to the supernatural character of his kingdom and its coming. In particular, the salvation of souls and peace on earth could not happen naturally in a world broken by human sin. Grimké also regularly underlined the supernatural character of Christ's mission in his teaching and ministry. Jesus was not merely a good moral example to be followed, and not merely a good teacher from whom to learn, but he himself accomplished salvation and promised eternal peace through his incarnation, life, death, resurrection, ascension, and promised return.

---

[29] Francis J. Grimké, "The Afro-American Pulpit in Relation to Race Elevation" (1892), in *Works*, 1:224.
[30] Francis J. Grimké, "A Special Christmas Message" (1918), in *Works*, 1:583–84.

One particularly memorable example of Grimké's confidence in the supernatural nature of Christ's mission occurs in a letter he wrote to Bessie Taylor Page. As Bessie's husband was dying, Grimké sat and prayed with them both during the man's final hours. After Mr. Page's death, Grimké wrote Bessie a letter of comfort that apparently led her to reflect upon Christian beliefs regarding life after death. She was struck by Grimké's confidence and his obvious concern for her, and after some weeks she sent him a letter in reply. She confessed that she struggled to believe in life after death and asked Grimké to send his honest views of the matter as well as his reasoning. Specifically, she asked him to present his views on the subject apart from appealing to the teaching of Scripture.[31]

Grimké replied with a letter of several pages outlining a variety of reasons for his confidence in eternal life. He did not refer specifically to the teaching of Scripture on the subject, but he did refer to the testimony of the historical Jesus. He pointed out that even philosophers and literary figures skeptical of the Christian faith, including John Stuart Mill, Leo Strauss, and Jean Paul (Richter) still respected Jesus and considered him to be a trustworthy teacher. If Jesus's teaching was respectable, he reasoned, then his teaching on eternal life was worthy of consideration. "Did he [the historical Jesus] have anything to say [about eternal life]? O yes, much; very much. Thought of the future is interwoven with all His teachings." Given the frequency of Jesus's teaching regarding eternal life, Grimké concluded that Jesus left only two options: "We must believe there is a future life on the basis of what Jesus says, or else we must give up our belief in the purity, in the loftiness of His character." He proceeded to give several more arguments for eternal life, but the most notable one was the resurrection of Jesus himself, which Grimké referred to as a "historical fact" resting upon "as good evidence as any other." Jesus was not only a "martyr to that mission," as Mill claimed; he rose from the grave to prove that he himself had power over life and death.[32] His mission was a supernatural one accomplished and vindicated by his resurrection from the dead.

Grimké not only believed that the supernatural mission of Jesus was a source of confidence; he also believed that the knowledge of Christ's mission was a source of personal transformation. He believed that a true understanding of who Jesus was and what he had done could not leave

---

[31] Bessie Taylor Page to Francis J. Grimké, December 11, 1916, in *Works*, 4:181–85.
[32] Francis J. Grimké to Bessie Taylor Page, December 1916, in *Works*, 4:185–89.

a person unchanged. Reflecting on the scriptural passages related to the death of Jesus commemorated in the Lord's Supper, he described the transforming power of the mission of Christ. Jesus promised to "transform" those who "heartily accepted" him and his mission, which are a "source of blessing to others." In fact, Grimké wrote, "It is impossible to realize fully what the great sacrifice on Calvary really means in the economy of grace, without being transformed by it, made into a new and better creature by it."[33]

In another place in his meditations, he tied this transforming power of the knowledge of Christ's mission to the life of service all Christians are called to lead. He expressed dissatisfaction with his own willingness to serve Christ, and he reminded himself of the mission of Christ to spur himself on to greater faithfulness. "The more we come to know him and to understand the nature of his mission, the greater will be our enthusiasm, the more sincere and earnest will be our devotion to him," he reflected. "If he had not come, and lived among us, and left us his noble example; and had not upon Calvary expiated the guilt of a lost world, how different the outlook for the individual and for humanity would be." The knowledge of what Jesus has done is wonderful and powerful. On the other hand, Grimké pointed out that failure to appreciate Jesus's mission has serious consequences, for "it is our failure to realize fully all that is involved in his coming, that will account for our lack of devotion, of consecration to him."[34] Growth in piety and Christian service depends upon the knowledge of the mission of Christ.

———————

Francis Grimké's hopeful understanding of the mission of the church fueled his fifty years of service as a pastor and buoyed him through the ups and downs of his ministry. He observed the ways in which the Scriptures identified the church with the kingdom of God, and accordingly the significance of the work drove him forward. He also called the church not to waver in its spiritual mission as it committed itself to the kingdom-building work of evangelism, discipleship, worship, and service. These spiritual priorities essentially intersected with daily life in the world, but he distinguished their pursuit from the materialistic view of the world that made the pursuit of worldly goods an end in itself. In this way he made Jesus's

---

33 *Works*, 3:587.
34 *Works*, 3:472.

admonition in the Sermon on the Mount to "seek ye first his kingdom and his righteousness; and all these things shall be added unto you" (Matt. 6:33) the foundation of his understanding of the church and its ministry, just as he allowed it to ground his understanding of the "paramount" importance of religion in the home.[35] Grimké exhorted his people, "Put the kingdom of God first and the other things will follow."[36] In his meditations he summarized this point powerfully:

> It is amazing how much time, strength, energy are put into the mere temporalities of our churches, and how little, comparatively, go into the higher, spiritual activities,—into the work of trying to make men better, to improve the individual life, and the home life, and the community life. The materialism of the age has invaded the churches and is paralyzing, more or less, all of its higher activities. It is a subversion of the Divine order, it is putting the temporal before the spiritual. In the Sermon on the Mount Jesus said: "Seek ye first the kingdom of God and his righteousness, and all these things shall be added unto you." And where that course is followed, the lesser things will always be taken care of. Keep the spiritual paramount, and have no fear for the material.[37]

Grimké's confidence in the consummation of the kingdom gave him hope for spiritual unity and racial equality, and chapters 10 and 11 illustrate not only the variety of ways in which this hope shaped his engagement in social concerns but also how it set him apart from the fundamentalists of his day. This chapter has demonstrated how Grimké's understanding of the relationship between Christ's mission and the kingdom of God also distanced him from the theological modernists who emphasized Jesus's teaching and moral example but minimized his divine nature, his miracles, and especially his resurrection and second coming. For Grimké, Jesus's kingdom mission to bring peace on earth could not be divorced from his work of saving sinners. His teaching could not be separated from his person and work as God in human flesh. Grimké believed firmly in the supernatural nature of the kingdom of God and the mission of Christ, and he grounded his understanding of the church's mission in these crucial scriptural teachings.

---

[35] Francis J. Grimké, "The Home as a Training School" (1917), in *Works*, 2:463.
[36] Francis J. Grimké, "The Things of Paramount Importance in the Development of the Negro Race" (1903), in *Works*, 1:387.
[37] *Works*, 3:520.

CHAPTER 8

THE MISSION OF CHRIST'S PEOPLE

The previous chapter explored the ways in which Francis Grimké built his understanding of the church upon the foundation of Christ's mission and the coming kingdom of God. Chapter 7 was generally positive, tracing the beliefs Grimké supported, though framed against fundamentalism and especially modernism, two theological movements that he held at a distance. These themes will continue to be important throughout the remaining chapters. Having considered the foundations of Grimké's ecclesiology, this chapter now turns directly to his understanding of the mission of the church.

As he taught and ministered, Grimké demonstrated and expressed wariness that the church would corrupt or lose the central thread of its God-given mission. He expressed this concern on many occasions, perhaps most powerfully in the address he delivered upon the death of Bishop Daniel Alexander Payne. Originally ordained in the Lutheran Church, Payne served the African Methodist Episcopal Church for over fifty years, including more than forty of those as bishop. Payne emphasized the importance of ministerial education and preparation, which Grimké highlighted at length. He believed such theological formation essential to the work of ministry as a safeguard against the most dangerous threats to the church and its mission. In the same message, he identified those threats as "ignorance" and "demagoguery," especially the latter.

Grimké highlighted Payne's legacy of calling the church to follow his example in facing both threats. In the past, ignorance was the "great obstacle" standing in the way of the "church's progress." Grimké narrated Payne's role in introducing and shepherding to fruition a rigorous plan of theological education in the early days of the African Methodist Episcopal (AME) Church, and he celebrated the rich harvest of the plan's fruits. In his own day, however, Grimké identified demagoguery as the new obstacle, calling for the next generation to take up Payne's mantle of leadership. Grimké defined this demagoguery as the work of "unprincipled men within the church" working together to "get control" for the sake of "power" and "personal aggrandizement." He called his audience both to celebrate Payne's legacy and to emulate his example by holding up both the knowledge of God and the importance of moral character in the church's ministry. The loss of either would prove fatal not only to the AME Church but to any church.[1]

These twin threats to the church's mission illustrate the contours of that mission. God called the church to preach the word and to make disciples for his glory. This chapter builds on the previous one by expositing Grimké's use of the Great Commission to articulate the church's spiritual mission to proclaim the gospel and to form Christian communities devoted to following Christ. For Grimké, this twofold mission to preach and to obey the word implied particular roles for the church as an institution along with its leadership, as well as for the people of God as they carried out their daily lives. The church gathered for worship and the church scattered in the world are the same church with the same twofold mission. Yet this twofold mission entails a more particular role for the church gathered in worship and more diverse roles for that same church when scattered in the world to live in faithfulness to God.

The Great Commission and the Mission of the Church

Throughout his ministry, Grimké relied on the Great Commission to formulate the mission of the church. He made this connection between the Great Commission and the church's mission in his sermons, public addresses, and personal reflections. He used the Great Commission not only to teach the church what it should do but also to draw boundaries around

---

[1] Francis J. Grimké, "Addresses Dealing with the Careers of Distinguished Americans," address 1, "Bishop Daniel Alexander Payne" (1893), in *Works*, 1:1–28. For the obstacles to the church's ministry, see pp. 13–14. For Payne's role in the development of theological education in the AME Church, see pp. 8–9.

the things, even otherwise good things, that exceed its purview. In so doing Grimké painted a picture of the church's mission centered on the proclamation of the gospel and obedience to the whole counsel of God.

Grimké's emphasis on the Great Commission tied the ministry of the new covenant church to that of Israel under the old covenant. The Great Commission that Jesus gave to his disciples, "Go ye into all the world and preach the gospel to every creature," was the same "purpose which God had in view in the training of the Jewish nation"—namely, the "dissemination of the gospel among all peoples."[2] The central mission of God's people was to announce God's purposes in the coming Messiah. Though the Great Commission gave a particular shape to the ministry of God's new covenant people, this ministry grew organically from the ministry of the old covenant with Israel. The Great Commission marked the foundation of the church, but the central mission of God's people is the same throughout the Scriptures, whether Old Testament or New, and it therefore belongs equally to all God's people in all times. Grimké's vision of the shared mission of God's people in all places put the coming of Jesus and its implications for all peoples in the center.

When he preached a series of sermons on the parable of the prodigal son, Grimké similarly highlighted the centrality of the proclamation of the gospel promises, and he tied this proclamation to godly living. He identified the Great Commission work of gospel proclamation with the ministry of his own church. "This very message" given to the disciples is the same message "which the parable so eloquently proclaims to us this morning." Here too he characteristically attached gospel proclamation to the appropriate response. He expected gospel preaching in accordance with the Great Commission to produce godly lives. For prodigals, he reminded his hearers, "coming home, don't forget, means coming under the rules and regulations of the home,—coming under the government of your heavenly Father."[3] The Great Commission of the church is to further the kingdom of God. Indeed, the church that preaches the gospel in accordance with the Great Commission can expect to make new citizens of God's kingdom.

In addition to setting the course for the church to pursue, Grimké believed that the Great Commission set boundaries limiting the church's activities. As he reflected on his career as a pastor toward the end of his life,

---

[2] Francis J. Grimké, "The Roosevelt-Washington Episode, or Race Prejudice" (1901), in *Works*, 1:335–36.
[3] Francis J. Grimké, "The Prodigal Son and Kindred Addresses" (sermon 12, 1923), in *Works*, 2:382, 386.

he attributed the "continued acceptance" of his ministry to the fact that he allowed his ministry to be limited by the Great Commission. He felt that his mission as a pastor was "to preach the gospel" and "to expound the Bible as the Word of God." For this reason, he studiously refused "to make the pulpit a platform from which to discuss all sorts of subjects." Because "the commission which Jesus gave his disciples was 'Go ye into all the world and preach the gospel unto every creature,'" therefore "it is the gospel [alone] which the minister is set apart to preach." The Great Commission to preach the gospel not only was the center of the church's mission but was its only mission. Thus, he concluded, "That is what I have tried steadily to do, in dependence upon the presence and power of the Holy Spirit."[4]

To be clear, limiting the church's mission to the proclamation of the gospel did not preclude the church from confronting moral issues. In fact, Grimké attributed the church's failure to confront race prejudice to its failure to follow the Great Commission:

> That real genuine Christianity is powerless in the presence of race prejudice, is not true; back of it is the mighty power of God. The gates of hell can not prevail against it. That the Christianity represented in white America is spurious, I am not prepared to say. That the church has failed to do its duty, in this matter, I am prepared, however, to say. Had it been true to its great commission; had it lived up to its opportunities; had it stood squarely and uncompromisingly for Christian principles, the sad, the humiliating, the disgraceful fact of which we are speaking, never would have been possible. The fact that in Christian America, in this land that is rolling up its church members by the millions, race prejudice has gone on steadily increasing, is a standing indictment of the white Christianity of this land—an indictment that ought to bring the blush of shame to the faces of the men and women, who are responsible for it, whose silence, whose quiet acquiescence, whose cowardice, or worse whose active cooperation, have made it possible. The first thing for the church to do, I say, is to wake up to the fact that it can do something. Its present attitude is a disgrace to it, is utterly unworthy of the name which it bears.[5]

Thus, the Great Commission did not limit the church from addressing matters of public moral concern. In fact, by not addressing race prejudice, the church was neglecting "to do its duty." Jesus commissioned his disciples to

4 *Works*, 3:265.
5 Francis J. Grimké, "Christianity and Race Prejudice" (1910), in *Works*, 1:463–64.

teach the church "to observe all things whatsoever I have commanded you" (Matt. 28:20). Therefore, the church must offer "careful instruction" in the biblical teaching regarding human equality and confirm that verbal testimony with the "testimony of the individual life, free from race prejudice."[6] The Great Commission enjoins moral instruction and moral example upon the church. Preaching the word means preaching the whole word.

In other words, for the church to fulfill its mission to be "the salt of the earth" and "Light of the world," it must repent of its failure to live in accordance with the teaching of Jesus. Grimké called the White churches of his day to "really become centers for the propagation of Christianity." He believed that if the White church reclaimed its Christian mission, both spiritual and social benefits would follow.

> The white churches, the white Sabbath Schools, the white Endeavor societies, must become centers, not professedly so, but really centers for the propagation of Christianity, pure and simple. They must teach and live the brotherhood of man. They must cease their cowardly silence and speak out in regard to this evil, and they must back up their teaching by consistent living. They must teach the gospel of love, of brotherhood,—the brotherhood of all men. It must be taught in the churches, in the Sabbath Schools, from the pulpits, in the homes,—taught to the children so that they will grow up, not as they are growing up now to hate others because they happen to be of a different hue from themselves. In less than a generation, all this sad, painful, disgraceful condition of things could be changed, if the Church was all right, if it did its duty, if it were half trying to fulfill its mission as the salt of the earth,—as the Light of the world.[7]

The church's mission to be "salt" and "light" in the world depends on the faithful proclamation of the gospel of God. If the gospel of God is the announcement of the person and work of Jesus Christ, and this announcement is for "all peoples," then a church that intentionally limits its witness to one class of people is a church in name only. Christians who refuse fellowship with other Christians are guilty of following another gospel. Just as Paul confronted Peter to his face when he refused to walk in a way that accorded with the gospel, Grimké confronted White Christians in America with their violation of the central implications of the Great Commission.

---

6 Grimké, "Christianity and Race Prejudice," 466, 469.
7 Francis J. Grimké, "The Race Problem—Two Suggestions as to Its Solution" (1919), in *Works*, 1:597.

The propagation of the Christian faith depends upon the proclamation of the gospel "in all the world," and the church therefore must be the equal home of all who respond with faith and repentance. Anything less is a fundamental failure of its very mission.

Grimké's reliance upon the Great Commission pushed in two directions. On the one hand, his understanding of the Great Commission limited the mission of the church to the spiritual activities of preaching of the gospel and making disciples. It precluded the pursuit of "other subjects," however worthy, by the church as a gathered institution under the authority of its leaders. On the other hand, Grimké depended on the Great Commission to illustrate the expansive implications of gospel proclamation. If Jesus commanded his disciples to go into the world and teach all people to observe "all things whatsoever I have commanded you," then a church that willfully refuses to teach and observe Jesus's truth regarding the equality and "brotherhood" of all followers of Christ unduly limits that mandate. Thus Grimké simultaneously limited the church's mission to spiritual activities and affirmed the expansive implications of this carefully proscribed mission by emphasizing that the preaching of Scripture often entails speaking to matters of public moral concern. He relied on the Great Commission to make both points.

The addresses, sermons, and letters published in Grimké's collected works are enough to illustrate both the "limiting" and the "expanding" sides of Grimké's use of the Great Commission. That said, the more expansive emphasis is the dominant note in these collections. Attention to Grimké's full body of work, however, demonstrates that he devoted significant energy to the more "limiting" side of the Great Commission as well. Therefore, readers of Grimké's collected works should recognize that these volumes are not necessarily representative of the full scope of his teaching emphasis. Especially toward the end of his career, he discerned that a careful line must be drawn between the public moral concerns that rightly demand the church's advocacy and the tendency to make the church a social or political organization just like any other. He called the church to find the delicate balance that rightly affirms the church's "spiritual" mission guided by the Great Commission and, at the same time, hangs on to the church's obligation to address the whole counsel of God in its teaching and example.

"Christ's Program for the Saving of the World" is a striking illustration of Grimké's desire that the Great Commission limit the church's mission to spiritual concerns. Published in his own lifetime, the address received widespread attention, but Carter Woodson chose not to include it in the four volumes of Grimké's collected works he published soon after Grimké's death. Benjamin Brawley, who served as dean at Morehouse College from 1912 to 1920, taught English at Howard University in the 1930s, and served as chair of the department beginning in 1937, wrote to Grimké in 1936 to commend him for the address and to seek "forty, perhaps even sixty copies" that he might "use to advantage" by circulating them at Howard. He also expressed interest in sharing the address with Benjamin Mays, the recently installed dean of the School of Religion, who he claimed "will want some copies, I know."[8] Brawley's optimism regarding Mays's enthusiasm for Grimké's articulation of Christ's "program" raises interesting questions in light of Mays's more progressive theological commitments, but Brawley's letter nevertheless attests to the prominent reception of Grimké's address. Grimké received similar letters about the address from other noteworthy figures and activists, including the prominent Baltimore Methodist Episcopal minister Daniel W. Hays, Hampden-Sydney College president J. D. Eggleston, and Dwight O. W. Holmes, the civil rights activist and author of *The Evolution of the Negro College* (1934).[9] In light of the prominent reception of this particular address given toward the end of Grimké's life, its absence from his collected works is noteworthy, and this gap also raises questions regarding Woodson's own agenda in superintending Grimké's legacy.

Consistent with his typical articulation of the Great Commission, Grimké's exposition of "Christ's Program for the Saving of the World" made careful affirmations and denials regarding the nature of the church's mission. On the one hand, he safeguarded the spiritual nature of the church's mission. Christ's program of salvation does not come through "philosophy, or science, or any special department of human knowledge; but teaching what is written in the Scriptures, the Word of God." He carefully distinguished general revelation from special revelation, and he located the

---

8 Benjamin Brawley to Francis J. Grimké, February 1, 1936, in *Works*, 4:38–39.

9 D. W. Hays to Francis J. Grimké, February 17, 1936, in *Works*, 4:541; J. D. Eggleston to Francis J. Grimké, February 5, 1936, in *Works*, 4:539; D. O. W. Holmes to Francis J. Grimké, March 4, 1936, in *Works*, 4:543–44. On Mays's more progressive social gospel commitments, see Gary Dorrien, *The New Abolition: W. E. B. Du Bois and the Black Social Gospel* (New Haven, CT: Yale University Press, 2015), 2–4, 8–11, 15, 484. Dorrien's work is complex, simultaneously arguing for a singular and recognizable "black social gospel" while also making the case that at least four streams—often diametrically opposed to one another—contributed to the existence of this recognizable movement. See chap. 10 for discussion of these figures and movements.

church's mission in the proclamation of the sacred doctrine of Christ based on special revelation.

> Nothing should be allowed to go on in it [the church] or under its direction, which has not one or both of these ends in view—the turning of men from their evil ways and attaching to them to Jesus Christ as their Lord and Saviour, or the bringing of them under the power and influence of some Bible truth.

Rather than churches devoted to any other good purpose, Grimké's bold vision was for the coming of God's kingdom solely through the ministry of the word of God. "When all of our churches and all of our ministers realize what the work is to which they are called, and get busy doing it, then, and not till then, will changes for the better take place; will the kingdom of God come, and come with power." Therefore, he continued, "What we need most of all is a faithful, courageous, consecrated ministry that will stick close to the Word of God in all their ministrations and in dependence upon the Holy Spirit to make effective the Word preached and taught."[10] Christ's program for saving the world promised the coming of God's kingdom exclusively through the carefully proscribed means of preaching and disciple making narrowly entailed in the Great Commission.

On the other hand, Grimké acknowledged that the spiritual mission of the Christian church cannot be separated from the material concerns of human beings living in the present age. The preaching of the gospel of spiritual salvation also entails "changes for the better of individuals and communities" that intersect with "the whole structure of human society" and "all human relationships." The spiritual nature of Christianity stands opposed to "other religions" and cuts across all ideologies, whether "Communism," "Nationalism," or "Capitalism."[11] A church committed to the narrow path set forth in the Great Commission cannot help but enable people to live more faithfully and fruitfully in every aspect of their lives. The truth of Christ stands supreme and pushes against every philosophical system, for every philosophical system developed by humanity is at least partially corrupted by sin. In Christ alone salvation is found, and full submission to the will of Christ is the path to full human flourishing. The breadth of

---

[10] Francis J. Grimké, "Christ's Program for the Saving of the World" (1936), box 40-6, folder 309, Francis J. Grimké Papers, Howard University Library, 11.
[11] Grimké, "Christ's Program for the Saving of the World," 9, 12.

Christ's program for saving the world encompasses moral concerns that intersect all aspects of daily life. Like the Great Commission, the ends of Christ's "program" for saving the world are incredibly broad.

Given the frequency with which he took up the topic, it is remarkable that Grimké's various addresses regarding the mission of the church do not appear in the four volumes of his collected works. The records of his preaching in the manuscript archives at Howard University reveal that this theme was crucial to his ministry and that his understanding remained strikingly consistent throughout his years of service at Fifteenth Street Presbyterian Church. Grimké shaped his life and work as a pastor with extreme care to carry out a finely principled understanding of the church's mission. He believed that the good efforts of Christians to effect moral and social change should not compromise the church's corporate spiritual mission of proclamation and disciple making, and he believed that this spiritual mission in turn forms disciples whose very lives are salt and light in a fallen world. If "Christ's Program for the Saving of the World" indicates his perspective at the end of his life, another sermon from the archives, "The Nature and Mission of the Christian Church," dates to a much earlier point, in the 1890s.[12] This early sermon communicated an understanding of the church's mission that also emphasized preaching and disciple making while outlining the public moral significance of genuine Christian discipleship.

Grimké organized his treatment of "The Nature and Mission of the Christian Church" to address two primary questions: "What is the church?" and "How does the church differ from other organizations?" He prefaced this material by reading the story of the church's founding on the day of Pentecost in Acts 2, emphasizing the church's international character as it spread from Jerusalem to Judea and Samaria, and then to the ends of the earth. He highlighted the presence of the early church in Syria, Antioch,

---

12 Francis J. Grimké, "The Nature and Mission of the Christian Church" (ca. 1889), box 40-8, folder 415, Francis J. Grimké Papers, Howard University Library. The page is torn in the manuscript copy, partially obscuring the precise dates. The portions of the two dates listed for the sermon on the last page indicate November 24 (year obscured), and April 27, 189— (last digit of the year obscured). The latter date is probably 1890, the only year in the 1890s in which April 27 occurred on a Sunday. Because the November 24 date is listed above the April 27 date, it probably is an earlier date. The two Sundays on November 24 between Grimké's assumption of the pulpit at Fifteenth Street and the April 27, 1890, date were 1878 and 1889. The latter date is more likely, given the subject matter. These years are conjectures that assume the sermons were preached on a Sunday, though it is possible they were given occasionally on different days of the week. Since the November date appears above the April one, Grimké almost certainly preached it before the 1890s. Thus, both sermons date to a point in the first twenty years of his ministry, very likely November 24, 1889, and April 24, 1890, soon after his return to Fifteenth Street from his brief sojourn in Florida. It appears he returned from Florida ready to cast a vision for his congregation's identity and ministry.

and Asia Minor more broadly before it arrived in Macedonia, Greece, and the rest of Europe. He pointed to the church's global expansion in "Europe, Asia, Africa, North and South America, and India, and in the Islands of the Sea." Despite the global presence of the church and its numerical explosion, which he precisely numbered as "138,885 distinct congregations, 94,457 ministers, and 19,790,328 communicants" in the United States alone, he lamented that "in the great majority of cases there is an almost total ignorance" of the "true nature and mission of the church."[13]

In relation to the first question about the church's identity, he outlined three principles. First, the church is an "organization made up of individuals without distinction of race or nationality, age, sex, or condition." Citing Revelation 7:9, he specified that in the church "are to be found all race[s] and nationalities, all ages, sex[es] and conditions, young and old, male & female, white, black and all the intermediate shades, rich and poor, high and low, educated and uneducated, bound and free." Second, the church is a "voluntary organization" in the sense that there is "no compulsion" to membership. "All who enter, enter because they want to. . . . No one is ever coerced." The church comprises those who "believe" in Christ. Third, the "bond of union, which unites together this complex and heterogeneous mob, is supreme allegiance to Christ." For Grimké this allegiance to Christ explains why the church may be referred to as the kingdom. Regarding church members' allegiance to Christ, he declared: "In this sense the church may be called the Kingdom of Christ. In it he is the King of Kings and Lord of Lords."[14] Thus, Grimké identified the church by these three principles. The church is the universal kingdom of all who willingly place themselves under the authority of Jesus the King. In this very precise sense it is the "Kingdom of Christ."

When it came to the second question about the church's purpose, he again outlined three principles unified by a common end. "Broadly stated," the end for which Jesus brought the church into existence is to "advance the cause of Christ in the earth"—in other words, "to carry forward the great work which he projected." "More particularly," this work could be described according to three principles. First, the ministry of the church includes proclamation. Citing the Great Commission, Grimké declared that the "aim of the church is to make known Christ, to publish the glad tidings of salvation, to diffuse far and wide a knowledge of the truth as it is in Jesus." The

---

[13] Grimké, "The Nature and Mission of the Christian Church," 3–4.
[14] Grimké, "The Nature and Mission of the Christian Church," 4–6.

second principle guiding the church's purpose in ministry is "winning" people to Christ. The Christian faith is a universal religion, and therefore Christians are to take the proclamation of Christ to all people in all places. "The great aim of the church is to bring every thought and imagination to the obedience of Christ—to make the religion of Jesus . . . the religion of the whole world." Third, the ministry of the church is to "destroy the works of darkness, to wage uncompromising war against all evil." Using military language, Grimké declared that "God intended the church" to serve as "propaganda for the truth" and an "offensive power against evil." By evil, he meant "all injustice" and "all oppression wherever committed and by whosoever committed." Such injustice and oppression "should always find in the church a stern and uncompromising enemy." Summarizing these three principles, Grimké declared that the "great aim" of the Christian church is "to make known Christ, and tell men of Jesus, and lead men to accept him, to love him, and obey him," and in this way "to destroy the works of Satan, to overthrow all evil and to enthrone righteousness."[15]

After naming these three aspects of the church's purpose, Grimké prophetically called the church to task for its failure to carry out its mission. "The church is not what it ought to be," he lamented. The sparsity of missionaries among the hundreds of millions of Christians around the globe illustrated the church's failure to proclaim the word. When it came to telling people about Christ and winning people to Christ, Grimké concluded, "In both of these respects the church is woefully deficient." Yet it was the third purpose, opposing evil and injustice, that he identified as the area in which the church was "most deficient."[16] Citing the abolitionist Theodore Parker, he called out church leaders for their failure to address the evils of slavery. How could it be that such leaders "are silent over such a sin?" The church should, rather, be the collective conscience that "thunders and lightens on this hideous wrong!" Sadly, he observed, "That is not so. The church is dumb, while the state is only silent; while the servants of the people are only asleep, God's ministers are dead!"[17]

The church needed to embrace its missionary purpose to tell people about Jesus and persuade them to believe in Christ, but Grimké identified

---

[15] Grimké, "The Nature and Mission of the Christian Church," 14, 17, 19, 20, 21.

[16] Grimké, "The Nature and Mission of the Christian Church," 20.

[17] Grimké, "The Nature and Mission of the Christian Church," 20–21: The quotation is from Theodore Parker, "The True Idea of a Christian Church. A Discourse at the Installation of Theodore Parker as Minister of the Twenty-Eighth Congregational Church in Boston, January 4, 1846," in Parker, *Speeches, Addresses, and Occasional Sermons*, vol. 1 (Boston: Horace B. Fuller, 1867), 41.

the third aspect of the church's ministry, its obligation to confront evil, as the place where the church in America fell especially short. The fault lay not only with church leaders but also with church members. Speaking of slavery and racial injustice, he grieved, "If the church had done its duty, if its members had spoken out, instead of remaining silent or in league with the enemies of righteousness, I believe that this . . . barbarism would long since have passed away."[18]

By naming both church leaders and church members Grimké championed an understanding of the church and its mission that took seriously its dual identity as a "gathered" institution and a "scattered" organism. The mission given to the institutional church is quite narrow. Because the church is the expression of the kingdom of Christ, it must submit to the missional purposes assigned to it by Christ the King. Those missional purposes, set forth in the Great Commission, include evangelism and disciple making—in other words, telling people about Jesus, winning them to Jesus, and teaching them how to follow Jesus in confronting evil and pursuing righteousness. Though this institutional mission of the gathered church is quite narrow, its reach is incredibly broad, because the people of God continue to be the church when they scatter into the world and live as faithful followers of Christ.

For this reason, as Grimké concluded his message on the nature and mission of the Christian church, he called the people to embrace their calling to "actively cooperate in furthering the great ends" of Christ's community. He bluntly stated—contrary to popular assumptions—that "the church is not a social organization . . . having as its object pleasure, recreation, mere entertainment." Rather, "it is a labor organization having a definite and specific work entrusted to it" and "all who enter it are supposed to be included in that work, and to be doing all in their power to push it forward." Therefore, membership in the church relates to both identity and activity, who someone is and what someone does. A church member must be growing in "character and life," and a church member must be "actively engaged in Christian work." That is the "idea of the church" and the "idea of a church member."[19] If the mission of the gathered institutional church is proclamation and discipleship, the mission of the church scattered is to live in accordance with the things proclaimed and discipled.

---

[18] Grimké, "The Nature and Mission of the Christian Church," 21.
[19] Grimké, "The Nature and Mission of the Christian Church," 25.

Thus, throughout his ministry, Grimké relied upon the Great Commission to teach the church both what it should do and what it should not do. He taught that the ends of the church are broad, affecting every aspect of the lives of its members, but he also taught that the church's means for pursuing these ends are narrow. On the one hand, Christ commanded the gathered, institutional church to proclaim Christ and disciple church members in following the commands of Christ. On the other hand, Christ commanded his people to believe and obey his commands. In this way, Grimké consistently and carefully distinguished the mission of the church as a gathered institution from the mission of the church as a scattered organism. In so doing he painted a picture of the church's mission centered on the proclamation of the gospel and obedience to the whole counsel of God.

The Mission of the Church Gathered

Francis Grimké relied on the Great Commission not only to detail the church's mission but also to determine the respective roles of church leaders and church members. Christ's teaching regarding the church's mission helped the church to know both what it should do and who should do it, and how. As Grimké put it in his mediations, "The great mission of the church is to preach the gospel and to live it."[20] Therefore, everyone in the church has a role to play in living out the mission that Christ gave to God's people, but not everyone possesses the same role.

This distinction in roles helps to explain how Grimké could put so much emphasis on the work of the minister in preaching the word faithfully—a cornerstone of his teaching and writings—without undermining the significance of the vocations of members. "If the church is to accomplish its mission in the world," both are crucial. On the one hand, the church "must stand squarely, uncompromisingly for the truth as declared in God's Word, the scriptures of the Old and New Testament: it must stand for Christian ideals and principles." This responsibility for standing uncompromisingly for truth belongs primarily to church leaders. On the other hand, the church also "must live what it preaches." In other words, "the life of its members must conform to its teachings." This duty of the church, which belongs to all its members, is "more important even than its correct verbal declarations." Grimké assigned such high regard to faithful

---

[20] *Works*, 3:312.

living because he believed that if the church "teaches one thing and lives another it will never be able to win the world over to Christian ideals and principles."[21] The church's faithful teaching is crucial and powerful, but the faithfulness of its members is also vital to its ministry.

Concerning the roles of church leaders, Grimké emphasized the importance of preaching the word of God. "As ministers," he wrote, "our duty is to preach what the Bible teaches, its ideals, principles, great truths concerning God and man, sin and righteousness, never mind what others may think or say, whether they believe or disbelieve in what is declared to be true in the Scriptures of the Old and New Testament."[22] The minister of God is a "divine representative" obligated to preach the Bible without fear of public opinion. In his meditations, Grimké recorded key insights into the nature and shape of preaching, he taught that the public ministry of the church must be regulated by the word of God, and he argued that the pulpit is the greatest power in the church.

The character of preaching is one of the most common themes of Grimké's meditations.[23] The goal of preaching is not merely the dissemination of information, and it certainly is not the sharing of personal opinions or even general wisdom. Rather, preaching is directed toward the winning of souls and the sanctification of God's people. Evangelism and discipleship in biblical holiness are the ends of preaching. In fact, these ends transcend the pulpit and should inform every aspect of pastoral ministry. Grimké put it this way with his characteristic passion:

> As ministers of the gospel, we ought to be all the time thinking and plan-
> ning to win men from their evil ways to Christ, and to build them up in
> faith and holiness. That is really our only business. . . . And, if our main
> concern is not in the direction of such winning and of such developing in
> them of Christian character, the sooner we get out of ministry the better.[24]

Grimké clearly distinguished material needs from spiritual, affirmed the importance of both, and yet regularly affirmed that the church and its leaders must focus on spiritual needs. "The great function of the Christian Church is to minister to a [person's] spiritual needs. . . . Only so far

---

[21] *Works*, 3:494.
[22] *Works*, 3:618.
[23] Interested readers can now consult the collection of Grimké's reflections on preaching gathered from *Works*, vol. 3, *Stray Thoughts and Meditations*, in Francis James Grimké, *Meditations on Preaching* (Madison, MS: Log College, 2018).
[24] *Works*, 3:420.

as it is doing this is it of any value," he wrote.[25] He instructed preachers to be confident that faithful biblical preaching would produce fruit, but one of the most frequent themes in his meditations relates to the role of the Holy Spirit in producing this fruit. In reminding pastors to depend on the Holy Spirit in their preaching, he urged them to aim at biblical faithfulness rather than results. Ultimately, spiritual fruit depends upon the work of God, not the work of the pastor. Preaching is God's chosen instrument, but the gracious work of regeneration and sanctification belongs to God alone.[26]

Because Grimké believed that preaching is a spiritual work oriented to evangelism and discipleship in dependence on the Holy Spirit, he also taught that sermons should be simple, serious, and carefully prepared. "The greatness of a sermon does not depend upon its literary qualities, or the profoundness of its thought, but the extent to which it is used by the Holy Spirit in bringing about spiritual results," he wrote. Citing Peter's great Acts 2 sermon on the day of Pentecost, Grimké celebrated it because it was "plain, simple, direct, pointed," and honest. Given the conversions that followed, Grimké characterized Peter's sermon as "one of the greatest, if not the greatest sermon ever preached."[27] He encouraged pastors to emulate Peter's simplicity. In addition to being simple, preaching should also be serious. Grimké also held that seriousness cannot be feigned. Preachers often fail "to impress their seriousness upon others" because they themselves are not affected by the seriousness of the matters at hand. "The truths we present ought first of all to lay hold of our own hearts. It is when we ourselves are fully impressed by them, that we are in a condition to present them effectively to others."[28]

Grimké also taught that sermons should be prepared carefully. The pastor convinced of the significance of his message should endeavor "as

---

25 *Works*, 3:76. Grimké regularly characterized spiritual needs as those connected to life with God, which he carefully defined as "life that has to do with God and our relation to him." The word of God and prayer are the nourishment needed for spiritual life. As he put it at length in one place: "I have just run across these words:—'The spiritual life needs nourishment every day.' And by the spiritual life is meant life that has to do with God and our relations to him, and the obligations growing out of those relations. And by nourishment is meant, a growing realization of the reality of God, and the value and importance of recognizing our relations to him, and of conforming to the requirements of his most holy and righteous laws. By saying that the spiritual life needs to be nourished every day means that this sense of the reality of God and what is required of us by him, needs to be quickened, intensified, every day. And the way to do that is by reading the scriptures every day, and thinking seriously upon what they teach about God, and our relations to him and our obligations under those conditions. It means also that we should daily cultivate the habit of prayer, of communion and fellowship with God, and with Jesus Christ and with the Holy Spirit. Every day this spiritual contact should be kept up, and there should be a growing sense of the value and importance of it. Yea, of the necessity of it. If the spiritual life is not fed, and fed daily, it will be sure to grow less and less, and finally entirely die out. This God-consciousness, or sense of his reality and of his presence with us, should be constantly cultivated, kept alive." *Works*, 3:173.
26 For a few examples of exhortations along these lines, see *Works*, 3:18, 56, 129, 276, 355, 357, and 509.
27 *Works*, 3:20.
28 *Works*, 3:21–22.

far as he is able by hard study and dint of perseverance, to feed his people on the finest of wheat." Reliance on the Holy Spirit and the pursuit of simplicity should by no means lead to slothful preparation. Speaking of his own ministry, Grimké admitted it required of him "hard, hard study, and the most careful preparation of my sermons."[29] Citing 2 Timothy 2:15, he encouraged his fellow ministers to fastidious attention to the word of God in sermon preparation: "Study to show thyself approved unto God, a workman that needeth not to be ashamed, rightly dividing the word of truth."[30]

Grimké adhered to a biblical model that placed a high value on the proclamation of God's word, and he also believed that the word of God should "regulate" the church's ministries by determining which programs the church should pursue and which topics the church should teach. He characterized the form of religion "dished out in most of the churches" as "perverted, one sided, distorted." He contrasted this form of religion with the "teaching and the spirit of Jesus Christ," which led him to bemoan the "conferences" and "elaborate programmes" religious leaders were "getting up, all on paper." Rather than condoning such flimsy programs designed to entertain, generate endless theoretical conversations, or raise money in the coffers of churches (especially their leaders), Grimké challenged the church to believe the gospel and obey the teachings of Scripture. He cast a vision for preaching and "squaring the life, the everyday conduct to what is preached." He lamented that many self-professed Christians apparently preferred "an opportunity of seeming to be doing something of a religious nature without doing what the religion of Jesus Christ really calls for," with its simple, biblical preaching and faithful worship and service. He prophetically portrayed the "so-called religious activities" of the church and parachurch organizations of his day as "mere camouflage."[31] He called churches to cease programs designed to entertain, attract crowds, generate finances, and start conversations. He challenged them to replace such programs with a simple biblical ministry of worship, ordinary scriptural teaching, and holy living.

Grimké also cast a vision for the Scriptures to regulate teaching topics. Positively, he encouraged church leaders to rely on the Scriptures in their teaching and preaching, and negatively, he warned church leaders

---

[29] *Works*, 3:180, 182.
[30] *Works*, 3:274.
[31] *Works*, 3:91. These comments came in the context of a discussion of the "Inter-denominational" and "Inter-Church Federation" efforts of his day.

of the dangers of building a teaching and preaching ministry on any other foundation. "A ministry that does not build on the word of God but which depends on other things, will be sure to be a barren one. On this point there can be no doubt." Citing a litany of Scripture passages, including John 8:31, John 17:17, Acts 20:32, Ephesians 5:2[6], 2 Timothy 3:16, and [1] Peter 2:2, he instructed ministers to "continue in the word," to "sanctify [believers] through thy [God's] word," to depend on the word "which is able to build you up," in order that the Lord "might sanctify and cleanse it, i.e. the church," and to trust the "sincere milk of the word" to feed the "new-born babes" of the church. He concluded that these passages are "sufficient to show what place the word of God occupies in the development of Christian character and life," and that the Scriptures alone are "the Divinely appointed food upon which the Christian must feed, and which the Christian minister must see that he gets." With characteristic zeal, he said of the minister who follows any other course, "His ministry is a farce."[32] According to Grimké, far too much preaching is "guessing, speculating, surmising, theorizing," especially when it comes to application to cultural issues. Preachers should spare congregations from such weak attempts to present themselves as armchair philosophers and cultural critics and instead stick directly and boldly to their texts and the more obvious implications of their texts. "As ministers, our duty is to preach what the Bible teaches, its ideals, principles, great truths concerning God and man, sin and righteousness, never mind what others may think or say," he wrote. Because the minister stands as a "Divine representative," he is "bound to declare" only what God reveals "in his inspired word." Such a sermon "may be relied upon with absolute assurance" because it "is not sand but rock" that the minister is building upon.[33] According to Grimké, both the programs and the topics of the church must be regulated by the Scriptures.

This emphasis on the biblical nature of the church's ministry helps to illustrate why he regularly spoke of the pulpit as the "greatest source of power for good in a church." For the ministry of the pulpit to be effective, however, the minister needs to be willing and able to preach God's word. God did not promise to use just any preaching. Rather, God promised to make the preaching of Scripture effective to his people through the work

---

[32] *Works*, 3:297.
[33] *Works*, 3:619. These comments came in the context of a critique of what Grimké took to be cultural engagement and analysis in college and university environments that replaced biblical teaching and actively undermined the kind of ministry taught in the Bible.

of the Holy Spirit. In this sense, Grimké held that faithfulness to the word of God ordinarily is necessary for effectiveness in ministry—faithfulness to the word both in the content of preaching and in the qualifications of the preacher. Preachers need to be "qualified" to teach by their devotion to God and by rigorous theological education. They need to apply their skills to the "sincere milk of the word" rather than "the husks of current happenings in newspapers and magazines."[34] In addition to preparation *for* the ministry, Grimké identified careful preparation *in* the ministry of God's word as necessary for effective preaching. "The time that ought to be given to preparation" should not be given to "other things," he declared, or "the flock is unfed, the services are not edifying, the people are not helped spiritually, the good work languishes, everything moves at a poor dying rate." He lamented the "kind of sermons that proceed from some of our pulpits" and their obvious "lack of preparation." He called ministers to "realize more fully than most of us do, that the business in which we are engaged is a serious one, involving the eternal interest of immortal souls," and therefore to "give a little more attention to our pulpit ministrations" in order to feed "the flock of God which he hath purchased with his own blood," an allusion to Acts 20:28.[35] The power of the pulpit demands that it receive pastoral priority.

These reflections are characteristic of Grimké's meditations. He frequently contemplated the nature and shape of preaching, the need to regulate the ministry of the gathered church according to Scripture, and the power of the proclamation of the word of God. His impulses on these matters signaled his commitment to allowing the Great Commission to direct his understanding of the church's mission. He believed that the mission of the church gathered is to proclaim Jesus to all peoples in order to make disciples by baptizing them into Christian communities and teaching them the whole counsel of God.

The Mission of the Church Scattered

Grimké also expected the fruit of a faithful ministry oriented by the Great Commission to be reflected in the vocations of God's people. He liked to emphasize that the people of God remain the church when scattered in the world to carry out their personal callings. Their ministry as a scattered

---

34 *Works*, 3:95.
35 *Works*, 3:164.

people is broader and more diverse than that of the gathered or institutional church. As Grimké put it in his meditations, "A Christian is one who believes in Jesus Christ, and who has joined hands with him to bring the world his way." For Grimké, this mission entailed not only a way of "thinking" but also a way of "feeling," and even a way of "acting." It belonged not only to those called to ordained office but to "every professing Christian." He concluded his evaluation of the mission with an exclamation, "And what a mission it is!" followed by a question, "Can there be a grander, nobler one?"[36]

This meditation reflects Grimké's twofold view of the church's mission. The mission of the church as an institution focuses narrowly on evangelism and discipleship, whereas the mission of the church as scattered Christians is as diverse as the gifts given to particular believers. Individuals are called to obey Christ and honor him in their thoughts, words, and deeds. This work too is appropriately described as the mission of the church, though it should not be conflated with the work of the church as a gathered institution.

Along these lines, Grimké envisioned every church as a "missionary center." The title of "missionary" belongs not only to ordained positions like "minister" or "church official" but also to non-ordained roles, including "Sunday school teacher," for example. Similarly, when it came to the question "Where is the church?" in addressing racism, Grimké looked to the membership. The church's failure to address racism was the failure of the "forty million professing Christians" in America. The church's silence was their silence. It was this church, its individual members, that he had in view when he spoke of the corporate whole "resting on its arms," and "doing nothing, or comparatively nothing" to address the problem of racism in America.[37] In his famous address "Christianity and Race Prejudice," he made this point repeatedly as he again identified the mission of the church with the mission of God's people. "The mission of the church, of Christian men and women is to mould, not be moulded by encircling influences of evil. To the shame of the millions of white Christians in this land, the brother in black is still a social and religious outcast."[38]

---

[36] *Works*, 3:85.
[37] Francis J. Grimké, "The Race Problem as It Respects the Colored People and the Christian Church, in the Light of the Developments of the Last Year" (1919), in *Works*, 1:612–13. See also his similar statements in Grimké, "Christianity and Race Prejudice," 462, 464.
[38] Grimké, "Christianity and Race Prejudice," 471. See the similar statements on pp. 462 and 464.

As noted above, Grimké often used the figure of faithful preaching to communicate the narrow mission of the corporate church, as distinct from the diverse giftings and vocations of scattered Christians. Perhaps the most notable illustration of this distinction occurs in the sermon he preached on the seventy-fifth anniversary of the founding of Fifteenth Street Presbyterian Church. That sermon recounts the history of the congregation, and the distinction between the singular mission of the gathered church and the diverse vocations of individual church members runs right down the middle of the sermon. As he recounted the church's history and its core principles, Grimké demonstrated a keen awareness that the congregation possessed a missional identity as a gathered congregation and also as individual Christians. For example, the Fifteenth Street Presbyterian Church "Resolved, That as a Christian Church, and as Individual Christians we feel bound to endeavor to promote the Redeemer's kingdom on the earth in every possible way." Some of those possible ways belonged to the church gathered, but others to a host of "missionary societies" and other institutions, as well as to their scattered lives as individual Christians.[39]

This distinction, though neat in principle, did allow for some flexibility in application. When Grimké returned to Fifteenth Street in 1889 after his sojourn in Florida, the session of the church established nine standing committees to deal with a variety of affairs. In addition to those dealing with the more obvious aspects of the gathered church's work, the church established committees to address temperance, missionary outreach to the poor, and "Systematic Benificence" [sic]. The nature of these committees and their work, how they were led, and the intersection of lay and ordained leadership in their activities are areas worthy of further study. It may be, as one study has concluded, that the church's decision was shaped by a "Social Gospel influence" emphasizing the importance of addressing "social wrongs in an institutional manner." On the other hand, it may have been an attempt on the part of the church's leadership to provide concrete avenues for its members to organize themselves according to their particular callings. It could also be evidence that even the sharpest of principles can become fuzzier in the context of real-world application. Further studies may provide clarity on the precise shape of this question, but either way,

---

[39] Francis J. Grimké, "Anniversary Address," delivered on the seventy-fifth anniversary of the Fifteenth Street Presbyterian Church, Washington, DC, November 19, 1916, in *Works*, 1:537.

it is clear, generally speaking, that Grimké put a great deal of emphasis on *both* the gathered and scattered church, even as he typically distinguished the tasks proper to each.[40]

At any rate, Grimké's regular exhortations to the people of God to embrace the diverse gifts and roles arising from their individual vocations enabled him to carefully protect the "spiritual" mission of the gathered church without unduly separating the spiritual life from material existence. He called Christians to live *in* the world but not to be *of* the world, and he understood the mission of the church to serve both ends. For Grimké, the church is a sanctuary into which God's people are gathered through evangelism and where they are then taught to be disciples. At the same time, as God's people worship together on Sunday, they are built up and prepared to scatter into the world, where they continue to be the church, living as salt and light the rest of the week.

Grimké's careful reliance upon the Great Commission to guide the church into its mission led him to walk a fine line between the tendencies of many of his contemporaries. Theological progressives despised his emphasis on the "spiritual nature" of the church's corporate mission, and they made their distaste known in letters to the famous preacher, as well as in print. They rejected Grimké's adherence to the exclusive claims of Christ, and especially to Grimké's emphasis on supernatural aspects of biblical teaching. His belief in the necessity of personal faith in Christ as the ordinary path to eternal life, his affirmation of biblical moral principles as the way to follow that path, and his unwavering conviction that the institutional church is the foretaste of God's kingdom all led him to emphasize evangelism and discipleship in a way that alienated theological progressives who sounded other notes.

On the other hand, Grimké's observation that the Great Commission requires the church to teach God's people "to observe all things whatsoever I have commanded you," combined with his recognition that God gave a

----

[40] See Jacqueline Moore, *Leading the Race: The Transformation of the Black Elite in the Nation's Capital, 1880–1920* (Charlottesville: University of Virginia Press, 1999), 76–77, for a discussion of these committees at Fifteenth Street Presbyterian Church. Moore's study is especially useful for pointing to the relevant sections of the church minutes in the archives of the Moorland-Spingarn Research Center at Howard University. Moore helpfully brings the approach at Fifteenth Street into conversation with that of Metropolitan AME Church around the same time. Her study invites further research along these lines.

diversity of gifts to his people, led him to stress that the mission of the church extends into the world through the lives of that diverse people. As he put it pithily in his meditations, "What we are will determine the use or uses to which what we have will be put."[41] He called people to a unified devotion to God as their sole purpose in life and to pursue holiness in accordance with biblical teaching rather than fleshly desires, but he also emphasized that this shared goal and moral vision should be pursued through means as varied as God's people.

Grimké's belief in the diverse means of pursuing God's mission was inseparable from his prophetic opposition to racism in the church. Just as he was convinced that God gave a diversity of gifts to a diverse people for service in God's mission, he was equally convicted that God's church should comprise this same diversity of gifts and people. These convictions led him to oppose vociferously the racism that proliferated in theologically conservative churches at least as much as, if not more than, in theologically progressive settings. Because of this, his understanding of the mission of the church was inseparable from his indictment of American Christianity (specifically) and Western Christianity (more generally) for allowing racial differences to exclude God's people and God's gifts from the church.

Thus, Grimké's use of the Great Commission to direct the mission of the church arose from his affirmation of the supernatural nature of the kingdom of God. The transformation of God's people can only come through the personal work of the Holy Spirit. God called the church to be the gathering place for the sanctification of this people, and God called this same church to be scattered back out into the world to live transformed lives. Grimké believed that if God's people would embrace both the narrow means given to the gathered church and the diverse means given to the scattered church, the world could not help but be affected by their salt and light in service of God's unifying kingdom. "We have a prophecy of what is sure to come. Christianity is not an evanescent, transient influence; it is here to stay until its mission has been fulfilled, until God's purpose has been fully accomplished through it," he wrote.[42]

Grimké's confidence in God's people, despite their present failures, arose from his belief in the kingdom promises of God to the church.

---

[41] *Works*, 3:517.
[42] *Works*, 3:219.

The question is sometimes asked, what is to be the future of Christianity as it comes into competition with other religions and with Communism, Nationalism, Capitalism, and all antagonistic forces? To my mind there is absolutely no need to worry about that matter. Jesus said, after hearing Peter's great confession, "Upon this rock I will build my church; and the gates of hell shall not prevail against it." [Matt 16:18][43]

---

[43] Grimké, "Christ's Program for the Saving of the World," 12.

CHAPTER 9

THE BLESSING OF THE ORDINARY MEANS OF GRACE

One of the primary themes in the chapters thus far has been Francis Grimké's emphasis on the spiritual nature of the Christian life. Previous chapters have also demonstrated that Grimké's spiritual vision strengthened his resolve for faithful Christian living in the present world. Chapter 10 will focus on his principles and practices regarding social engagement, and certainly this vision for Christian engagement in the world distinguished his approach to the Christian life. Even more notable, however, was how he found strength for his vigorous social engagement through his regular pattern of worship. Gathering together with God's people for worship gave him life. Therefore, before moving on to consider his approach to social engagement, this chapter underlines one further aspect that ties together his views on the individual and the church—namely, the importance of corporate worship in the Christian life.

In his meditations, Grimké repeatedly emphasized the importance of communion with God. Grimké considered this communion an individual experience that should be ever present. As he put it, "The Christian life ought to be a life of communion, of fellowship with God daily—better still, moment by moment."[1] Even more often, however, he emphasized the importance of participation in the church's worship as the source and center of communion with God. In doing so, he not only pointed to the benefits

---

[1] *Works*, 3:79.

of joining his brothers and sisters in prayer and worship generally but also particularly emphasized the benefits of the corporate reading and preaching of the word of God and the celebration of the Lord's Supper. Grimké regarded these ordinary means of grace, especially experienced in the context of corporate worship, as crucial to a strong and healthy Christian life.

The Christian Life as Communion with God

On the occasion of his seventy-sixth birthday, Grimké recorded a pensive reflection in his meditations. Looking back on his life, and despite his bodily aches and pains, he could say, "It seems wonderful how God has led me all these years." Always the activist, he observed that the only way to get any "benefit out of our religion" is to live a life wholly devoted to the "work of serving God." In other words, "it is only when it is Christ for us to live, that we come into possession of [religion's] many rich and unspeakable blessings." The Christian life is not one of "casual" living or "occasional" contact with Christ but is "constant, daily, loving fellowship with him."[2]

He went on to write that such a life of total devotion and constant commitment is impossible without spiritual sustenance. "The spiritual life needs nourishment every day," he noted, defining spiritual life as "life that has to do with God and our relations to him, and the obligations growing out of those relations." The most striking aspects of his reflection relate to his definition of the Christian life, on the one hand, and his description of spiritual nourishment for that life, on the other hand. Though a true Christian life is one of service, it would be a mistake to focus on the service itself rather than the one being served. The Christian life has, first and foremost, to do with God and our relation to him and only secondarily to the obligations that flow out of that relation.

Therefore, it is not surprising that Grimké emphasized Scripture and prayer as the nourishment needed for a life in relationship with God. Christians must regularly feed on God's word and cultivate a healthy diet of prayer. Grimké made this explicit, writing that "the spiritual life needs to be nourished every day," and the way to do that is "by reading the scriptures every day," and by a daily "habit of prayer," which for him was synonymous, with "communion and fellowship with God, and with Jesus Christ and with the Holy Spirit." According to Grimké, the consequences of a poor diet in

---

[2] *Works*, 3:172–73.

this regard are dire. "If the spiritual life is not fed, and fed daily, it will be sure to grow less and less, and finally entirely die out."[3]

In contrast to such nourishment, he went on to lament that many of his contemporaries offered harmful advice by focusing more on material well-being than on spiritual well-being. In his opinion, their bad advice represented a concession to the spirit of the age. He argued that "modern civilization" is a "beastly civilization," too focused on "the almighty dollar" and "brute force." Not only was he devoted to a different spiritual vision throughout his ministry, but he became even more convinced by the goodness of that alternative vision toward the end of his life. "The longer I live, the less patience I have with the lack of interest in things which really count," he wrote. He was certain that the obsession with material concerns can have "no real and permanent value." Material things and material betterment are only worthwhile if they do not cause "neglect" of, or make subordinate, the "things of the spirit."[4]

Grimké's emphasis on communion with God as the heart and soul of the Christian life also informed the way he thought about scriptural teaching on eternal life. In a reflection on Titus 1:2, he wrote, "Eternal life here means blessed fellowship and communion with God." Though such communion is "begun here," it also will continue on, "growing in sweetness and blessedness throughout all countless ages of eternity." According to Grimké, the life of repentance and faith in Christ is "the one great thing to be desired." It is not only best for "this life" but also the sum of all that is best in "the life to come."[5]

Word and Sacrament as Means of Grace for the Christian Life

It is important to note that Grimké emphasized communion with God not only as a personal experience but also as the apex of the church's corporate worship. "All the services in the church are designed, or should be, to help people Godward and heavenward." He ruthlessly criticized churches that lost focus on communion with God and focused instead on other things, even good things. For Grimké, such churches had "no value" at all. Indeed they possessed "no reasonable ground for existing." Just as Jesus knew the absolute necessity of "communion and fellowship with his Father," so the

---

[3] *Works*, 3:173.
[4] *Works*, 3:175–76.
[5] *Works*, 3:373.

church also must be convinced of the same thing and design its services to lead people to desire it in their personal lives.[6]

The high value Grimké placed on corporate worship as the venue for Christian formation grew out of his emphasis on the word and sacraments as the "means" of God's grace. The previous chapter already demonstrated Grimké's high esteem for the reading and especially the preaching of God's word. Here it is worth adding that his reason for this high esteem was the status of preaching as the means of God's grace. Faithful attendance to "the regular ordinances of God's grace," especially the preaching of God's word, can make even a minister with poor leadership gifts a faithful servant, his ministry "blessed of God" and "helpful to the people."[7] Grimké believed that the single most important characteristic of an effective sermon is its faithfulness to God's word. In a reflection upon effective preaching, he wrote, "It is never amiss to expound the word of God." For Grimké, sticking close to the "inspired record" was the thing that mattered most. He even demonstrated a humble willingness to critique his own preaching in this regard, recounting his own failure in a recent sermon. Rather than sticking to the most important things that would be of use to his listeners, he veered off course to address another matter of scientific concern. While "in some respects" the matter itself was very important, involving the demands that his scientific, materialistic age was making upon the church, he acknowledged that "it would have been better if I had taken another line of thought."[8] He believed that the text, its central meaning, and its application are always the most important things a congregation needs to hear.

In addition to preaching, Grimké held the sacrament of the Lord's Supper in high regard as a means of grace. His meditations contain numerous accounts of Communion services and reflections on their significance and effect. One extended commentary he wrote toward the end of his life stands out. There he noted that a Communion service is "impressive for several reasons." As a reminder of the suffering of Christ, it illustrates the "hideousness of sin" and the deep need for forgiveness. A Communion service also depicts the nature of God and his "infinite justice" by revealing the wrath of God against sin, which must be punished. In addition to these difficult realities, the Lord's Supper demonstrates the love of God by revealing to us "the extent to which God was willing to go in his efforts to bring

---

6 Works, 3:577–78.
7 Works, 3:386–87.
8 Works, 3:515–16.

deliverance to the sinner from the guilt and power of sin." The "patient sufferer" on the cross is none other than God's only begotten Son, his well beloved Son." Finally, the Supper also reveals not only the divine nature, in general, and the mission of the Father, in particular, but also the "love" and powerful will of the Son. It declares that Jesus "was not obliged to do what he did. It was a purely voluntary act on his part." Communion is a means of grace that sets forth human sin, God's justice, and the divine love of the Father and the Son.[9]

For Grimké, the benefits of the Lord's Supper correspond to the truths it depicts. It produces sorrow and repentance for sin, awareness of the holiness of God, and a deepening sense of the love of God. In turn, this awareness of God's love leads to "a new determination to consecrate ourselves more fully to his service." For all these reasons, Grimké wrote, "The communion or celebration of the Holy supper may be made a source of great spiritual benefit to all who come to it in the right spirit, and who make the proper preparation for it." He declared that "no one should miss" a Communion service, that it should be "greatly prized" by all true believers. Indeed, he concluded, "It is where, in a peculiar, special sense, we meet with the Lord."[10] According to Grimké, and in line with 1 Corinthians 10:16, participation in the celebration of the Lord's Supper is more than a mere remembrance; it is a communion with the Lord Jesus Christ himself.

Along these lines, elsewhere in his meditations Grimké reflected on his participation in the Lord's Supper one Sunday morning. He noted in retrospect the Supper's purpose as a "remembrance" meant, moreover, to "draw us nearer" to Christ and "to consecrate" his people to his service. Reflecting on the words of the hymn "When I Survey the Wondrous Cross," Grimké noted that the service of Communion deserves celebration and proper preparation. As a "means of grace," the Lord's Supper is a "source of great spiritual blessing to us."[11]

As a result of his high view of the sacrament and his conviction that Sunday services should be regulated by God's word, Grimké strongly objected to the common tendency to replace or supplement God's divine ordinances with other celebrations and remembrances of human invention. On one occasion he recorded a strongly worded objection to the celebration of Mother's Day during the Sunday morning worship service. "No one thinks

---

9 *Works*, 3:620.
10 *Works*, 3:621.
11 *Works*, 3:633–34.

more highly of Mother's Day than I do," he noted. "As highly as I think of the day, there is no reason, however, so far as I can see, for putting it in the place of services appropriate for a communion season." He deemed it wrong to substitute the celebration of Mother's Day for the "regular morning service," and even more so on a Sunday planned for a Communion service. "The celebration of the Lord's Supper should be kept sacred." According to Grimké, the Sunday service belongs to Jesus, and therefore "his service" should "be kept in remembrance of him." His conclusion was terse: "A talk about mothers can wait for another time."[12]

Weekly Worship as a Help for Daily Faithfulness

Francis Grimké highly valued corporate and personal Christian piety. Just as he refused to choose between personal spirituality and a life of public service, he also held on to both the individual and the communal aspects of Christian worship. In fact, as he saw it, the public worship of God's corporate people functioned as a school of formation for daily life. He believed that setting aside Sundays as a sacred time did not devalue the worldly concerns of other days but rather served to orient the Christian believer to a proper disposition toward those things.

One Sunday morning, as he prepared himself for the worship service, he did not know whether the sermon would be "helpful." But he reassured himself with the expectation that he would be "quickened spiritually" and "brought nearer to God" through worship nonetheless. He believed that he would go away "refreshed" and with, as he put it, "renewed purpose and determination to be more faithful and earnest in my endeavors to live a full-fledged Christian life." The reasoning behind his high expectations was simple: "Attendance upon the public ordinances of religion will always be a help to us if they are properly prepared, and conducted, and we come in the right spirit, desiring to be helped, and giving careful attention to what takes place." He believed that carefully attending to the singing, Scripture reading, prayer, and preaching would ordinarily be a great blessing to the believer.[13]

Grimké's high view of the importance of Christian worship correlated closely with his high view of the "Lord's Day" or "Christian Sabbath." Sundays should be "set apart" for personal and (especially) corporate public

---

12 *Works*, 3:638–39.
13 *Works*, 3:535.

worship. "The Sabbath and the church are institutions of incalculable benefit in keeping us on the higher levels of life," he wrote. Therefore, he believed it was a "great mistake" to neglect the public ordinances of worship or to "desecrate the day" by "allowing other things to come in and absorb our time and attention." Other things belong to "other days of the week." Grimké believed that "God knew what he was doing when he set apart the Sabbath day, especially, as a day of rest from the cares of the world." He noted that if Christians would attend more faithfully to the true purpose of the Sabbath, it would be "better for us" and for "all with whom we come in contact." As a result, the whole world needs Christians to be more faithful in observing the Sabbath day for rest and worship. "What the world greatly needs in order to assure its uplift, is a Sabbath properly observed. The farther it gets away from the divine conception of the Sabbath, the worse it will be for it, the less hope there will be for it."[14]

Though Grimké believed the Sabbath is good for the world, and this inclined him to think it would be good for all people to keep it, he also rejected the idea that the Sabbath should be enforced by political or coercive means. The day should be "kept by all Christians," but "as to others," there is "no warrant for coercing them." The Sabbath day is a matter best left to the individual conscience. Certainly, people will answer to God for their adherence to God's moral law. "We cannot violate any of God's laws without suffering, without sooner or later paying the penalty," he wrote. However, Grimké rejected the idea that the state should regulate Sabbath observance.[15]

Grimké's view on Sabbath enforcement differed from the teaching he would have received at Princeton Theological Seminary, but the difference was subtle. For example, Charles Hodge, professor of theology, taught that if the government fails to honor the Sabbath and does not rest from ordinary civil, legislative, and legal work, it makes it difficult for Christians to function as civil servants. On this basis, Hodge argued that the government should rest on Sunday. Grimké did not disagree about the need to rest from such labors on the Lord's Day, but his perspective presumed less about the establishment of Christianity in the nation.

Hodge held that there was a significant sense in which America was a Christian nation, but he distinguished between the "principle" and the description of the matter. As he put it, the description of America as "a

14 *Works*, 3:333–34.
15 *Works*, 3:611.

Christian and Protestant nation" was "not so much the assertion of a principle as the statement of a fact."[16] In other words, Hodge did not believe that America was a Christian nation in the sense that it formally established Christianity as a state religion, but he did believe that the nation's Christian majority was free to, and even possessed an obligation to, instantiate its moral views, including its view of the Sabbath, in civil law. He believed that the majority of Americans were Christians, and his position led him to expect that this majority would be effective advocates for morality in society through the promulgation of good laws. While Grimké agreed with Hodge that America was not a Christian nation "in principle," he disagreed with Hodge about the extent to which Christian virtue held sway in America. Grimké was less confident that America was a Christian nation as a "statement of a fact." He therefore was more sensitive to the importance of protecting Christian morality from the majority than was Charles Hodge.

Grimké's impression that Christian virtue was not widespread also led him to a different perspective on the legislation of the moral law. On the one hand, it led him to lean more on persuasion and less on the presumption that the majority of Americans would establish Christian moral viewpoints. On the other hand, it opened his eyes to the need for civil governments to protect the rights of minority religious viewpoints wherever possible. A good system of government should be workable both if Christians are in the majority and if Christians are in the minority, so that Christians are free to practice their faith in either scenario. Therefore, Grimké did not believe that the role of government is to legislate every moral good, but rather it should protect those moral goods essential to defending life and basic rights while avoiding the violation of religious and moral consciences wherever possible.

These convictions led Grimké to a positive assessment of the form of government of the United States. He believed that the government should defend basic rights like those enshrined in the Constitution and Bill of Rights. But other moral goods should be pursued by persuasion. Not every moral good need be legally established. Some are more basic than others. Grimké's perspective as a minority led him to see that government should make every effort possible to allow for different religious communities to practice their faiths insofar as they do not violate basic human rights; and he also believed that some moral laws are better perpetuated by persuasion

16 Charles Hodge, *Systematic Theology*, 3 vols. (New York: Scribner, Armstrong, 1874), 3:343.

than by legislation. He saw the danger of creating a form of government that would not allow Christians to participate as a moral minority.

While the Sabbath was not under the jurisdiction of the state as a matter of coercion, Grimké did see its observance as a great good. The weekly rest and worship of God's people could have a profound effect on their daily lives and on the good of the nation. Therefore, Grimké believed that the observance of the weekly Lord's Day should be carefully ordered by churches and their ministers. "What an opportunity the minister has, under the guidance of the Holy Spirit," he exclaimed, "to help those who come up to the house of the Lord, Sabbath after Sabbath." Therefore, every service should be "a kind of mount of vision," to help them see God and to see things from a "Divine standpoint." Through the careful design of Sunday worship, and through the ministry of the Holy Spirit, Grimké believed that ministers possessed the opportunity to "lift" people to a "higher plane," which also "strengthened and fortified" them for the "immediate tasks" of daily life before them.[17]

––––––––––––

At the end of his life, Grimké looked back to his ordination and his fifty years of service in gospel ministry. At the age of seventy-eight, he was "weak in body" and, by his own account, "no longer capable of long and strenuous effort physically or mentally. The "frost of many winters" rested on his head. In such a state, his only explanation for his ability to carry out his pastoral obligations over his many long years was that he had "relied upon God." His labors had been great, but, he wrote, "Had I not been sustained by a living faith in God, and the abiding sense of his all-sufficiency, I could never have gone through with it." He acknowledged not only his need for God's help but also his own shortcomings. "No one knows better than I do," he admitted, "how far [I fall] below the noble ideal of what a Christian ought to be; and no one can more sincerely deplore it than I do." He rejoiced that his only hope was in "the perfect righteousness of the Lord Jesus Christ, imputed to us and received by faith alone."[18]

Despite his shortcomings, he also reflected with joy on the fruit of his ministry. Here too, he expressed humility. Though his ministry touched "thousands of people," only God knew the effect. The ordinary means of

––––––––––––

17 *Works*, 3:54–55.
18 *Works*, 3:264–65.

grace belong to God, and they depend upon God. Francis Grimké knew that any fruit of his ministry ultimately belonged not to him but to God. And therefore, the last Sunday he preached at his church, he requested that there be no "parade" or "demonstration of any kind." Instead, he wished the end of his ministry to be marked "by a simple sermon by myself, from the text John 12:32, expressive of my ministry from the beginning." He closed his ministry, he said, "by calling attention to the fact that I began my ministry with the old, old story of Jesus and his love." Similarly, he ended his ministry with "the same old gospel of the grace of God in Christ Jesus."[19]

Francis Grimké's meditations reveal a firm conviction regarding the power of a simple church ministry that relies on the work of God through the Holy Spirit. He believed that communion with God is the most important part of the Christian life. He believed that the word of God, sacraments, and prayer are the ordinary means God promised to use to bring people into this communion. He believed that the corporate worship of the church should lead people to daily reliance on God's word and prayer, and he also believed that people so formed will be blessed in their daily Christian lives. Francis Grimké believed that participation in the weekly life of the church is crucial to the everyday Christian life. It was this vision of Christian ministry that drew him closer to the Lord and prepared him for service in the world day by day for fifty years of ministry as a pastor.

---

[19] *Works*, 3:266.

PART 4

SOCIETY

Christians and Social Engagement

CHAPTER 10

PRINCIPLES FOR COLLABORATIVE ACTIVISM

In June of 1934, *The Crisis*, the publication of the National Association for the Advancement of Colored People, published an article by Francis Grimké decrying the evils of race segregation. The primary purpose of the article, however, was not to lament White racism but to respond to the recent statements of fellow NAACP collaborator and editor of *The Crisis*, W. E. B. Du Bois, who endorsed separate Black institutions despite his aversion to segregation. According to Grimké:

> Segregation produces a condition that is not conducive to the best interest of either race. It tends to build up a false or artificial sense of superiority in the one, and is sure to create or engender in the other, feelings of resentment, of hatred, of discontent, out of which no good can come to either, but will continue to be a source of friction, of irritation.[1]

Grimké went on to declare, "No race, with any self-respect, can accept the status of a segregated group for itself." He argued that such acceptance would be an admission of "inferiority," and he pronounced that doing so would be wrong in both "principle" and "spirit." As a pastor, he supported his argument with an explicit appeal to his theological belief that

---

[1] Francis J. Grimké, "Segregation," *The Crisis*, June 1934, 173.

segregation "violates every principle of right and is contrary to the spirit of Jesus Christ and to the noble ideal of brotherhood."

Grimké was responding to Du Bois's "Postscript" from the previous issue of *The Crisis*. There Du Bois likewise had argued against the evils of segregation by race, but he had added an account of his own failed attempt to convince the board of directors of the NAACP to state that it "has always recognized and encouraged" distinct Black institutions and endeavors, including "the Negro church, the Negro college, the Negro public school, Negro business and industrial enterprises." According to Du Bois, the success of such distinctly Black institutions and endeavors would prove "Negro efficiency," show "Negro ability and discipline," and demonstrate "how useless and wasteful race segregation is." Despite his appeals, the board of directors did not approve his motion, nor even a modified version of it. Instead, the NAACP approved an alternative statement, which merely expressed its continued opposition to segregation and did not take a position on the utility of separate Black enterprises.[2]

Apparently, Du Bois felt that the NAACP's refusal to explicitly endorse the merits of Black churches, schools, and businesses was a hill on which to die, for on June 11 he resigned his position as editor of *The Crisis*. He respectfully expressed his disagreement with Francis Grimké in that month's issue, and on June 26 he wrote a letter to the directors to clarify that his reason for resigning was not the disagreement per se, but rather the board's refusal to allow criticism of its officers and policies in *The Crisis*.[3] The very next day, Du Bois wrote a letter to inform Grimké that he could not print Grimké's subsequent response to his June comments in *The Crisis* as a result of his pending resignation, and he also respectfully yet forcefully told Grimké that "I naturally resent" some of the things that you have written.[4] Grimké's reply was equally forceful and also dramatic:

> This is no time for dividing our forces. We must present an undivided front to the enemy. Your leaving the Association, I hope, doesn't mean that you are stacking your arms, that you are giving up the fight. As long as you live I hope that you will continue to speak out bravely as you have

---

[2] W. E. B. Du Bois, "Postscript," *The Crisis*, May 1934, 149.
[3] W. E. B. Du Bois to the Board of Directors of the National Association for the Advancement of Colored People, June 26, 1934, in *Works*, 4:508–10; Du Bois, "Postscript," *The Crisis*, June 1934, 182–84; Du Bois's direct response to Grimké is found on p. 174.
[4] W. E. B. Du Bois to Francis J. Grimké, June 27, 1934, in *Works*, 4:508.

for so many years in behalf of our rights as men and as American citizens. This you owe to yourself and to the race.[5]

Grimké also expressed his lament that Du Bois was leaving the NAACP, and offered a half-hearted appeal that he remain, but it was to no avail. Du Bois remained steadfast in his decision to leave the organization he helped to found. His public exchanges with Grimké illustrated the contours of the ideological chasm separating him from the board and leadership of the NAACP on the issue of segregation. To Du Bois, the chasm seemed unbridgeable.

Francis Grimké's Role in the Formation of the NAACP

Perhaps it was fitting that this exchange between Francis Grimké and W. E. B. Du Bois should have marked the close of Du Bois's affiliation with the NAACP. Their working relationship was instrumental in founding the organization in the first place. Many narratives of the NAACP's formation rightly emphasize Du Bois, along with Ida B. Wells-Barnett, Mary Church Terrell, Moorfield Storey, William English Walling, and others. Yet the historical record indicates that the roles played by Francis Grimké and his brother Archibald were also crucial, and that they have been underappreciated.

In the months leading up to the famous Carnegie Hall Conference in January 1904 that led to the break between Booker T. Washington and Du Bois, Grimké received confidential letters from both men. Washington's letter contained not only an invitation to the meeting but also the exhortation that "the whole matter should be held absolutely confidential. Each one who has been asked to attend, has been requested to speak on the subject to no one else."[6] Apparently, Du Bois had a different sort of confidentiality in mind, for his letter came with an attached memorandum marked "confidential," which listed each participant by name, broke participants into categories according to the relative strength of their loyalties to him and to Washington, laid out the "platform" of the "Anti-Washington men," and offered tactical advice for the handling of the meeting.[7] It is notable that of the twenty-eight names he listed, Du Bois placed only four other

[5] Francis J. Grimké to W. E. B. Du Bois, July 13, 1934, in *Works*, 4:511.
[6] Booker T. Washington to Francis J. Grimké, November 19, 1903, in *Works*, 4:89.
[7] W. E. B. Du Bois to Francis J. Grimké, December 28, 1903, in *Works*, 4:90–91.

names besides his own and Grimké's as solidly aligned with his cause. Grimké was a trusted member of a very small circle. Ultimately Francis did not attend the meeting but instead ensured that Archibald was invited to go in his place.[8]

Archibald and Francis remained instrumental in the years that followed the break between Washington and Du Bois. Though Archibald maintained a working relationship with Washington for a few more years, his rhetoric and increasingly his allegiance lay more with Du Bois. His influence in Boston made him an important figure, and Du Bois continued to court him for further involvement with the Niagara Movement—which formed after the Carnegie Conference—whose leaders were also central to the creation and early leadership of the NAACP. Francis remained instrumental as well. In 1909 a call was issued for a national conference to address the unequal treatment of people of color in the United States and advocate for civil liberties. The call was sent to prominent social leaders for their signatures of support, and Francis Grimké was one of seven African Americans to sign it. This call led to the Negro National Conference, held on May 31 of the same year. Out of that conference, a steering committee was created to form the NAACP. Archibald was one of a handful of Black members on that committee.[9]

The Grimkés continued to play major roles in the early years of the NAACP. By 1913, Archibald moved to the nation's capital and became the president of the chapter in Washington, DC. Soon thereafter, he was named vice president of the national organization during the period of concerted effort to transition NAACP leadership positions to people of color. Around the same time, a 1916 conference was held in Amenia, New York, for the express purpose of putting to rest factionalism like that between Washington and Du Bois. Francis Grimké's name appeared on the guest list of select leaders invited to the conference.[10] Though he often worked to place Archibald in formal positions of authority, Francis also consistently worked informally behind the scenes from the formative years of the

---

[8] Washington in fact did not want to invite Francis and did so only at the insistence of Du Bois. In turn, Archibald was invited at the suggestion of Francis only after significant wrangling via a series of letters among the three. Washington finally relented and invited Archibald after Francis declined to attend. See Dickson D. Bruce, *Archibald Grimké: Portrait of a Black Independent* (Baton Rouge: Louisiana State University Press, 1993), 104–5.

[9] Mark Perry, *Lift Up Thy Voice: The Grimké Family's Journey from Slaveholders to Civil Rights Leaders* (New York: Viking, 2001), 332–33.

[10] Roy Nash, "Amenia Conference acceptances for three days, August 7, 1916," W. E. B. Du Bois Papers (ms. 312), special collections and university archives, University of Massachusetts Amherst Libraries.

NAACP through Du Bois's resignation in 1934. In the early 1900s, Francis was courted by various leaders, including both Washington and Du Bois himself. Francis's influence in Washington, DC, made his support essential to the early success of the NAACP, both because of the prominence of Fifteenth Street Presbyterian Church and as a result of the stature of his public ministry more generally. His pull remained significant throughout the first third of the twentieth century.

Grimké's Ongoing Support of the NAACP and Assessment of W. E. B. Du Bois

Speaking in 1921 on behalf of the NAACP's membership drive and anti-lynching crusade, Francis Grimké offered four primary reasons for his "hearty support" of the organization. These reasons included, first, the "source" of the appeal, the NAACP itself, which he characterized as "the one, big, effective organization in this country today that has for its object the maintenance of or safeguarding our rights, civil and political, as American citizens." In addition, Grimké cited his American citizenship and his status as a person of color as two additional reasons for his support. Given the prevalence of lynching, his own very life and safety depended on the work of the NAACP.

> No member of our race, either as to life or property, is safe in any community where the mob spirit prevails, as it does all over the South, and as the great mass of our people are in the South, we all ought to be interested in this appeal for our own sake and for the sake of the millions of our brethren.

As a fourth and final reason for supporting the NAACP, Grimké appealed to the second table of the decalogue: "I believe in God Almighty and in the great moral laws which He has prescribed for our government. One of those laws, as set forth in the Sixth Commandment, is, 'Thou shalt do no murder.'" As Grimké went on to write, "No one can believe in God, can have a spark of true religion in his heart, and not wish to have this horrid record of lynching stopped."[11] His endorsement was grounded in his identity as an American citizen, as a person of color, and as a Christian. For Grimké, even if the cause of the NAACP was imperfect, it was generally righteous

---

[11] Francis J. Grimké, "The National Association for the Advancement of Colored People: Its Value, Its Aims, Its Claims" (1921), in *Works*, 1:618–21.

and therefore worthy of the support not only of all people of color but of all Americans and all Christians.

Grimké continued to give unqualified public support to the NAACP throughout his ministry.[12] His personal views of the organization's leadership were more nuanced, however. His private reflections and letters regarding W. E. B. Du Bois offer an important window into how Grimké handled his partnerships in the pursuit of social good. He made careful distinctions between sacred and secular goods, on the one hand, and public and private advocacy, on the other; and these principles enabled his strong, unwavering public support for what he took to be the generally righteous cause of the NAACP during the years of his ministry.

In public, Grimké chose to celebrate the aspects of Du Bois's leadership and teaching that were consistent with his own beliefs. For example, in his well-known 1903 address "God and the Race Problem," Grimké referred to Du Bois's new book *The Souls of Black Folk* as "masterful" and "one of the most remarkable contributions that has yet been made on the Negro question." Grimké carefully highlighted Du Bois's intellect, culture, and rhetoric. He explicitly endorsed Du Bois's emphasis on education and his affirmation of equal rights.[13] In a 1905 address, Grimké similarly praised Du Bois's "splendid" prose poem *Credo*, highlighting Du Bois's assertion that all human beings are created in the "image which their Maker stamped" on their souls, and his observation that "the Devil and his angels" constantly "work to narrow the opportunity of struggling human beings, especially if they be black."[14]

Regarding other theological and religious views, however, Grimké was more critical, especially in later years, and particularly in private. In his personal reflections he noted that the philosophers of the age could be followed when what they said was consistent with God's word. Socrates, Newton, Hegel, Kant, and others all had much wisdom to offer. But when it came to theology, Grimké was not ashamed to say that he was happy to faithfully follow Jesus when those great minds departed from him. He made the same point about influential social activists, including those involved in the NAACP. If Du Bois or Clarence Darrow, the famous atheist,

---

[12] Francis J. Grimké to Wendell Phillips Stafford, November 30, 1911, in *Works*, 4:124; see the description of Grimké's financial support for the NAACP in Roy W. Wilkins to Francis J. Grimké, June 7, 1933, in *Works*, 4:487; Grimké to Du Bois, July 13, 1934; see the sermon attached to Grimké's two letters to President Woodrow Wilson in *Works*, 1:518.

[13] Francis J. Grimké, "God and the Race Problem" (1903), in *Works*, 1:367–68.

[14] Francis J. Grimké, "The Negro and His Citizenship" (1905), in *Works*, 1:398.

said something true, as they often did, it should be celebrated and followed, but if they said something false, especially if it was related to their religious views, then it was important to swallow the meat and spit out the bones.[15]

For example, Grimké recounted a time Du Bois spoke at Howard University. According to Grimké, Du Bois was willing to "scoff at religion" and "ridicule prayer." In response, Grimké did not mince words, declaring that "such sentiments ought to have been, there and then, publicly rebuked." In fact, he continued, "Such sentiment ought not to have been allowed to be uttered from the rostrum of the university without a protest of some kind." He reasoned that such comments were out of touch with both "history" and "the teachings of Christianity," and therefore they were not what the university could "afford to sponsor." Instead, he argued, "What the race needs more than anything else are moral and spiritual leaders." Universities should be "helping to make" such leaders instead of "affording opportunities for blind leaders to propagate their views."[16]

Grimké then went on to offer an instructive summary of his views of Du Bois:

> Men, like DuBois, when they speak on economics, or on the civil and political rights of the Negro as an American citizen, speak with authority and may be safely followed; but when it comes to religion and morality, they are sadly in need of guidance themselves. They are far, far out of the way as tested by the Word of God and the ideals and principles of Jesus Christ.[17]

These words clearly indicate the principles at stake for Grimké. He was willing to follow the political and economic wisdom of those who held very different religious views from his own, even unbelievers. For Grimké, the Scriptures offered general principles for how societies should be ordered, but they did not provide details. These details needed to be drawn from general revelation, and Grimké felt that Christians and non-Christians both have access to this revelation. In fact, to the shame of Christians, it frequently was non-Christians who thought more deeply about temporal concerns. For these reasons, Grimké deemed it important to listen to others—even nonbelievers—"when they speak on economics" or on "civil

---

15 *Works*, 3:464–65.
16 *Works*, 3:464–65.
17 *Works*, 3:465.

and political rights." Yet Grimké expressed discernment regarding the spiritual views of these same figures, and he thought it possible to distinguish religious matters from political ones.

Grimké also demonstrated willingness to disagree with these figures when they expressed political views he found contrary to Scripture, and he was willing to do so both publicly and privately. If the exchange between Grimké and Du Bois in the pages of *The Crisis* in the 1930s on the role of exclusively Black institutions offers an instructive example of Grimké's public advocacy, it is not hard to find examples where he chose to engage privately. For example, he networked extensively with other prominent clergy, including the Episcopalian minister and longtime Howard University professor William Tunnell. The two exchanged letters criticizing the position of Du Bois on segregation.[18]

Similarly, Grimké did not hesitate to lobby NAACP leaders behind the scenes. In the fall of 1932, he objected to the reported comments of NAACP officer Robert Bagnall in support of Bill Thompson, a Chicago mayor well known for his corrupt connections. According to Grimké, Bagnall advocated for the election of corrupt politicians if their politics worked in the favor of African Americans. Grimké could not abide such rank pragmatism, and he wrote to Walter White, the executive secretary of the NAACP, in order to lodge his protest in regard to the comments and to inquire formally into the position of the NAACP on the matter.[19] The prompt replies from both White and Bagnall assuring Grimké that the comments had been misreported and that the NAACP in no way stood for corruption in politics are as much evidence of Grimké's stature as they are clarifications of the organization's position. When Grimké in turn responded to their comments with further exhortations and requests for clarifications, Bagnall replied quickly with further assurances, and a few weeks later he wrote to Grimké yet again to express his thanks for his ongoing support.[20]

Grimké was forceful and adamant, yet also tactful, in handling matters privately when there was sufficient evidence that his collaborators shared his basic principles and were operating in good faith. He also distinguished

[18] William V. Tunnell to Francis J. Grimké, December 10, 1934, in *Works*, 4:521.
[19] Francis J. Grimké to Walter White, October 24, 1932, in *Works*, 4:461.
[20] Walter White to Francis J. Grimké, October 25, 1932, in *Works*, 4:462; Robert W. Bagnall to Francis J. Grimké, October 25, 1932, in *Works*, 4:462–63; Francis J. Grimké to Walter White, October 27, 1932, in *Works*, 4:463–64; Francis J. Grimké to Robert W. Bagnall, November 1932, in *Works*, 4:464–65; Robert W. Bagnall to Francis J. Grimké, November 7, 1932, in *Works*, 4:466; Robert W. Bagnall to Francis J. Grimké, November 17, 1932, in *Works*, 4:466.

between Bagnall's freedom to hold "any view [he] may see fit on any phase of the Negro question" as a private individual and the obligation of the NAACP as an institution to stand "only on the highest moral grounds." In addition to his ability to distinguish religious versus secular matters, and situations warranting public versus private dispute, Grimké also exhibited the ability to distinguish the personal from the political. The proper functioning of the NAACP required its membership to agree on the importance of racial equality and justice. Grimké did not believe it necessary for every member to hold the same understanding of racial identity. Members might have similar goals related to equality and justice and different conceptions of racial identity underlying those shared goals. Differing personal views were acceptable so long as the broader political platform remained shared.[21]

This chapter has explored Grimké's collaboration with and assessment of W. E. B. Du Bois, paying close attention not only to his public statements but also to his personal correspondence and private journals, including those published in his collected works and those in the manuscript collections at Howard University Libraries. These sources demonstrate not only the depth of collaboration between these two figures in the formation of the Niagara Movement and the NAACP but also the rise and fall of their collaboration with Booker T. Washington and the Hampton Institute, as well as their participation in the American Negro Academy alongside Alexander Crummell and other significant figures. In particular, this chapter has focused on Grimké's expression of his points of commonality and difference with Du Bois. Grimké was quite critical of Du Bois's religious views, and yet he expressed a nuanced but general appreciation not only for Du Bois's famous *The Souls of Black Folk* but also for his economic and political activities more generally. It was only when Du Bois shifted his broader political platform to endorse self-imposed segregation that Grimké began to voice his political opposition publicly.

Francis Grimké's role in the early civil rights movement remains worthy of further study. Alongside Ida B. Wells-Barnett and W. E. B. Du Bois, Francis was one of seven African American signers of the call for the Emancipation Conference that led to the formation of the NAACP. His brother

---

21 Grimké to Bagnall, November 1932.

Archibald served on the committee that established the organization and
went on to serve as its vice president. Francis felt that his role as a pastor meant that it was more appropriate and more effective for Archibald
to take on a leadership role while he, himself, kept his own participation
more informal but no less committed. Though he chose a less formal role,
his personal support for Du Bois at the expense of Booker T. Washington
was crucial to the success of the Niagara Movement and ultimately the
NAACP itself. The influence of the Grimkés led Du Bois to go to considerable lengths to ensure their commitment to the cause. Their collaboration
is interesting on many levels and worthy of further study.

Francis Grimké's role in the formation of the NAACP is particularly
remarkable, considering his traditional theological commitments, as well
as his emphasis on the spiritual mission of the church and the Christian
ministry discussed in chapters 7 and 8.[22] This consideration of Grimké's
collaboration with Du Bois confirms the conclusions of recent scholarship
that call into question facile binary distinctions between "conservatives"
and "liberals," or "evangelicals" and advocates of the "social gospel."[23] It
also builds upon recent work by Barbara Savage, demonstrating the shortcomings of historiographical categories that emphasize the political at the
expense of the religious when it comes to the role of African American
churches in American society.[24] Grimké engaged in the work of social activism in part because he believed that the American church's racial failures were an affront to the gospel of Jesus Christ and a hindrance to the
kingdom of God.

Here again, recent historical work demonstrates the need to recover
the full breadth of voices among African American Christians in America.
Chapter 7 already demonstrated that, in addition to White fundamentalists
who tended to affirm supernatural Christian beliefs and to ignore or even
oppose racial equality, and in addition to the social gospelers who tended
to advocate for racial equality but were ambivalent with regard to supernatural Christianity, there were Black fundamentalists who were conservative theologically but socially progressive on matters of race.[25] Yet even this

[22] See, e.g., Francis J. Grimké, "Christ's Program for the Saving of the World" (1936), box 40-6, folder 309, Francis J. Grimké Papers, Howard University Library.
[23] Mary Beth Swetnam Mathews, *Doctrine and Race: African American Evangelicals and Fundamentalism between the Wars* (Tuscaloosa: University of Alabama Press, 2017).
[24] Barbara Dianne Savage, *Your Spirits Walk Beside Us: The Politics of Black Religion* (Cambridge, MA: Belknap Press of Harvard University Press, 2008).
[25] Daniel R. Bare, *Black Fundamentalists: Conservative Christianity and Racial Identity in the Segregation Era* (New York: New York University Press, 2021).

additional category of Black fundamentalism, explored so well by historians like Daniel Bare, still does not account for the approaches of prominent voices like that of Francis J. Grimké. He was extremely traditional in his affirmations of biblical authority, the person and work of Christ, and other historical Christian doctrines, yet he never self-identified as a fundamentalist or collaborated significantly with fundamentalism as a movement. But he did collaborate with Clarence Darrow and W. E. B. Du Bois, and he was instrumental in the establishment of the NAACP. Grimké's place in the story requires categories beyond the limited options of modernists, social gospelers, and fundamentalists.

Francis and Archibald Grimké's collaboration with Du Bois is not only noteworthy because two of the primary movers and shakers in the early NAACP were a theologically conservative Presbyterian minister and his brother. The Grimkés' collaboration with Du Bois is also noteworthy because it provides an example of an approach to faith and life capable of distinguishing the civil and the political from the religious and the moral without separating them, Such an approach to political collaboration refuses to make "all or nothing" judgments on the basis of personal religious or ideological disagreements between collaborators when those differences do not relate to the central platform. It is an approach to political discourse that carefully distinguishes circumstances requiring public intervention from those where private engagement might be more appropriate. Emphasizing Francis Grimké's role in the formation of the NAACP thus offers a more holistic picture of the organization's founding in the past and suggests a pattern of political engagement worthy of consideration in the present.

CHAPTER 11

PREACHING THE GOSPEL AND FIGHTING RACE PREJUDICE

Francis Grimké demonstrated a remarkable pastoral ability to hold multiple truths in tension, seeking a synthesis that honored each facet of complicated subjects. This sensibility required him to grasp a wide range of specific biblical and theological commitments clearly, to systematize and order those principles, to strive for a proper balance among them, and to allow his ongoing experiences in life and ministry to push him to return time and time again to the Scriptures to sharpen his theological reflections and vision. Though Grimké was neither omniscient nor free from his own sins and blind spots, his reputation for integrity and fastidiousness was well earned. One of the more interesting examples of this ability to carefully hold multiple truths in tension comes from his reflection on his ministry at the end of his life. Writing to the alumni of Princeton Theological Seminary, he reminisced:

> During these forty years two things I have tried to do with all my might:
> (1) To preach the gospel of the grace of God, to get men to see their need of
> a savior, and to accept of Jesus Christ as the way, the truth, the life. If I had
> to live my life over again I would still choose the ministry, I could not be
> satisfied in any other calling. (2) I have sought with all my might to fight

race prejudice, because I believe it is utterly un-Christian, and that it is doing almost more than anything else to curse our own land and country and the world at large. Christianity, in its teachings, and in the spirit of its founder, stands for the brotherhood of man, calls us to do by others as we would be done by, to love our neighbor as ourselves.[1]

This letter illuminates a combination of key insights central to Grimké's ministry and vision for social engagement. He believed in the primacy of the gospel of Jesus Christ and the spiritual ministry of the church, he distinguished this message of the gospel from the fight against race prejudice, and he refused to separate the two. This precise formulation was characteristic of his ministry and social engagement, it set him apart from many of his contemporaries in the late nineteenth and early twentieth centuries, and it is a thought-provoking distillation of these issues worthy of careful consideration today.

Grimké's "Framework" for Preaching Social Christianity

The preceding chapters have demonstrated that the scriptural narrative of the coming of God's kingdom richly informed Grimké's understanding of the mission of the church. His understanding of the kingdom also crucially informed his engagement with social issues. Just as he applied kingdom theology to the church with careful nuance, he applied his understanding of the kingdom to social issues with essential refinement. In one fascinating passage of his meditations, he recorded a multifaceted exposition of his views regarding the implications of kingdom of God for social issues, and he framed his reflections in relation to notable contemporary works.

First, he cited a sermon by Clarence Edward Macartney, pastor of First Presbyterian Church in Pittsburgh, teacher of homiletics at Princeton Theological Seminary, and close associate of J. Gresham Machen. Machen famously led the split of Princeton Seminary to form Westminster Theological Seminary in 1929 as a result of concerns regarding theological modernism. Macartney's national reputation put him in a similar position closely connected to his public criticism of Harry Emerson Fosdick's famous 1922 sermon "Shall the Fundamentalists Win?" The Pittsburgh preacher, whose sermons received a wide distribution over the radio, replied to Fosdick's

---

[1] Francis J. Grimké to the members of the class of 1878 of Princeton Theological Seminary, April 27, 1918, in *Works*, 4:215.

sermon with his own equally provocative message, "Shall Unbelief Win?" The General Assembly of the northern PCUSA elected Macartney moderator in 1924. This position allowed him to support the ecclesiastical prosecution of Fosdick and push for the deeper embrace of the inerrancy of Scripture, the virgin birth and deity of Christ, substitutionary atonement, the bodily resurrection of Jesus, and the historical and supernatural nature of Christ's miracles. The denomination originally endorsed a version of these "Five Fundamentals" in 1910 and reasserted them in the Auburn Affirmation, ultimately passed by the 1924 General Assembly under Macartney's leadership.[2] These doctrines were common themes in Grimké's preaching as well, but the sermon he cited in the context of his discussion of Christ's kingdom was Macartney's "Your Fellowship in the Gospel," which impressed Grimké for a different reason. Grimké appreciated that sermon's affirmation of the necessity of "a living faith in Jesus Christ as the only hope of a sin-cursed world," as well as the "duty of spreading that faith, and of living it, exemplifying it." He lamented that more pulpits did not proclaim the kind of message endorsed by Macartney's sermon. He declared that pastors possessed no calling for "ransacking papers, magazines, and periodicals" to "entertain," nor to "keep [members] informed as to secular matters," but rather were called to "feed their souls with the bread of life" and to "keep before them the things of enduring value"—namely, things that "build them up in holiness and comfort."[3]

Second, Grimké cited *The Christ of the Indian Road*, by E. Stanley Jones, the famous Methodist missionary to India. Jones's writings became extremely popular in American Christian circles associated with the civil rights movement, and Martin Luther King Jr.'s quotations from Jones's later work on Mahatma Gandhi eventually became especially well known.[4] If Grimké appreciated Macartney's advocacy of a living faith, he expressed appreciation for Jones's "indictment of Western Christianity" along exactly these same lines. Grimké valued Jones's affirmation of the necessity of "living" the "principles and ideals of Jesus Christ." He also appreciated his refusal to dissociate the ethical and social aspects of the Christian faith from those related to salvation. Yet this strong affirmation of the ethical and social implications of following Jesus should not be taken as an unqualified

2 Bradley J. Longfield, *The Presbyterian Controversy: Fundamentalists, Modernists, and Moderates* (New York: Oxford University Press, 1991), 6, 11, 104–27, 162–80.
3 *Works*, 3:187–88.
4 On King's use of Jones, see Keith D. Miller, *Voice of Deliverance: The Language of Martin Luther King, Jr., and Its Sources* (Athens: University of Georgia Press, 1992), 204.

endorsement of the social gospel movement. Later in his ministry, Jones offered particularly explicit support for some social gospel ideas that simultaneously revealed the liabilities of a mere social gospel. He refused to choose between "an individual gospel" and a "social gospel." According to Jones, "an individual gospel without a social gospel is a soul without a body." And "a social gospel without an individual gospel is a body without a soul." Therefore, he concluded: "One is a ghost and the other a corpse. I don't want one of them. *I want both.*"[5] Grimké's citation of Jones's work moved in precisely the same direction. Apparently, *The Christ of the Indian Road* stuck with him, for many years later he described the prophetic nature of Jones's message, noting its "authority" and its "conviction," and observing that "the truth as he presents it is vitalized, made living."[6]

Grimké carefully framed his exposition of the social implications of the kingdom of God in relation to these two works. Though both authors affirmed the importance of a "living faith," they represented dramatically different communities of discourse. This framing illustrates how Grimké carefully connected his understanding of the kingdom to figures associated, on the one hand, with conservative theological opposition to modernism and, on the other hand, with progressive social and cultural views related to racial and economic equality. He notably avoided reference to one without the other. He also carefully utilized this framework to present a vision of living faith that affirmed a strong belief in the supernatural essence of the Christian faith, the Christian God, and Christian revelation. This supernatural faith drew comfort from the eternal promises of the Scriptures, the emphasis on the individual soul, the need for the gift of salvation in response to personal sin, and the hope of heavenly mindedness. At the same time, this same supernatural faith called forth a life of service, neighborly love, personal sacrifice, and social concern. Grimké consistently held such affirmations together, drew from diverse thinkers to formulate and commend them, and boldly pushed against those who tried to pit one set of affirmations against the others as if they were contradictory or mutually exclusive.

Grimké's own definition of the implications of the kingdom of God for social engagement closely traced these same outlines. He began by

---

[5] E. Stanley Jones, "Christ of the Asbury Road," "Faculty/Staff: Dr. E. Stanley Jones Day, May 8, 1942," in "600 Faculty/Staff: E. Stanley Jones Literary Productions," Asbury University Archives, cited in David R. Swartz, "Christ of the American Road: E. Stanley Jones, India, and Civil Rights," *Journal of American Studies* 51, no. 4 (2017): 1134, emphasis original.
[6] *Works*, 3:388–89.

emphasizing the spiritual nature of the kingdom of God. He chastised those people of Israel in Jesus's day who made the mistake of "looking for a Messiah who was to set up a temporal kingdom that was to bring under it all the kingdoms of the world." Contrary to this temporal expectation of some of the people of Israel, Grimké noted that the present expression of the "true Messianic kingdom, however, was to be spiritual" rather than political. This kingdom "was to be set up in the hearts of men" and "designed to set them free from the galling yoke of sin and Satan." According to Grimké, "it is this kingdom of righteousness that is needed in the individual heart and life, and when it is fully set up [it] will dominate the world." He then doubled down on the error of identifying the kingdom of God in the present age with political or temporal rule. What the people of Israel ultimately needed "was not freedom from the Roman yoke, but from the yoke of sin, from the bondage of their corrupt, evil hearts." This need for the forgiveness of sins belonged not only to Israel; "that is what we all need," and "there is no way of getting that relief except by surrendering ourselves to Jesus Christ, by coming under his reign, the true Messianic King, the king of righteousness." According to Grimké, the proper expectation of the kingdom of God in the present age is a spiritual rule, set up in the "hearts" and "souls" of individuals, and made manifest through repentance and faith, leading to the forgiveness of sins. "Outside of this kingdom there is no hope for any one."[7]

Up to this point, Grimké's reflections on the social implications of the kingdom of God echoed his employment of the same motif in relation to the church. In stark contrast to many progenitors and popularizers of social gospel ideas, Grimké comfortably emphasized individual salvation, the forgiveness of individual sin, the distinction between soul and body, the centrality of eternal life, and the hope of heaven, while he explicitly warned against conceptualizing the kingdom in "secular," "temporal," or purely social terms. In other words, and as will become even clearer below, Grimké expressed the individual and social, the eternal and temporal, the spiritual and the material, the salvific and the ethical as both–and rather than either–or categories. He also placed in them in a particular order relative to one another. Both "bread" and "the bread of life" are right, good, and important, but one clearly receives priority and gives shape and direction for thinking about the other. Before we turn to the other half of the equation,

---

7 *Works*, 3:189.

Grimké's emphasis on the social implications of these spiritual doctrines, it is worth thinking a bit more deeply about his historical context.

The Context of Grimké's Social Christian Preaching

Popular conceptions regarding the nature and definition of the social gospel make it difficult to evaluate the relationship between Grimké's teaching, ministry, and activism and these ideas. Older histories often treated the social gospel as the response of liberal, mainstream Protestantism to "the challenge of modern industrial society."[8] On the contrary, some recent studies emphasize the "evangelical overtones" of the social gospel and its reliance upon the "American pietist, evangelical tradition" in order to characterize the social gospel as a "fusion" or "unique synthesis" of "evangelical and liberal American Christianities."[9] This awareness of the diversity of social gospel ideas is not absent from some older works on the subject, though. Henry May, for example, argued in 1949 that the success of social gospel tropes was the result of their popularization in moderate forms by novelists; they were not as radical as the theologians whose outright denials of the traditional understanding of the divinity of Jesus were less palatable to the American public.[10] May's assessment indicates that there were more- and less-radical social gospels rather than one simple set of ideas, but this nuance is not always present in the histories or in the popular treatments of these subjects. The pervasive tendency in popular and even some academic conversations to refer to "the" social gospel, as if it were a well-defined doctrinal position or set of positions, obscures the contours of the conversation and Grimké's place within it.

Similarly, the tendency to categorize American Protestants, such as Grimké, according to binary distinctions between "liberals" and "fundamentalists" or "liberals" and "evangelicals" also fails to make sense of his views and influence. Christopher Evans's recent biography of Walter Rauschenbusch, the famous author of *A Theology for the Social Gospel* and a self-professed leader of the social gospel movement, makes this point well. Not only does Evans's research reveal that "what historians call 'the social gospel' was never a unified social or theological phenomenon"; it

---

[8] C. Howard Hopkins, *The Rise of the Social Gospel in American Protestantism, 1865–1915* (New Haven, CT: Yale University Press, 1940), 318.

[9] Matthew Bowman, "Sin, Spirituality, and Primitivism: The Theologies of the American Social Gospel, 1885–1917," *Religion and American Culture* 17, no. 1 (2007): 96, 100.

[10] Henry May, *The Protestant Churches and Industrial America* (New York: Harper, 1949).

also challenges significant aspects of the "two-party thesis" that relies exclusively on a division between theological "conservatives" and "progressives" to understand the story of American religion.[11] Evans's exposition
of Rauschenbusch's career and reception makes clear that sharp divisions
occurred within conservative circles as well as within liberal circles, and
not just between conservatives and progressives. Whatever uses the "two-
party thesis" may have for illustrating the breakdowns in specific denominations at particular moments, differing perspectives on a whole host of
theological, social, and cultural issues cannot be summarized according
to merely two "camps."

If this was true for White Protestants, it was true for Black Protestants
as well. Gary Dorrien's recent work on W. E. B. Du Bois helpfully narrates
the diversity of social gospel advocates among African Americans. Dorrien
identifies at least four distinct "versions" of what he refers to as "black social Christianity." Though he identifies Francis Grimké most closely with
the group tied to advocacy for social justice, careful readers of this book
will notice that Grimké's friendships, partnerships, and correspondents
included members of all four groups.[12] Along these lines, paying attention

[11] Christopher H. Evans, *The Kingdom Is Always but Coming: A Life of Walter Rauschenbusch* (Waco, TX: Baylor University Press, 2020), xxiii–xxiv. Evans identifies Martin E. Marty, *Righteous Empire: Protestantism in the United States* (New York: Dial, 1970), as one prominent articulation of such a "two-party thesis" worthy of reconsideration.
[12] Dorrien associates the first group with Booker T. Washington, with whom he links important denominational leaders in the AME and AME Zion Churches, including Wesley J. Gaines, Abram Grant, and George Clinton, as well as Baptists like E. C. Morris and R. H. Boyd. These figures sought, alongside Washington, to bargain with White elites for a "season of peace and economic opportunity," and created a powerful national following among White and Black people. Dorrien identifies a second group of "socially active Black Christians" with Henry McNeal Turner and the cause for Black nationalist separation and/or African emigration. He places the Episcopal missionary and intellectual leader Alexander Crummell, as well as James T. Holly and Alfred L. Ridgell, in this group, figures who argued for biological and/or ontological national belonging associated with various conceptions of Black identity, authenticity, and distinctiveness. A third group focused on calls for racial justice and adamantly opposed Washington's willingness to pacify White elites. Du Bois attached himself to these figures, including Archibald Grimké's close associate William Monroe Trotter, as well as a host of church leaders and prominent lay people like Reverdy Ransom and Ida B. Wells-Barnett in the AME Church, Baptist leaders like James R. L. Diggs and Peter James Bryant, the Congregational minister Byron Gunner, and Episcopal priests Robert W. Bagnall and George Frazier Miller. Dorrien includes Carter Woodson (editor of Grimké's collected works) in this group and identifies Francis and Archibald Grimké as its allies. In addition to these Black nationalists and Black justice advocates, Dorrien characterizes a fourth group as those who attempted to combine Du Bois's advocacy for civil rights with the diplomacy of the Booker T. Washington group. Among the litany of figures Dorrien names in this fourth cluster, some friends of Grimké stand out, including Howard University dean Kelly Miller. Dorrien's emphasis on the diversity of these streams of "black social Christianity" is rigorously researched and thought provoking.
     In addition to this broadly construed "black social Christianity," Dorrien identifies a more narrow "black social gospel" that he argues developed primarily from the third stream of figures, though with contributions from the fourth stream, as well as a small group of contemporary socialists. He associates this "black social gospel" with Du Bois and describes this "full-fledged black social gospel" as a combination of features including "an emphasis on black dignity and personhood," "protest activism for racial justice," "a comprehensive social justice agenda," "an insistence that authentic Christian faith is incompatible with racial prejudice," "an emphasis on the social ethical teaching of Jesus," and "an acceptance

to Dorrien's method and definitions leads to a mixed assessment of his narrative. On the one hand, his description of the diverse groups of figures who
utilized Christian social teaching to form a coalition or movement to advocate for civil rights and other social concerns is compelling. On the other
hand, his description of a "Black social gospel" is fundamentally a theological description when he claims it is not, and it is a theological description
that many of his cast of characters, Francis Grimké not least, would have
rejected. As Dorrien notes, the "Black social Christianity" of Grimké's day
represented a diverse coalition that held a spectrum of social and theological views, including many figures who were not self-professedly Christian.
It would be a mistake to identify this coalition with a coherent preaching
of a "Black social gospel." To understand the preaching ministry of Francis
Grimké, it is crucial to pay close attention to these dynamics.[13]

The primary point is that Grimké's social preaching of the kingdom
of God is obscured by two overlapping problems pervasive in popular narratives of American religious history. First, his preaching confirms the
criticisms that many historians level against the simplistic binary choice

---

of modern scholarship and social consciousness." See Gary Dorrien, *The New Abolition: W. E. B. Du Bois
and the Black Social Gospel* (New Haven, CT: Yale University Press, 2015), 3–4.

[13] Much of Dorrien's presentation is helpful, and historians interested in Grimké's life and ministry can
learn much from *The New Abolition*. At the same time, there is an inconsistency in the framework. This
inconsistency calls into question Dorrien's attempt to utilize a singular, "narrow" definition of the social
gospel. On the one hand, Dorrien argues in the introduction to the book that "the social gospel was fundamentally a movement, not a doctrine, featuring a social ethical understanding of the Christian faith."
On the other hand, later in the book he argues, "The theologians of the black social gospel had to make
a case that the church was still relevant to the struggle for civil rights and social justice, even as this
struggle increasingly employed ideological, political, and cultural modes of discourse that marginalized
Christianity." Dorrien, *The New Abolition*, 3, 295.

That sounds like more than just a movement; it sounds an awful lot like a theological argument
made by, as Dorrien points out, theologians. Therefore, it is inconsistent for him to cast the "black social
gospel" as a movement rather than a doctrine or a set of doctrines. The Black social gospel movement was
more diverse than he acknowledges, and his use of the phrase "black social gospel" not only is explicitly
theological but makes evaluative judgments about which views count as more central and which ones
are more peripheral. While Dorrien's "broad" description of Black social Christianity is helpful even if it
lumps together a wide range of approaches and views, his "narrow" definition of a "black social gospel"
is more theologically laden than he admits.

In other words, Dorrien's narrative self-consciously moves beyond historical description to theological
advocacy for his own preferred understanding of social gospel ideas. He is especially interested in the method
by which a marginalized Christianity could make itself relevant, a method that relies on his own interpretation of the Gospels. According to Dorrien, Christian relevancy could be obtained by preaching "the religion of
Christ," which entails despising prejudice, associating with the poor, and following the Golden Rule. No doubt
these all were crucial teachings of Jesus neglected by many American Christians. Dorrien's claim is stronger,
however. These things, he says, were "exactly what the black social gospelers preached as the touchstone of
good religion. They were gospel-centered theological progressives committed to the inward and outward
flourishing of God's kingdom." These, rather obviously, are doctrinal claims about the relative importance of
various Christian teachings. In other words, Dorrien's definition of the Black social gospel is manifestly doctrinal. It includes the moral teachings of Jesus ("love your neighbor as yourself," Matt. 22:39 ESV) but not the
teachings of Jesus that were metaphysical ("I and the Father are one," John 10:30 ESV), historical ("the Son of
Man must be delivered into the hands of sinful men and be crucified and on the third day rise," Luke 24:7 ESV),
or exclusive ("no one comes to the Father except through me," John 14:6 ESV). Therefore, many specific attributes of Dorrien's notion of a Black social gospel are like square pegs that do not fit the round hole he describes.

between "liberal" or "evangelical" Christianity. Second, his preaching fits within the very broad rubric of "Black social Christianity," but it very clearly does not fit at least one prominent historian's definition of a "Black social gospel." Grimké's social preaching of the kingdom of God was simultaneously ethical, historical, and metaphysical. It involved the proclamation of Jesus's divine person, his supernatural work, and his moral teachings, refusing to choose between them. It also entailed all of Jesus's moral teachings, irrespective of whether society found them "conservative" or "progressive." Grimké's preaching demands categories for Christian ethical preaching, and indeed Black social preaching, that refuse the binary choices between theological liberalism and evangelicalism or social liberalism and conservativism. Grimké's vision for a social Christianity that affirmed historic orthodox Christian theological commitments does not fit such categories.

Social Christianity versus "the Social Gospel"

Grimké's use of Clarence Macartney and E. Stanley Jones to situate his reflections on the kingdom of God signaled a conscious effort to set forth a vision for a living Christianity that cut across so-called liberal and conservative theological and social proclivities. Appealing to one author or the other might allow him to be co-opted for a particular agenda, whereas appealing to both allowed him to affirm aspects of the Christian faith defended by opponents of modernism as well as aspects of the Christian faith defended by cultural progressives in favor of racial equality. Grimké's social preaching of the kingdom of God cut across the theological and political spectrum of his day, and his preaching regularly gave attention to both the substance of a matter and its framing in order to accomplish this goal.

In fact, Grimké's preaching of the social implications of God's kingdom can be seen as a careful effort to preserve a fully orbed gospel as the motivation for a holistic social conscience. The previous chapter demonstrated how he aligned himself and participated actively in coalition movements advocating for "Black social Christianity." Careful attention to his preaching makes clear that he also found it necessary to critique and respond to key doctrines associated with self-identified advocates of the social gospel, whether Black or White. His critique of contemporary expectations of a temporal messianic kingdom, his affirmation of the spiritual nature of the kingdom, his emphasis on the individual heart and soul, not to mention his persistent defenses of scriptural inspiration and authority and Christ's substitutionary atonement, all directly contradicted some of the most prominent social gospel preachers. Grimké firmly advocated the temporal faithfulness of God's people and refused to disassociate the spiritual claims of the gospel from the material implications of obedience to God's revealed law. He drew direct connections between racial equality and this faithfulness and obedience. His preaching sought to communicate these matters as both–and rather than either–or relationships.

By contrast, Walter Rauschenbusch notably and frequently communicated these relationships in mutually exclusive terms or gave priority to the other side of the equation. Rauschenbusch's publications—*Christianity and the Social Crisis* (1907), *Christianizing the Social Order* (1912), and *A Theology for the Social Gospel* (1917), together with his popular *For God and the People: Prayers for a Social Awakening* (1910)—made him a prominent and self-proclaimed mouthpiece of social gospel ideas. Recent historical work rightly emphasizes that Rauschenbusch blended evangelical pietism and revivalistic urgency with modernist theological impulses in a way that made his work more accessible than that of academics like Shailer Mathews at the University of Chicago Divinity School.[14] For many American Christians, it also made his ideas more persuasive.

It may be true that Rauschenbusch blended evangelical or revivalistic *piety* with modernist theological convictions, but it is important to emphasize that his theology departed dramatically from classical Protestant beliefs. Whereas Grimké held the spiritual and the temporal together, Rauschenbusch either pulled them apart or redefined spiritual matters in exclusively material terms. For example, in *Christianity and the Social Crisis*, he placed eternal life and the kingdom of God, the very same terms Grimké held closely together, in opposition to one another:

> But as the eternal life came to the front in Christian hope, the kingdom of God receded to the background, and with it went much of the social potency of Christianity. The kingdom of God was a social and collective hope and it was for this earth. The eternal life was an individualistic hope, and it was not for this earth. The kingdom of God involved the social transformation of humanity. The hope of eternal life, as it was then

---

[14] Prominent examples of such scholarship include Evans, *The Kingdom Is Always but Coming*, and Bowman, "Sin, Spirituality, and Primitivism."

held, was the desire to escape from this world and be done with it. The kingdom was a revolutionary idea; eternal life was an ascetic idea.[15]

To be sure, Rauschenbusch stated a belief in life after death, but he emphasized such different notes in doing so that the result was dissonance rather that harmony. Rauschenbusch accused the Christian tradition of choosing eternal life over the kingdom of God, but rather than holding both scriptural notions together, he just reversed the error. In doing so, he explicitly criticized the teachings of both the Gospel of Luke and the Gospel of John. According to Rauschenbusch, sometimes Luke and John were right and sometimes they were wrong. His own theological system functioned as the grid for judging the authenticity of Jesus's sayings.[16]

Rauschenbusch also communicated directly that his conception of salvation was different from both Catholicism and Protestantism. In his

---

15 Walter Rauschenbusch, *Christianity and the Social Crisis* (New York: Macmillan, 1907), 162.

16 Rauschenbusch not only separated the kingdom of God from traditional notions of eternal life but also downplayed its relationship to the individual soul and expressed skepticism regarding scriptural passages that affirmed that connection. He acknowledged that Jesus "worked on individuals and through individuals" but said that "his real end was not individualistic, but social, and in his method he employed strong social forces." For Rauschenbusch, Jesus's end "was not the new soul, but the new society; not man, but Man." He called into question the statements of Jesus recorded in the Scriptures about "his return and final consummation of the kingdom," arguing that likely they were corruptions of Jesus's actual words by the early church. Scholars may point out that the Scriptures contain affirmations of both the present and future presence of the kingdom of God, but Rauschenbusch argued that the present expressions were more authentic and that John's use of the present tense to describe the kingdom was more trustworthy than the use of the future tense in the other Gospels. Though Rauschenbusch found John more trustworthy on the timing of the kingdom, he thought that John was less trustworthy than the other Gospels regarding the nature of God's kingdom. Whereas John put "eternal life" in the center of Jesus's teaching, and his interests were "religious and theological," Rauschenbusch preferred Luke's emphasis on the kingdom, and so he characterized Luke's treatment of the nature of the kingdom as more reliable. Rauschenbusch, *Christianity and the Social Crisis*, 60–61, 62–63. 80.

The opening portion of this chapter observed that Grimké criticized first-century messianic expectations of the political alignment of God's kingdom with any contemporary nation. According to Rauschenbusch, however, Israel's error was not related to their "national, social, and religious" expectations but merely in their use of violence to pursue them. In making this evaluation, Rauschenbusch repeatedly used either–or language: "It is not a matter of saving human atoms, but of saving the social organism. It is not a matter of getting individuals to heaven, but of transforming the life on earth into the harmony of heaven." Any expression of "spiritual force" only "proved his [Jesus's] sagacity as a society-builder." In all these ways, Rauschenbusch privileged the temporal, earthly, and the social as the primary purposes of God's kingdom (64–65).

Just as he redefined eternal life and disassociated it from the kingdom of God, Rauschenbusch made similar moves in *A Theology for the Social Gospel* when discussing salvation more broadly. He did not directly deny the salvation of the individual. But his statements affirming that "the salvation of the individual is, of course, an essential part of salvation" came in the immediate context of acknowledgments that his goal was to redefine what salvation means. Having affirmed the salvation of the individual, he went on to write that "our understanding of personal salvation itself is deeply affected by the new solidaristic comprehension furnished by the social gospel." After defining sin in social terms, he defined salvation as "the voluntary socializing of the soul." Faith also received a new definition as "an energetic act of the will, affirming our fellowship with God and man, declaring our solidarity with the Kingdom of God, and repudiating selfish isolation." Rauschenbusch also marginalized the word, the sacraments, and prayer as the basic tools of growth in holiness. In fact, he declared, "Those who believe in the social gospel can share in any methods for the cultivation of the spiritual life, if only they have an ethical outcome." In this way, Rauschenbusch articulated a system with a great deal of coherence. A social understanding of salvation demanded a similarly social understanding of initiation and growth in the Christian faith. Walter Rauschenbusch, *A Theology for the Social Gospel* (New York: Macmillan, 1917), 96, 97, 99, 102.

system, "the fundamental theological terms about the experiences of salvation get a new orientation, correction, and enrichment through the religious point of view contained in the social gospel." He claimed that this notion of salvation was superior to Catholic and Protestant views, for it returned to "the spirit and outlook of primitive Christianity."[17] It is not hard to see why many readers of the Scriptures and other early Christian writings, whether Catholic or Protestant, were not convinced.[18]

In sum, for Rauschenbusch the kingdom of God functioned as the central dogma of the Christian faith. It was the source, substance, and goal of religion. Indeed, "the doctrine of the kingdom of God . . . is itself the social gospel." He contrasted this central dogma with what he took to be other options chosen by other theologians. When it came to the "marrow of the gospel," "just as the incarnation was to Athanasius, justification by faith alone to Luther, and the sovereignty of God to Jonathan Edwards," the kingdom of God "was just as dear to Jesus." Therefore, "the newer manuals [of theology] not only make constant reference to it in connection with various doctrines, but they arrange their entire subject matter so that the Kingdom of God becomes the governing idea."[19] By contrast, while Grimké certainly did not object to giving proper attention to the kingdom of God, he was less inclined to define it in a way that would marginalize or redefine the incarnation of Jesus, justification by faith, or the sovereignty of God. Rauschenbusch thought his teachings contained unifying doctrine, because, as he put it, "The social gospel is believed by trinitarians and unitarians alike, by Catholic Modernists and Kansas Presbyterians."[20] According to Rauschenbusch, what people believed about the nature of God, the revelation of God, and the acts of God mattered far less than whether they shared the same ethical understanding of God's kingdom.

It is hard not to see Rauschenbusch's social gospel preaching as a central target of Grimké's preaching ministry. Grimké's earlier sermons, including "The Nature and Mission of the Church," communicated positive

---

[17] Rauschenbusch, A Theology for the Social Gospel, 105.
[18] In addition to shifting the goal of salvation and the means of salvation, Rauschenbusch relied on different sources for his theological views. The chapters above have illustrated Grimké's deep reliance on the Scriptures as the source of his doctrine and his preaching. In place of Scripture, Rauschenbusch elevated the role of personal experience. He argued that the Scriptures themselves were the result of the "personal experiences" of the prophets. The "ethical monotheism" and "God-consciousness" of the biblical writers "grew" from their own experiences, just as Jesus "reinterpreted and perfected" their teachings "in his personality." Rauschenbusch cited Friedrich Schleiermacher, Albrecht Ritschl, and the philosopher Josiah Royce as his theological forebears, together with Otto Pfleiderer, whom he quoted regarding their views. Rauschenbusch, A Theology for the Social Gospel, 107, 125–27.
[19] Rauschenbusch, A Theology for the Social Gospel, 131, 138.
[20] Rauschenbusch, A Theology for the Social Gospel, 148.

preaching of the social implications of Christian teaching while advocating for the necessity of preaching the person and work of Christ, including the metaphysical and historical aspects of the Gospel narratives. Grimké pointed out that the Gospels clearly teach Jesus's "miraculous conception and birth," and his "crucifixion, burial, resurrection, and glorious ascension," and they promise his return in "power." Similarly, the church is different from other institutions and is uniquely an expression of the kingdom of God. The church is "not a man made but a heaven born institution." It is "not the result of human reason" or the product of "man's ingenuity." According to Grimké, therefore, "the church is not to be confounded" with any other organization. "It belongs to a higher category," which Grimké explicitly affirmed is informed by a notion of personal salvation. Its members must "accept of the Lord Jesus Christ as the Lamb of God, as a Personal and all sufficient Savior from the guilt and power of sin."[21]

Grimké's later sermons, especially those preached after Rauschenbusch, targeted the ideas he expressed in *Christianity and the Social Crisis* and *A Theology for the Social Gospel* even more explicitly. Grimké's 1936 sermon "Christ's Program for the Saving of the World" specifically blamed the loss of faith in the inspiration of Scripture and the failure to preach about the reality of personal sin and the personal work of Christ for what he took to be the declining influence of Christianity. Christian ministers, he lamented, "have, to a very large extent, been recreant with the trust committed to them." They have not been following "faithfully and earnestly the program here laid down by the master." What was the measure of this assessment? The measure was how "faithfully" they have "been preaching the gospel." In fact, he cried: "They have preached on almost everything except Jesus Christ as the Lamb of God whose blood alone cleanses from sin. The thought of sin, from which we need to be saved, has largely dropped out of most of our preaching." Instead they should have made their chief task "to expound the Word of God, setting forth clearly before the people the teachings of the inspired volume concerning character and conduct, line upon line, precept upon precept, here a little, and there a little, in season and out of season?"[22] By the end of his life, Grimké clearly thought it important to emphasize the inspiration

---

21 Francis J. Grimké, "The Nature and Mission of the Christian Church," box 40-8, folder 415, Francis J. Grimké Papers, Howard University Library, 6–9. See chap. 8, n. 12 regarding the dating of this sermon.
22 Francis J. Grimké, "Christ's Program for the Saving of the World" (1936), box 40-6, folder 309, Francis J. Grimké Papers, Howard University Library, 10.

of Scripture, the supernatural nature of the person and work of Christ, the reality of personal sin, and individual salvation in the context of his preaching of social Christianity.

While these themes were present in his early preaching and became more explicit and focused at the end of his life, there is evidence that the second decade of the 1900s, the height of Rauschenbusch's populariza-tion of *A Theology for the Social Gospel*, played a role in the development of Grimké's voice. In March 1918, the year after the publication of that book, Howard University organized a conference entitled "Effective Christianity in the Present World Crisis" and invited Grimké to preach. Grimké deliv-ered a message with the same title, in which he offered, on the one hand, a definition of Christianity and, on the other hand, a perspective on the nature of the present crisis. His definition of Christianity held up Jesus as "prophet, priest, and king" and the Bible as "the word of God, the only in-fallible rule of faith and practice." He went on to affirm Jesus's divinity, his substitutionary atonement, his authority, and the inspiration of the Scrip-tures. After offering a definition of the Christian faith directly opposed to the type offered by figures like Rauschenbusch, he proceeded to express skepticism regarding the unique nature of the present social crisis and, in particular, the need for Christianity to change to address it. "Christianity is the same under all conditions," he noted flatly. "Its principles are the same; the gospel which it preaches is always the same: its standard of mor-als is always the same." Therefore, he concluded simply, "The only thing to do under all circumstances is to live it, is to be faithful to its principles."[23] Grimké's sermon cut to the heart of Rauschenbusch's notion of the social crisis and the theology needed to address it.[24]

---

[23] Francis J. Grimké, "Effective Christianity in the Present World Crisis" (1918), box 40-7, folder 342, Francis J. Grimké Papers, Howard University Library, 1–2, 4.

[24] This chapter utilizes Rauschenbusch's work as an obvious foil for Grimké's preaching. See chap. 7 for the ways in which Grimké opposed similar ideas when they appeared in the works of Black authors like William Stuart Nelson, a member of the theology faculty at Howard University. Since the studies of Ralph E. Luker and Ronald C. White Jr., historians have increasingly recognized that White proponents of the social gospel did not ignore racial injustices. Building on their work, Gary Dorrien argues that "black social gospelers" could "live with a variety of theologies, especially in ecclesiology and biblical interpre-tation, but the crucial thing was to build strong black institutions through which religious commitments effected social change." In this way, he claims these advocates of a Black social gospel represented a "distinct tradition" with "its own problems, figures, history, and integrity." Dorrien, *The New Abolition*, xii–xiii; Ralph E. Luker, *The Social Gospel in Black and White: American Racial Reform, 1885–1912* (Chapel Hill: University of North Carolina Press, 1991); Ronald C. White Jr., *Liberty and Justice for All: Racial Reform and the Social Gospel, 1877–1925* (Louisville: Westminster John Knox, 1990). It is beyond the scope of this book to evaluate Dorrien's claims fully, but Francis Grimké is clearly an example of a prominent Black advocate of social Christianity who repeatedly warned against theological diversity and ecclesiological innovation, and he based his arguments on traditional biblical interpretation. He did not distinguish between White and Black opponents in setting forth this vision. His popular reception and prominent institutional location invite further consideration of the extent to which voices like his have been unduly

Grimké not only commended a different theological system in his social preaching but also encouraged different spiritual disciplines. Indeed, in setting forth traditional Christian practices like Bible reading, prayer, and corporate worship, he explicitly distinguished the "spiritual life" from the "physical life." In a tract entitled "The Spiritual Life," he wrote: "The spiritual life, like physical life, must be cared for. A failure to read the Bible, to pray, and to attend upon the public ordinances of religion will soon make themselves felt in our lessening spirituality."[25] Throughout his ministry, he distinguished the spiritual from the physical or material, and he never placed his holistic vision of the social and ethical implications of the Christian faith in opposition to traditional Christian spirituality or beliefs. On the contrary, he believed that it is just this traditional Christian spirituality that supports and enables a healthy public faith.

The Necessity of Social Christianity

Though Grimké framed his social preaching to explicitly oppose central beliefs of self-identified social gospel preachers, in view of the previous chapters of this book it should not be surprising that he also framed his preaching to advocate for the importance of drawing concrete social and ethical applications from the Scriptures, and he was not afraid when his applications overlapped those of his theological opponents. Grimké believed that theological opponents could often agree on social issues and that all Christians, including pastors, should care deeply about those social issues. Indeed, his own statement of his ministerial vocation included his calling not only to "preach the gospel of the grace of God" but also to engage socially to "fight race prejudice."[26]

His quotations from Clarence Macartney and E. Stanley Jones enabled him to frame the importance of such a "lived Christian faith" as a calling endorsed by prominent figures with a spectrum of cultural and political views. While he chastised God's people for their error of confusing God's kingdom with any temporal political entity, he nevertheless boldly communicated the social, cultural, and political relevance of the advancement of God's kingdom through the church's ministry. Joining the church

---

marginalized by historical categories that minimize theological distinctives or continue to hang on to the "two-party thesis" regarding American Christianity.

25 Francis J. Grimké, "The Spiritual Life" (undated), Francis J. Grimké Papers, box 40-10, folder 491, Howard University Library, 1–2.

26 Grimké to the class of 1878 of Princeton Theological Seminary, April 27, 1918.

through faith and repentance means "coming under" the reign of Jesus, "the true Messianic King, the king of righteousness."

Holding together personal salvation and social concern, Grimké declared that "Jesus is seeking primarily to get men into right relations with God," but he identified this goal with Jesus's work "to awaken within them and to set up in their hearts and minds the thought that it is their first, their chief duty so to order their lives as to meet his approbation." These thoughts culminated in a declaration of the relationship between the "kingdoms of the world" and "the kingdoms of the Lord and of his Christ." The kingdoms of the world are to become the kingdoms of the Lord "by the men in whose hearts this kingdom of righteousness has been set up getting control of them and ministering their affairs." Therefore, according to Grimké, no one temporal earthly political kingdom can claim a special identification with the kingdom of God; no kingdom in the present age can claim to express the kingdom of God fully; and the means of kingdom advancement are spiritual—namely, evangelism and discipleship in the way of Christ. The "kingdom of God will be established on earth" by establishing righteousness in the hearts of people.[27]

The kingdom themes in Grimké's preaching not only underwrote his social and ethical vision; they also enabled him to emphasize simultaneously the gracious character of God's kingdom and the importance of good works in relation to its coming. On the one hand, Grimké emphasized the works of the believer as the instruments of God's kingdom. Because Christians may count themselves "members" of the kingdom of God, they must also count themselves subject to the "rules and regulations" of God's kingdom, the moral teachings of Scripture. Therefore, he reasoned, one explanation for why the church, "which is the visible representative of the kingdom of God on earth" is "weak," is that "there are so many weaklings in it, so many half-hearted, worldly-minded, careless, indifferent followers." In fact, "it never will be strong" he declared, "until Christian obligations are regarded more seriously than they are."[28]

On the other hand, such "Christlikeness" is an "effect" rather than a "cause." The effect of "Christlikeness" is "but the unfolding of a life that has been implanted in the soul by the Spirit of God." It is a "fruit" of God's grace; its "roots" are "in God" and its nourishment is found "by abiding in

---

[27] *Works*, 3:189–90.
[28] *Works*, 3:233.

him." The good works of the believer are the "fruit" or "glorious result" of regeneration, which is the gift of God.[29] This connection between God's grace and the coming of his kingdom through the preaching and faithfulness of the church explains how he could say, "What the world needs is the Gospel of the grace of God in Christ Jesus; and that Gospel preached by men who believe it, and who know from personal experience that it has power to save." It is not accidental that he recorded this statement immediately after a reflection on the ministry of the apostle Paul in "bringing others into the kingdom."[30]

Because Grimké tied the gracious coming of God's spiritual kingdom to the ministry of the church, he called the church to rise up and oppose social injustices, especially racism. He cited, as a foil, Lothrop Stoddard's infamous White supremacist treatise *The Rising Tide of Color against White World-Supremacy* (1920). Whereas Stoddard called White people around the globe to unite to defend their "continued hegemony," despite their numerical disadvantage, Grimké presented a starkly different vision informed by the "kingdom which was set up by Jesus Christ." The design of Christ's kingdom is "not to array race against race, class against class" but, rather, to "break down walls of separation."

> God's plan for the future of humanity, as set forth in Christianity, is not to make white men, or black men, or red men, or brown men, or yellow men,—is not to make Americans, or Englishmen, or Frenchmen, or Germans, or Russians, or men of any other nation; but to make out of them all, Christians, to put upon them all the stamp of Jesus Christ, to make them all over into the image and likeness of Jesus Christ. And if they are all made Christians, if they all accept his ideals and principles, and imbibe his spirit, they will be no trouble, the fact that they are not all of the same race stock will make no difference. A man who is really, truly a Christian will be a good American, or a good Englishman, or a good Frenchman, or a good Chinaman, or a good Japanese,—he will make good in any nationality, and will play the part of a brother wherever he may be found. The universal man, the man that fits in anywhere is the Christian. And so, instead of all this tomfoolery about races, and about keeping races apart, and keeping one above another, if we gave ourselves to the work of setting up the kingdom of Jesus Christ in the world, of sowing the seeds

---

[29] *Works*, 3:190.
[30] *Works*, 3:26.

of brotherhood, of justice, of truth, of love,—how much better it would be, how much brighter would be the outlook for the future.

The aim of all should be, not for the supremacy of white, or black, or brown, or red, or yellow, but the supremacy of Jesus Christ, the supremacy of his great ideals and principles which can be realized just as fully in one race as another. When men begin to think less about race, and more about building the world's manhood and womanhood after the measure of the stature of the fulness of Christ, there will be fewer books written like this one of Mr. Stoddard. Men will be ashamed to put forth such a document as that. The aim of Jesus Christ is to set all the forces of righteousness against the forces of evil, but not whites against blacks, or blacks against white. And it is wicked for anyone to do it, or ever to suggest it.[31]

Grimké's social vision affirmed the goodness and beauty of ethnic diversity shorn of any pretense to ethnic supremacy. The advancement of the kingdom of God makes more Christians, faithful followers of Christ comfortable in their national or ethnic heritage and willing to pursue justice, truth, and love that crossed national and ethnic lines. Grimké did not view such attitudes and ideals as optional for Christians, and so he boldly called the church to pursue the social implications of God's moral law personally and politically. Anything less would be a "perverted one sided, distorted Christianity."[32]

The church's obligation to engage in social and ethical issues raised thorny tensions though, for Grimké also believed that the church's power is spiritual rather than temporal, and that church leaders do not possess the right to bind the consciences of church members to vote for specific candidates and policies. These dynamics informed Grimké's reflections on the actions of "some of our bishops in the churches" who publicly endorsed the Democratic Party presidential candidate Al Smith over the Republican nominee, Herbert Hoover, in the 1928 election. In these reflections, Grimké carefully distinguished the personal political convictions of the pastor from the pastor's obligation to minister God's word. Along these lines, Grimké recorded his own personal reservations with the political wisdom of voting for Democratic candidates. For pragmatic reasons, he did not feel that the racial shortcomings of the current Republican Party warranted a shift in party allegiances to the Democratic Party, especially

---

31 *Works*, 3:89–90.
32 *Works*, 3:91.

in light of their dubious record on a host of racial and moral issues. Similarly, because of his support for the temperance movement and the priority he gave to the issue, he thought it better to vote for a supporter of the movement rather than a "wet" advocate for overturning the Eighteenth Amendment, like Smith. For these reasons and others, Grimké personally felt that Hoover was a better presidential candidate than Smith. Yet, despite his personal political convictions, Grimké also objected to church leaders who attempted to control the political actions of their members. Churches that told their congregants how they must vote failed to respect "the freedom of thought" of members and wrongfully sought to "cultivate a spirit of subserviency to the priesthood." In Grimké's view, such attempts by the church "to get within its grasp all power, ecclesiastical as well as civil," are a "menace to all free governments." In fact, "no church can be an asset in a free state that dictates to its members how they shall vote."[33]

It is worth considering the extent to which Grimké's comments here were influenced unwittingly by his political commitments and what may have been anti–Roman Catholic sentiments. Furthermore, a case can be made that he was not himself consistent in following his own counsel, particularly when it came to the temperance issue. At the same time, there were also clear principles at stake that Grimké sought to follow with integrity, whatever his shortcomings in doing so. First, Grimké called the church to distinguish morality from politics, however entangled they might be. The institutional church possesses a calling to engage moral issues but to avoid political advocacy. Second, his twofold conception of the church also informed his approach. While the church possesses a calling to engage politically, this calling belongs to its individual members. The church as a gathered institution is called to teach God's revealed moral will but not to dictate pragmatic political conclusions about the most effective way to pursue moral good.

These two principles—the distinction between the moral and the political, and the distinction between the political role of the church gathered and that of the church scattered—should not be confused with political indifference, on the one hand, or political individualism, on the other. On the contrary, Grimké regularly advocated for political "agitation" and even civil disobedience in pursuit of righteous moral causes. As the previous chapter narrating his own involvement with the NAACP demonstrates, Grimké also

---

[33] *Works*, 3:292–95.

endorsed the organization of Christians for political purposes. Christians can align themselves, as members of the church scattered, with a variety of organizations.

With these caveats in mind, Grimké saw these two principles as the necessary implications of the nature of church power regulated by the Scriptures, but they clearly did not lead him to political complacency or naivety. He instructed the church gathered to teach biblical morality and the church scattered to draw practical insights from this morality and to pursue them politically. The church as an institution is called of God to teach the whole counsel of God, and the preaching of God's revealed moral will must not be divorced from its political relevance. At the same time, the application of scriptural morality to most specific political questions requires a chain of inferences too long to deem them "necessary." Grimké saw a difference between teaching that murder is wrong and declaring how to reduce or punish murders. The church (gathered) has a clear command from Jesus to teach the moral principle that murder is wrong. On the political questions of how to reduce or punish murder, the church has no explicit precept, but individual Christians (the church scattered) have an obligation to employ wisdom alongside non-Christians to form better human laws. A church or pastor who adds a "thus saith the Lord" to such political matters goes beyond God's calling. But a church or pastor who fails to encourage a congregation to form convictions about political matters, and certainly a church or pastor who fails to preach the moral teachings of Scripture, is a church or pastor who fails to perform a God-given duty. For Grimké, a socially engaged Christianity was not optional; it was necessary. The question was not whether the church should engage politically but how.

While it is not hard to trace these principles in Grimké's mature reflections, there also is evidence that his views on the nature of the church's political and social role may have developed over time. Early in his ministry, he endorsed the practice of the (institutional) church petitioning the civil government on specific political issues. In 1899 he wrote a public letter to the New York *Independent* observing the hypocrisy of the willingness of "all the Presbyterian churches in this city" to sign a petition protesting the practice of polygamy by a member of the House of Representatives. "I have no objection, of course, to these petitions," he wrote. In fact, he said, "I am heartily in favor of the object which they seek to accomplish." Grimké observed that polygamy was a moral evil that ought not to have been tolerated in a public official. His objection, rather, was to the lack of petitions regarding far greater moral evils. Citing the brutal and unprosecuted murders of Black people in the South amid the racist political revolution in Wilmington, North Carolina, he expressed shock at the lack of political concern on the part of Christians. "Why is it that the church waxes warm in the one case voicing its protest in the form of petition for redress, and in the other is as silent as the grave?" He called out the church's hypocrisy and complacency. "If duty requires silence in the one case, it requires it equally in the other; if it is right to speak in the one case, it is equally right to speak in the other."[34]

The tension between this letter and his later meditations may be evidence that Grimké's understanding of the church's political role changed over time, or it may just be that the obvious hypocrisy of the church's racial failures called for an appropriate expression of moral outrage. Another possibility is that Grimké deemed—to use the language of his church's confession of faith—both matters to be "cases extraordinary" and so worthy of such petition.[35] At any rate, it is not hard to sympathize with Grimké's assessment of the church's hypocrisy in petitioning against polygamy while failing to oppose race-motivated murder and political oppression. It would not be surprising if his views developed over time, and the complexity and moral gravity of these issues militate against hasty conclusions regarding his degree of consistency.

If Grimké's theological convictions led him to oppose the theological modernism characteristic of the most prominent leaders of the social gospel movement, these same beliefs led to him preach a form of social Christianity opposed to the racism pervasive in White fundamentalist circles. In 1917 he wrote a letter to the Great Commission Prayer League noting the hypocrisy of the organization's acceptance of racial discrimination, given its expressed mission to intercede for the world. Grimké felt that an organization that allowed for racial discrimination was not "fit" to appeal for prayer in the name of Jesus Christ. He also declared that tolerance for such racism gave him little faith in "American Christianity." Whereas Jesus came to "break down walls of separation," the "American Church," by contrast, "has been, and is now doing all in its power to produce the very

---

[34] Francis J. Grimké to the New York *Independent*, April 6, 1899, in *Works*, 4:58–60.
[35] See the Westminster Confession of Faith, 25.2.

opposite effect." According to Grimké, it was "white churches" who were primarily in need of intercession. Because "white Christians in America, as a body," never accepted racial equality, they should not "dare to call themselves Christians." To this he added that the racism of "white Christians in America" was a violation of a "fundamental" principle of Christianity. The failure to embrace this principle was a "cancer," and Grimké called for a "revival of religion" characterized by repentance for racism.[36]

The timing and language of Grimké's letter is intriguing. He called opposition to racism a "fundamental principle" of Christianity in 1917. He was a keen follower of denominational politics and would have been well aware of the doctrinal deliverances of the 1910 General Assembly that became known as the "Five Fundamentals" (discussed in the previous chapter). He also would have been aware of the publication of the *The Fundamentals*, the collection of ninety essays spread across twelve volumes released between 1910 and 1915. According to his obituary, Thomas E. Stephens, the director of the Great Commission Prayer League and the recipient of Grimké's letter, was also the business manager under whose leadership the Testimony Publishing Company funded and distributed three million copies of *The Fundamentals* to pastors, missionaries, and other ministry leaders around the world.[37] It is hard to imagine that Grimké's choice of words was coincidental. His letter can be read as an indictment not only of racism but also of the incomplete nature of *The Fundamentals* for failing to include basic anthropological and ethical Christian convictions addressing racism.

Grimké's vision for the intersection of fundamental Christianity with matters of social concern also led him to confront hypocrisy within his own Reformed circles. In 1924 he sent a letter to the Witness Bearing Committee of the Reformed Presbyterian Church. This committee had circulated an invitation to pray for the nation. Grimké's scathing letter suggested that the committee instead should invite prayer for the church. American unwillingness to acknowledge Jesus as "Divine Ruler" was "regrettable," Grimké acknowledged, but the church's allegiance to Christ "except in name only" was far more problematic. Grimké declared that the church should get its own house in order before claiming the right to pray for the nation. "When the Church ceases its empty, hypocritical cant about the Kingship of Jesus Christ and courageously stands up for Christian princi-

36 Francis J. Grimké to the Great Commission Prayer League, July 2, 1917, in *Works*, 4:191–93.
37 "The Death of the Director of the Great Commission Prayer League," *Reformed Presbyterian Advocate* 61 (November 1927): 244.

ples in the midst of this degenerate age and nation, we may expect a change for the better," he declared, "but not until then. The place for judgment to begin is at the house of God." He closed the letter by acknowledging the difficult substance and tone of his words and expressing shared concern for the acknowledgment of Jesus as Lord: "Pardon me for writing as I have. I am now, and have been for a long time, deeply interested in the matter of which you have spoken."[38]

Grimké received a response thanking him for his "kind and thoughtful" letter. For at least one leader within the Reformed Presbyterian Church, Grimké's words struck a chord, for this respondent wrote, "I am inclined to agree with you that Jesus Christ has not been accepted as the Divine Ruler of the Nations, nor in any real way as the Divine Ruler of the Church." The author made two further points, related to the church's teaching and discipline. On its discipline, he wrote: "I believe that the Church of Jesus Christ has one tremendous power in her hands which she seldom uses, and that is the power of discipline. If she would put out rank offenders against the principles of her profession, she would stir this whole country." Regarding its teaching, he wrote, "I am a firm believer also in the power of the truth boldly, frankly, plainly preached. If the preachers in this country would stand boldly for the truth, we know the whole moral aspect of affairs would be changed at once."[39] One cannot help but imagine what the church would be like if more Christians would respond similarly to Grimké's call.

Grimké's willingness to follow scriptural teaching wherever it led and to take countercultural stands that pushed in every direction make his approach to life and ministry a fascinating, challenging, and encouraging study. His ability to hold multiple truths in tension and his willingness to work out a coherent approach capable of incorporating the diverse and complex strands of theology, piety, and ethics make him stand out among his contemporaries. It is not surprising that he developed such a reputation as a careful reader of Scripture and morally upright and ethically engaged pastor. His ability to communicate his painstakingly worked-out theological conclusions to a broad audience also was remarkable. Theologians, social activists, and community members all highly valued his voice and support. Even when he failed to persuade his opponents, they had to reckon with his considerable influence. He may at points have been inconsistent or overly

---

[38] Francis J. Grimké to the Witness Bearing Committee of the Reformed Presbyterian Church, July 19, 1917, in *Works*, 4:193–94.
[39] W. J. Coleman to Francis J. Grimké, July 24, 1917, in *Works*, 4:195.

shaped by the cultural sensibilities of his day, but the record of his public words and private reflections indicates that he strove continually to grow in faithfulness, consistency, and self-awareness. This chapter demonstrates that though he carefully distinguished the message of the gospel from the fight against race prejudice, he arduously refused to separate the two, and he devoted his life to pursuing both. True Christianity must be a socially engaged Christianity, even as it remains committed to the "unadulterated" gospel of personal salvation.

REFLECTIONS ON FRANCIS J. GRIMKÉ'S VISION OF THE CHRISTIAN LIFE

Francis Grimké taught and practiced the Christian life amid complex and difficult circumstances, and his spiritual legacy is worthy of consideration today. This book only scratches the surface of that legacy, and one of my primary hopes in writing it is that it will inspire others to dig deeper into his written works and the archives to fill out the story and perhaps even correct the one told here, where needed. Much work remains to be done to recover the story of the early civil rights movement and the various Christian figures and groups left out of the dominant narratives in American religious history, as the lack of scholarly and popular attention given to Francis Grimké thus far makes abundantly clear.

In tracing Grimké's understanding of the Christian life and his exposition of the individual, the family, the church, and society in relation to it, this study has identified some important themes. First, Grimké comfortably distinguished between the "sacred" and the "secular," the "spiritual" and the "material," and the "eternal" and the "temporal." Second, though he made these distinctions and even identified a priority of things deemed sacred, spiritual, and eternal over those deemed secular, material, or temporal, he relentlessly pursued them all. His "heavenly" vision of the Christian life made him more rather than less desirous to do "earthly" good. He distinguished without separating the different facets of the Christian life.

This holistic, yet differentiated, vision of the Christian life led him to take a nuanced approach to the theological and political movements of his day. He freely utilized expressions from a variety of sources, and he freely collaborated with a variety of figures and organizations. As he relied upon the Holy Spirit working through Scripture to shape his convictions, he also embraced what he took to be a Christian obligation to work within a particular church and its ecclesiastical apparatus, despite its rather obvious shortcomings and corruption. His choice of an ecclesial location was the result of his theological convictions, and those same theological convictions fueled his relentless challenges to his colleagues to confess and practice what they professed to believe.

We have seen that Grimké sought to affirm (all) the ethical teachings of Jesus, as well as his metaphysical and historical claims to be God in human flesh, the fulfillment of Israel's promises, and the one who lived, died, rose, ascended, and will return to consummate all things. Because of this, Grimké does not fit well into the story of American religious history as a conflict between liberals and fundamentalists or between "private" and "public" conceptions of Christian faith and practice. It should be beyond all doubt that he most certainly was not a moderate either. Further studies of Grimké's life and context could very well provide further evidence that would support the growing desire of historians to nuance, fill out, and diversify the various "two-party theses" of American religious history.[1] Grimké happily subscribed to the "old faith" consistent with the

---

[1] The desire to diversify the two-party thesis dates as far back as the original reviews of its most famous instantiation, Martin E. Marty, *Righteous Empire: Protestantism in the United States* (New York: Dial, 1970). In a thoughtful reflection, Marty acknowledged the usefulness of the critiques in those reviews, as well as those in Douglas Jacobsen and William Vance Trollinger, eds., *Reforming the Center: American Protestantism: 1900 to the Present*, and he pointed out his own more "pluralistic model" in Marty, *A Nation of Behavers* (Chicago: University of Chicago Press, 1976), and Marty, *Pilgrims in Their Own Land: 500 Years of Religion in America* (New York: Penguin, 1985). Nevertheless, as Marty himself points out in that essay, the approach in *Righteous Empire* continues to characterize his work and its reception. See Marty, "Righteous Empire Revisited," *The Proceedings of the American Antiquarian Society* 117, no. 1 (2007): 37–60. Similar binary approaches characterize other highly influential studies in a variety of fields, including Robert N. Bellah, *The Broken Covenant: American Civil Religion in a Time of Trial* (Chicago: Chicago University Press, 1975); James Davison Hunter, *Culture Wars: The Struggle to Control the Family, Art, Education, Law, and Politics in America* (New York: Basic, 1991); George Marsden, *Fundamentalism and American Culture* (New York: Oxford University Press, 1980); Robert Wuthnow, *The Restructuring of American Religion* (Princeton, NJ: Princeton University Press, 1988). While binary approaches and narratives certainly have some merits and create useful categories for introductory students and popular audiences, Marty's commendation

summaries of biblical teaching in his Presbyterian Westminster Confession of Faith and Catechisms, but he did not align himself wholeheartedly with fundamentalism as a movement any more than he did with theological modernism.[2] When it came to the social, cultural, and political views of his own day, this study has demonstrated that some of his views were quite progressive and others quite conservative, though all sought to follow divine revelation. Perhaps contemporary Christians, just like historians, ought not feel the pressure to choose between these options either. Perhaps the Christian faith often cuts across our typical cultural categories and sensibilities, challenging them all.

To be sure, Grimké's attitude toward the relationship between the law of God and the gospel of God informed his sensibilities in these matters. He believed that the gospel of God could meet humanity's deepest needs, and he also thought it impossible to preach the good news of the gospel without preaching the moral law of God. He affirmed that God reveals his law in nature as well as the Scriptures, and in practice he distinguished between the extent, scope, and purposes of these two types of revelation. His sermons drew from the Scriptures, but his public arguments frequently drew from natural law. He viewed all of God's law as harmonious, regardless of its form, though the second half of the Ten Commandments particularly demonstrates the overlap between natural and divine law, and therefore it proved a rich well for his social activism.

His nuanced understanding of God's law related to his terminology for the gospel. Because calling people to repentance and faith in the person and work of Christ for salvation also requires the preaching of the law of God, there is a broad sense in which preaching the law is part of preaching the gospel. In this sense, he characterized the White church's refusal to preach the racial equality of all people as an affront to the gospel of Jesus Christ. But there is also a narrow sense in which the notion of the gospel can be limited to the "pure, unadulterated" message of the person and work of Christ, including his virgin birth, miraculous life, death as an atoning sacrifice, and resurrection, ascension, and second coming. This gospel alone can provide assurance of salvation to those awaiting Jesus's glorious return. In this way, narrowly speaking, the law and gospel of God

---

of his own more nuanced conclusions in his other works also is instructive regarding the downsides of such methods.

2 For his views on the "old faith" and its opposition to the views of "Higher Critics" and "Modernists," see *Works*, 3:501.

are fundamentally distinguishable but also inseparable. These themes, set forth in chapter 2, can be traced throughout the pages of this book, and they informed the way Grimké thought about the Christian life in relation to the individual, the family, the church, and society.

Because of these things, though he placed the preaching of the Scriptures in general and the proclamation of the gospel in particular at the center of the Christian ministry, he also believed deeply in the importance of social activism. Grimké developed careful principles for the pursuit of social good. These principles rise to the surface in chapter 10's exploration of his involvement in the founding of the NAACP especially, but they may be discerned in the other chapters as well. First, he carefully distinguished the theological and religious views from the social and political views of his partners in social activism. He readily cooperated with those who shared the latter even if they did not share the former. The shared pursuit of social and political goals did not require a corresponding theological alignment.

Second, he carefully distinguished situations warranting public debate from private disputes. When he shared basic principles and believed that his partners were acting in good faith, he frequently chose to address differences—even significant ones—in private. He reserved public criticism for addressing the violation of basic principles.

Third, and related to these first two principles, he carefully distinguished the personal from the political. If someone shared his platform, he readily overlooked significant ideological differences and joined them in their cause. He believed it was more effective to build multiple coalitions with different people and groups rather than to expect ideological alignment on every issue. Even within in the NAACP, he supported allowing a diversity of approaches to racial identity and identification, so long as there was agreement on the basic platform of racial equality and justice.

While Grimké earned a reputation for integrity in practicing what he preached in his own day, it is understandable that his moral stridency led to resentment that carries over into the present day. At various points, this study has attempted to narrate Grimké's relationship to the "respectability politics" that historians describe, in both the Reconstruction and the early civil rights eras, and the years since. Chapters 3 and 4 address these issues directly by narrating his attempts to distinguish himself explicitly and self-consciously from those who assimilated or otherwise acceded to the expectations of White society. Recent historical works that narrate

Grimké's ministry and that of Fifteenth Street Presbyterian Church in terms of accommodation to White middle-class values could attend more directly to his own words and the historical records of his personal and public life, as well as the archives of the church. Historical figures who include statements like the following in their personal notebooks may not always be perfectly self-aware, but they are not always liars or deluded either:

> I have been preaching now for nearly forty years. During all that time, there are certain things that I can truthfully say of myself:
>
> 1. I have never been afraid of anybody. I have always spoken fearlessly what I believed to be right, whether it agreed with the views of others or not.
>
> 2. I have never sought to curry favor with anybody. I have always tried to do my duty and to treat everybody with due consideration, not, however, with a view of reaping some personal benefit, because I thought they might do me a good turn some day, but because I felt it was the right thing to do.
>
> 3. I have never been influenced by the financial or social standing of those with whom I have come in contact. I have never been able to bring myself to think more of a man simply because he had money and lived more expensively than others. I have always made it a rule to estimate people by their moral and spiritual worth rather than by their material possessions.[3]

Not every attempt to pursue moral excellence is reducible to a concession to respectability politics.

Similarly, some accuse Grimké of elitism motivated by colorism.[4] Such accusations would be more credible if they also engaged his public statements, personal memoirs, and the vast archival records, especially the frequent meditations in his own private notebooks along these lines:

> GOD IS NO RESPECTER OF PERSONS. What does that mean? It means that God, in dealing with us, is entirely uninfluenced by our outward condition, by the fact that we are rich or poor, high or low, educated or uneducated, white or black. A rich man will receive no more consideration from

---

[3] *Works*, 3:31–32.
[4] E.g., Kerri K. Greenidge, *The Grimkes: The Legacy of Slavery in an American Family* (New York: Liveright, 2022), 238–39.

him than a poor man, or a poor man than a rich man; a white man will fare no better at his hand than a black man, nor a black man than a white man. With God it isn't what your color is, what race you are identified with, what your material condition is, whether you have much or little education, but what your principles are. It is character that God takes account of. If your character is not pure, upright, if your principles are not what they ought to be, *it doesn't make any difference how white you are, or how black you are,* how rich you are or how poor you are, however highly educated you are or how ignorant you are, you will be treated as you deserve to be treated. Your race, your money, your influence, your high social standing will count for nothing.[5]

Grimké's ministry is best interpreted as an attempt to consistently adopt and implement a biblically informed and confessionally Protestant view of the Christian life that self-consciously and intentionally sought to push against the politics of respectability, classism, and colorism.

While approaching Grimké's thought and practice on its own terms may free it from anachronistic or reductionistic interpretations, this does not mean that his ministry was fully consistent or faultless. For example, his engagement with the temperance movement is an instance where his desire to follow the teaching of Scripture regarding the abuse of alcohol led him to at least two conclusions in tension with his other principles. First, his advocacy for total abstinence from the use of alcohol rather clearly went beyond the teaching of Scripture and the example of Jesus.[6] Second, his counsel that "every church, and every member of every church, ought to be actively and aggressively opposed" to the sale of liquor contradicted his typically more nuanced position regarding the relationship between morality and politics.[7] Even if it were granted that the consumption or sale of alcohol is immoral in itself, Scripture does not offer direct teaching regarding the best political means to reduce the drinking of alcohol or disincentivize its market. Therefore, Grimké's explicit statements in his meditations, letters, and especially his many sermons on the temperance issue run counter to his counsel regarding the inferential application of

---

[5] *Works*, 3:196, emphasis added. Grimké explicitly and relentlessly opposed racism, colorism, and classism. His references to "race, color, and class" as a set of (distinguishable) equally unacceptable reasons for determining status are so pervasive that it seems unnecessary to list them all.

[6] For example, he wrote in one place, "There is no single force or agency that Christian men and women should feel impelled to fight with all their might, as the use of alcoholic liquors as a beverage." *Works*, 3:277.

[7] *Works*, 3:337.

Scripture to political issues considered in chapter 10.[8] While the rampant abuse of alcohol may prompt sympathy for Grimké's overwrought conclusions, these nevertheless seem like rather straightforward inconsistencies in his teaching.

If accusations of respectability politics or classism miss the mark, that is not to say Grimké was without cultural blind spots. Therefore, the lack of evidence for respectability or classism as *motivations* in his thought and ministry should not foreclose consideration of the extent to which the social, cultural, and intellectual assumptions of his time and place not only formed the context but also shaped the substance of his theological conclusions. Perhaps future studies of Grimké's life and context can explore these questions more deeply.

In the meantime, this study maintains that courage, resilience, and hope were among the most notable characteristics of Grimké's approach to the Christian life. These virtues arose from his trust in God's faithfulness rather than a vain or superficial optimism that earthly circumstances would improve anytime soon. In the summer of 1929, he reflected upon an article in *Harper's* magazine by Oswald Garrison Villard entitled "The Crumbling Color Line." In contrast to what he took to be Villard's attempt to "lighten . . . the otherwise dark outlook" for Black people in America, Grimké considered the article "too optimistic." He then offered some reading advice for anyone who "thinks the color line is crumbling," which included less-cheerful social commentary.[9] The publication dates of his alternative readings were from the same year, indicating that even in his semiretirement he kept close tabs on the latest research in a variety of fields. His conclusion was stark: "The color line may be crumbling, but if it is it is barely perceptible. There are influences at work looking to that end, but the result, so far, is very meagre."

His pessimism regarding racial progress is understandable for a Christian minister who experienced the rise of Jim Crow, attempts to make racial intermarriage illegal, and race riots in a city where the vast majority of residents professed to be Christians. Yet his pessimism did not prevent him from acknowledging the benefits of looking on "the bright side," as he also pointed to a source of hope and a reason to keep fighting that was even stronger. His source of hope was not first and foremost the glimpses

---

[8] For Grimké's temperance sermons, see, e.g., *Works*, 2:483–527.
[9] His recommendations included Robert Russa Moton, *What the Negro Thinks* (Garden City, NY: Doubleday, Doran, 1929) and Scott Nearing, *Black America* (New York: Vanguard, 1929).

of social progress but, rather, the "certainty of the fact that God is on the throne, that Right is bound ultimately to triumph; that the spirit of Jesus Christ is in the world, and that his noble principles and ideals are at work in the hearts of men and will go on working 'until man to man shall brothers be.'" Times may be dark now and for the foreseeable future, but "there is always light ahead, if we keep our eyes on God and on the great immutable principles of his moral government."

Grimké pressed on not because he believed that social improvement was imminent but because God is ultimate. On the one hand, he saw no reason for naive optimism, for premature declarations of the end of racism or other moral evils, or for simplistic statements about the gospel being the only answer needed for social ills in the present age. On the other hand, he saw no reason for pessimism, despair, or rejection of the power of God working through the gospel either. There is "no reason to become discouraged, though at times things may look pretty dark," he wrote. Rather, "we are hopeful, and will ever be" because "Jesus Christ has set his kingdom up in the world," and the gates of hell will not prevail against it. Grimké's view of God's coming kingdom was multifaceted. He believed that the kingdom is both already and not yet, and he drew courage, resilience, and hope from both truths. "The triumph of the Messiah's kingdom is assured," he concluded.[10] In this way he refused both the inordinate optimism of what might be called kingdom presentism and the inordinate pessimism of kingdom futurism. It would not be inaccurate to describe his view as a form of kingdom realism. This realism lent itself to simple faithfulness in the Christian life. As he exhorted his congregation, "Let us stop worrying about the future of Christianity and get down to the hard work in carrying out the instructions of the Lord."[11]

Though life "may look pretty dark," Francis Grimké called God's people to look to "the reign of Jesus Christ" as "the solution of all the dark problems of earth." The Christian's spiritual life in Christ brings light and joy in the face of the darkness.

> The Christian life, where it is really, truly lived, is a most blessed life,— a life full of joy, full of sunshine, full of peace; it is a life that keeps us ever moving in the direction of all that is best and noblest in character

---

10 *Works*, 3:330–31.
11 Francis J. Grimké, "Christ's Program for the Saving of the World" (1936), box 40-6, folder 309, Francis J. Grimké Papers, Howard University Library, 13.

and conduct: it is a life that keeps us in loving sympathy with those about us who need to be cheered, comforted, blessed. It is a life which not only steadily lifts us to higher levels of thought and sentiment, but which also sends us out on missions of love to others.[12]

The light and joy of Christ fueled Francis Grimké's vision for spiritual and social vitality. They can fuel ours as well.

---

[12] *Works*, 3:90.

GENERAL INDEX

nature and nurture, 108–9, 115
Nearing, Scott, 133n26
Negro National Conference, 178
Nelson, William Stuart, 74n40, 125, 200n24
Niagara Movement, 12, 178, 183, 184
nonbeliever, speaking on economics or civil and political rights, 181–82

obedience to God, 141, 149, 151, 154, 157, 196
oppression, 149
original sin, 109, 110

Page, Bessie Taylor, 136
parable of the prodigal son, 66, 104, 105, 134, 141
Parker, Theodore, 149n17
patriotism, 56
Paul
  on the centrality of love, 39
  on preaching the gospel, 19–20
Payne, Alexander, 139–40
peace, 135
Perry, Mark, xvii n1, 84n14
perseverance, 37
personal experience, 198n18
personal identity, 37–38
  and the image of God, 42
personal righteousness, 113
personal transformation, 136–37
Peter's sermon at Pentecost, 153
Pfleiderer, Otto, 198n18
philosophers, wisdom of, 180
pietist churches, 57
Pitts, Helen. See Douglass, Helen Pitts
poetry, 31
"politics of respectability," 45–49
polygamy, 206–7
poor, outreach toward, 158
popularity, 49
prayer, 63–64, 164
preaching, 140, 146
  centrality of, 214

on cultural issues, 155
faithfulness in, 156, 166
not for sharing personal opinions, 152
power of, 155–56
qualifications for, 156
simplicity of, 153–54
see also gospel proclamation
preaching against the evils of racism, 21
preaching the gospel, 19–20, 29–30
preaching the law, 22–23, 39
Presbyterian Church in America, xv
Presbyterian Church in the United States (PCUS), segregation in, 9
Presbyterian Church of the United States in America (PCUSA)
  segregation in, 9, 10–11
  toleration of racism, 22
Princeton Theological Seminary, 4, 16, 22, 63, 169, 187
  toleration of racism, 22
"Prodigal Son and Kindred Addresses" (sermons), 104, 134n28, 141
proper respect, 47–48, 50–52, 55
Psalms, encouragement from, 53
public and private, 180, 214
public school system, 110–11
Purvis, Harriet Forten, 84
Purvis, Robert, 84

race prejudice, 11, 16–17, 44, 61–62
  in the church, 29, 50–52, 68, 142
  fight against, 76, 188, 201, 210
race riots, 10, 25–26, 43, 53, 54, 217
racial identity, 47
racial intermarriage. See interracial marriage
racial stereotyping, 44
racial uplift, 105–6
racial violence, 13, 43–44, 53
racism, 17, 22
  church's failure to address, 157
  intractableness of, xiii

228   *General Index*

SCRIPTURE INDEX

WISDOM FROM THE PAST
FOR LIFE IN THE PRESENT

Theologians on the Christian Life

AUGUSTINE
by GERALD BRAY

BAVINCK
by JOHN BOLT

BONHOEFFER
by STEPHEN J. NICHOLS

CALVIN
by MICHAEL HORTON

EDWARDS
by DANE C. ORTLUND

GRIMKÉ
by ANDREW J. MARTIN

LEWIS
by JOE RIGNEY

LLOYD-JONES
by JASON MEYER

LUTHER
by CARL R. TRUEMAN

NEWTON
by TONY REINKE

OWEN
by MATTHEW BARRETT &
MICHAEL A. G. HAYKIN

PACKER
by SAM STORMS

RYLE
by ANDREW
ATHERSTONE

SCHAEFFER
by WILLIAM EDGAR

SPURGEON
by MICHAEL REEVES

STOTT
by TIM CHESTER

WARFIELD
by FRED G. ZASPEL

WESLEY
by FRED SANDERS

The Theologians on the Christian Life series provides accessible introductions to the great teachers on the Christian life, exploring their personal lives and writings, especially as they pertain to the walk of faith.

For more information, visit **crossway.org.**